# Early Feminists of Colonial India

# Early Feminists of Colonial India
## Sarala Devi Chaudhurani and Rokeya Sakhawat Hossain

Bharati Ray

YMCA Library Building, Jai Singh Road, New Delhi 110 001

Oxford University Press is a department of the University of Oxford. It furthers the
University's objective of excellence in research, scholarship, and education
by publishing worldwide in

Oxford   New York
Auckland   Bangkok   Buenos Aires   Cape Town   Chennai
Dar es Salaam   Delhi   Hong Kong   Istanbul   Karachi   Kolkata
Kuala Lumpur   Madrid   Melbourne   Mexico City   Mumbai   Nairobi
Sao Paulo   Shanghai   Singapore   Taipei   Tokyo   Toronto
and an associated company in Berlin

Oxford is a registered trademark of Oxford University Press
in the UK and in certain other countries

Published in India
By Oxford University Press, New Delhi

© Oxford University Press 2002

The moral rights of the author have been asserted
Database right Oxford University Press (maker)
First published 2002

All rights reserved. No part of this publication may be reproduced,
stored in a retrieval system, or transmitted, in any form or by any means,
without the prior permission in writing of Oxford University Press,
or as expressly permitted by law, or under terms agreed with the appropriate
reprographics rights organization. Enquiries concerning reproduction
outside the scope of the above should be sent to the Rights Department,
Oxford University Press, at the address above

You must not circulate this book in any other binding or cover and you must
impose this same condition on any acquirer

ISBN  0 19 565697 0

Typeset by Jojy Philip
Printed by Roopak Printers, Delhi 110 032
Published by Manzar Khan, Oxford University Press
YMCA Library Building, Jai Singh Road, New Delhi 110 001

*For Sukhendu*

# Acknowledgements

Sarala Devi Chaudhurani and Begum Rokeya Sakhawat Hossain on whose writings this volume is based.

The Rockefeller Foundation which granted me a Residency at the Bellagio Centre for Conference and Research where this volume was written.

The Indian Council of Historical Research for a research grant.

The authorities of the Rabindra Bhavan Archives, Visva Bharati, for generous permission to use photographs for publication.

The Librarian and staff of the National Library, Calcutta; Sahitya Parishad Library, Calcutta; West Bengal State Archives, Calcutta; Parliament Library, New Delhi; Nehru Memorial Museum and Library, New Delhi; Rabindra Bhavan Archives, Visva Bharati; Dhaka University Library, Dhaka; and Bangladesh High Commission Library, Calcutta, for ungrudging co-operation and help.

Professor Tapan Ray Chaudhuri, Professor Gautam Bhadra, Dr Isha Ray, and Dr Raka Ray for perceptive comments.

Dr Rimi B. Chatterjee, Professor Basudeb Chatterjee, and Ms Joyee Deb for reading the manuscript and offering helpful suggestions.

And Shri Prabir Mukhopadhyay for assistance in research.

# Preface

It was a hot July day in 1984 at the National Library, Calcutta. I had sent my manuscript entitled 'Hyderabad and British Paramountcy' to Oxford University Press for possible publication, and was awaiting their response. For my next book, I was considering turning from colonial history to the history of gender in colonial India. In an almost unplanned, random search, I immersed myself in writings by women, preferring to look at indigenous literature rather than at Anglo-Indian works. It was in this process that I encountered a somewhat slim and worn-out volume, *Motichoor*, volume 1, by R. S. Hossain. I knew of her as the founder of the Sakhawat Memorial Girls' School in Calcutta where my sister had once studied. I picked it up, and started reading. I was certainly not prepared for what I found. In truth, I was amazed, almost shocked. How could a Bengali woman, a Muslim woman, in the first decade of the century have written like this? More importantly, what had made her think like this? It was revolutionary thinking even by the standards of the late twentieth century. The more I read, the more fascinated I became. I decided to join the battle she had begun eight decades ago.

Later, I encountered a second important book, *Jibaner Jharapata*, by Sarala Devi Chaudhurani. Of course I had heard the name—who had not? The intelligentsia in Bengal adore the Tagores and Sarala belonged to the Tagore family from her mother's side. Had she however been such a forthright, dynamic, and courageous woman? The autobiography was not a major work of literature; it was often jumbled, confused certain dates, and occasionally even gave the impression of being somewhat exaggerated. That notwithstanding, there was a directness and a simplicity about the woman it portrayed. Why did Rabindranath Tagore, her uncle, not give her the recognition she deserved? Why did the emerging nationalists of Bengal adore her? Finally, why has Bengal all but forgotten her today? Such queries led me into the life of another remarkable Bengali woman.

This research was undertaken twelve years after I had come across

*Motichoor* and *Jibaner Jharapata*. Closer acquaintance with their life and work made their limitations and political manoeuvres more apparent. Certain orthodox utterances and actions compromised their otherwise liberal approach. Sarala and Rokeya were, simultaneously, ahead of their time and products of it. In a period of nation-building which tended to dwarf the individual, they were both remarkable women in terms of their personalities and contributions—pioneers on several counts—and rendered significant services to the country and the community.

This study is a historical assessment of Sarala Devi and Begum Rokeya, identifying the similarities and differences in the ideas and activities of these two women from two different communities in colonial Bengal, one Hindu-Brahmo, the other Muslim. The focus throughout is on their concern about, and their work around, women's issues.

This book comprises five short chapters. In the first, I briefly sketch the lives of the two women; in the second, I provide an overview of the age, and the condition of women, both Hindu and Muslim, during that period. In this process, I also explore the question that had struck me at the very outset: what made it possible for these two women to be who they were. In the third chapter, I look at the steps they advocated or adopted to improve the lives of women. The fourth chapter tells the story of their efforts at organizing women; each was the first woman in her respective community in Bengal to initiate such a step. The final chapter is an assessment of Sarala and Rokeya. How did their contemporaries view Sarala and Rokeya, and how are they regarded today?

This is the story of two outstanding Bengali women fighting for a cause, so similar and yet so strikingly different at multiple levels. If this generates further interest and research in the subject, this slim volume will have served its purpose.

Bharati Ray
Calcutta

September 2001

# Contents

1. Sarala and Rokeya: Brief Biographical Sketches — 1
2. The Age and its Women — 28
3. Sarala and Rokeya: Women's Issues — 57
4. Organizing Women — 78
   Conclusion — 97
   *Notes and References* — 114
   *Biographical Notes* — 140
   *Bibliography* — 155
   *Index* — 169

# 1. Sarala and Rokeya: Brief Biographical Sketches

### Introducing Sarala Devi and Begum Rokeya

It was 26 December 1901. The session of the Indian National Congress was being held in Calcutta. At its inauguration, a young woman, educated and unmarried, led a chorus with a deeply stirring song she herself had composed and set to music. Over fifty girls assembled from different parts of India accompanied her. The response it evoked from the public was supremely enthusiastic. The young woman was Sarala Ghosal (1872–1945), known after marriage as Sarala Devi Chaudhurani. The reputed newspaper *Bengalee* had reported on the previous day,

SING HINDUSTHAN ... the patriotic song to be sung at the opening of the Congress proceedings is being actively rehearsed by about 50 musicians, representing all classes and creeds of the vast continent of India ... specially composed by that great lady, Miss Sarala Ghosal.[1]

Sarala made her debut in India's political world through the medium of music. Her purpose was not only to sing, but to inspire a nation in deep slumber under the yoke of foreign masters. Indeed, the key quality in her character was this desire to inspire. In whichever field she turned her attention, whether it was politics, or literature, or music, or the women's question, she attempted to stimulate, to activate, to arouse.

About four years later, in 1905, another young woman, married and without any formal education, handed over a few pieces of paper to her husband, Sakhawat Hossain. Rokeya, or Mrs R. S. Hossain (1880–1932) as she called herself, later recounted the incident.

We were then stationed in Bhagalpore. My husband was away on tour, and I was left alone at home. He returned after two days and asked me what I had been doing during his absence. I then showed him the draft of 'Sultana's Dream', which I had just written. He promptly read through the whole book without even bothering to sit down, and remarked, 'A terrible revenge!'[2]

Sakhawat was wrong. It was not revenge; it was rebellion. The principal characteristic of Begum Rokeya Sakhawat Hossain *was* rebellion: against the evils of a system that kept women subjugated, humiliated, and subservient, and 'Sultana's Dream' was symbolic of that protest.

These two outstanding women, Sarala Devi Chaudhurani and Begum Rokeya Sakhawat Hossain, lived and worked in twentieth century colonial Bengal. They were contemporaries, and were both concerned with the condition and status of women and their advancement, looking at the issues from their respective points of view. This study attempts to explore these, and understand the social, political, and cultural compulsions that constructed and shaped their ideology and work. It also aims at clarifying the differences and similarities between the perspectives of the two women and, in the process, to shed some light on contemporary Hindu and Muslim societies, their pattern of change during the colonial encounter, and the emergence among both the communities of a new generation of women. The term 'women' is used in this study in a restricted sense, to refer to only women of the middle and upper middle class in urban Bengal.

What was the situation of women's lives in contemporary colonial Bengal? How was the notion of *unnati* (progress) constructed by Sarala and Rokeya in their particular contexts? How did they diagnose the ills responsible for women's *abanati* (degradation)? What issues did they prioritize? How did they conceptualize the responsibilities of women? What was the significance of their contributions in terms of the women's movement of today? These are some of the questions that will be investigated in this work, which will use the literary oevres of the two women as the primary data. In order to comprehend how the mentalities of Sarala Devi and Begum Rokeya were formed, and what forces created their personalities, characters, and particular visions, it is necessary first to examine their lives and activities.

They came from well-to-do families, and their lives had certain similarities. Both were born Bengalis, married non-Bengali widowers outside Bengal, lived in their husbands' states, were widowed and then returned to live and work in Bengal. Both wrote profusely, strove for women's education, advocated advancing the social position of women, and built women's organizations. Nevertheless, there were major differences in their ideas and actions, and vast disparities in their cultural contexts. One of them came from a privileged and relatively 'progressive' background, and the other from one with a more stifling atmosphere; they belonged to two different religious communities, one was a Hindu–Brahmo, the other was a Muslim, and they chose separate philosophies to serve a common cause: the advancement of women. Throughout the discussion, I have chosen to talk of Sarala Devi before Begum Rokeya, because she was the older of the two women.

## Sarala Devi

### Family

Sarala belonged to the Hindu–Brahmo community, which had played a leading role in the nineteenth century reform movement in Bengal. She was related to the Tagores, unquestionably the most illustrious family in Bengal. The principal family seat was at Jorasanko, which had become veritably *the* centre of creative culture and new ideas in India and a meeting ground of the thoughts of the East and the West.

Two sisters: Sarala and Hironmoyee

Sarala's mother, Swarnakumari Devi (1855–1932), the daughter of Maharshi Debendranath Tagore (1817–1905), and the elder sister of Rabindranath Tagore (1861–1941), the greatest poet of Bengal of all time, was herself an author of repute. Although married at an early age (1867), Swarnakumari was not illiterate at the time of marriage, as it was the custom in her family to impart education to the daughters primarily through the help of 'Vaishnavis', who were women belonging to the Vaisnava Hindu religious sect.[3] Swarnakumari became one of Bengal's earliest successful female writers. She wrote numerous poems, essays, short stories, and novels,[4] and edited the prestigious journal *Bharati*,[5] launched by her elder brother Jyotirindranath Tagore (1849–1925), for several years from 1291 BS to 1301 BS (1884–94) and from 1315 BS to 1321 BS

(1908–14). She was close to Annie Besant, and became the President of the women's branch of the Theosophical Society in Bengal. When this women's branch was closed down, Swarnakumari founded Sakhi Samiti (Women's Friendly Association) in 1886, the first women's organization in Bengal to be set up by a woman, with a view to providing assistance to indigent widows and helpless women.[6] She also devoted herself, along with her husband, to the cause of nationalism, working for the Indian National Congress. She and Kadambini Ganguli (1861–1923) shared the unique distinction of becoming the first female delegates to the Indian National Congress at its Calcutta session in 1890. Swarnakumari Devi was the president of Bidhaba Shilpashram (The Centre for Arts and Crafts for Widows), founded by her daughter Hironmoyee Devi (1870–1925).[7] She organized annual fairs called Mahila Shilpamela (Women's Arts and Crafts Fair) where cottage industry products made by women from different parts of India were displayed. In every sense, therefore, Swarnakumari was one of the pioneering women of late nineteenth and early twentieth century Bengal.

Sarala's father, Janakinath Ghosal (1840–1913), the son of a local zamindar of Krishnanagar, and a latter day nationalist leader of the Indian National Congress, was a man of independent will. When he married Swarnakumari, whose father Maharshi Debendranath Tagore was by then a very distinguished Brahmo leader, he refused to stay in the Tagore household in Jorasanko, although all Maharshi's sons-in-law had had to become *gharjamai* or sons-in-law living at the father-in-law's house.[8] Janakinath was 27 years old and Swarnakumari only 12. They set up their own household, but when Janakinath went to England, Swarnakumari returned to Jorasanko with her children. Much of Sarala's childhood was, therefore, spent there. Janakinath became one of the earliest and chief supporters of the Congress, and contributed greatly to nurturing its early phase. It was probably from him that Sarala inherited her sense of nationalism, and her strong will and independent spirit.

Sarala's elder sister, Hironmoyee Devi, studied at Bethune College, wrote poems and stories that appeared in *Sakha*, *Balak*, and *Bharati o Balak*. She edited *Bharati* along with Sarala Devi for two years.[9] One of her principal social services was the formation of the Bidhaba Shilpashram in 1906 in aid of widows. She thus at once manifested social concern and literary talent. She was married to Phanibhusan Mukhopadhyaya (1860–1927), who was a professor, wrote books and essays on science, and assisted Hironmoyee in her social activities. Jyotsna Ghosal, the only brother of Sarala and Hironmoyee, joined the Indian Civil Service.

The family of Sarala's mother, the Tagores, deserve special mention. Apart from Raja Rammohan Roy (1772–1833) or Iswar Chandra Vidyasagar

(1820–91), there were perhaps few Bengalis who could claim to have contributed as much to the cultural efflorescence in contemporary Bengal as members of the Tagore family did. Prince Dwarakanath Tagore (1794–1846) was a pioneer industrialist; his son, Maharshi Debendranath, was the leading Brahmo figure after Rammohan. Almost all Debendranath's sons rose to fame. The eldest, Dwijendranath (1840–1926), was a philosopher, a nationalist, a writer, and the first editor of *Bharati*, which he edited for six years. He was also an enthusiastic patron of the Hindu Mela.[10] The second son, Satyendranath (1842–1923), was the first Indian member of the Indian Civil Service, and a champion of women's 'liberation' from confinement within the four walls of the home.[11] He took his wife Gyanadanandini Devi (1852–1941) to live with him in England, Bombay and in various towns in western India. The third son of Debendranath, Hemendranath (1844–84), was a businessman, and a fervent supporter of women's education.[12] The fourth son, Jyotirindranath (1849–1925), was a man of many interests: a writer, musician, industrialist, nationalist, the Secretary of Adi Brahmo Samaj, and a champion of women's 'liberation'. The publication of *Bharati* was his idea, and he edited it for one year. However, outshining all the brothers and reigning over the cultural terrain of India as long as he lived, was Rabindranath (1861–1941), Nobel laureate in literature, creator of Rabindrasangeet, a new genre of music, and an excellent painter. Thus, Thakurbari, as the Tagore family home at Jorasanko was known, was the meeting point of many a brilliant contemporary mind. Indeed, to all the intellectuals of the nineteenth century, Thakurbari was almost a place of pilgrimage. Not only were there animated discussions on social, political, and scientific subjects, and a prolific flow of creative writings, but quite often plays were staged and enacted by members of the family themselves.

The women of the Tagore family proved to be the vanguards of women's 'progress' and education. Apart from Swarnakumari Devi, who has already been mentioned, there was a galaxy of brilliant women. Debendranath's wife, Sarada Devi, knew how to read and write, and was often found reading a book during her spare time. Their daughter, Saudamini Devi (1847–1920) was admitted at the age of five to Bethune School (founded in 1849), and was one of the earliest Bengali upper middle class girls to go to school.[13] Swarnakumari Devi was, however, the most famous of Debendranath's daughters.

Of Debendranath's daughters-in-law, Gyanadanandini Devi, the wife of Satyendranath, became one of the most 'modern' women of her time.[14] She lived with her husband in Bombay for two years, and when she returned in 1866, violated family custom by publicly alighting from a carriage at the family home at Jorasanko, a step that moved the old family retainers to tears of shame.[15] An innovator on dress reform, she, on returning from Bombay, introduced a new way of wearing the sari which solved for upper middle class women the problem of how to dress appropriately when going out of the privacy of the home. Swarnakumari Devi commented that the 'civil and elegant attire', designed in imitation of Gujarati women, was 'an integral combination of indigenousness, decorum, and modesty'.[16] Gyanadanandini Devi also left her mark in the literary field by starting a children's magazine, *Balak* (Boys), in order to encourage the children of the family to start writing. Another memorable daughter-in-law of Debendranath was Kadambari Devi, the wife of Jyotirindranath Tagore. Along with her husband she often used to ride on horseback, wearing tailored clothes, violating traditional Bengali norms. She was an inspiration for the young poet Rabindranath, and was a highly accomplished actress, participating in the family plays that were enacted in the sprawling Jorasanko home. Mrinalini Devi, Rabindranath's wife, was an actress of some talent. In the next, that is Sarala's, generation, Satyendranath's daughter Indira Devi (1873–1960), and Hemendranath's daughter Pratibha Devi (1860–1922), became reputed for literary and musical talent.[17] Thus, in terms of education and culture, and of dress reform that made it possible for women to go out, the Tagore women set an example of 'progress' to other women of Bengal.

It was among such a galaxy of men and women and in an atmosphere of cultural excellence that Sarala had the good fortune of growing up. Although her mother had moved out of Jorasanko with her father after marriage, Sarala had the opportunity of spending the years of her childhood in the Jorasanko ambience, as her mother returned while her father was away in England. Sarala recalls those happy, uninhibited times.

During my father's absence in England when I was about five or six years of age, we went to live with my mother's family at no. 6 Jorasanko for a longish period. Counting the children of my many aunts and uncles (sisters and brothers of my mother), we cousins formed quite a large contingent. Understandably, there were age-wise groupings amongst the children. My elder sister Hironmoyee's group was just above ours, but even though my elder brother Jyotsna's group consisted entirely of boys, we were on fairly good terms with them. Our sister's group was somewhat condescending towards us, but without any inhibitions, we often used to engage ourselves in fights and fisticuffs with the boys in my brother's group.[18]

Hironmoyee Devi too recalls the joys of childhood. Those were wonderful days at Jorasanko, when Jyotirindranath, Rabindranath, and Swarnakumari were together, composing new songs, writing stories, and organizing dramatic performances. The children emulated their elders.

Once on our mother's birthday, we invited the elders for a tea party. We staged a play without telling any of them before. They all acclaimed our acting as well as the stage decorations ... . On the drop-scene was painted the face of uncle Rabindranath surrounded by a garland. Each flower was the face of a child actor or actress.[19]

Clearly, Hironmoyee and her sister Sarala grew up in a happy, free, and culturally rich environment.

*Education*

Her family encouraged Sarala to opt for institutional education. She was admitted to Bethune School at the age of seven. Bethune was at the time *the* centre of learning for the girls from 'enlightened' and 'progressive' families. Here Sarala came in touch with other future celebrities like Lajjabati Basu (1870–1942), the daughter of the Brahmo leader Rajnarayan Basu, who never married, devoting herself to the cause of education and literature. Another close friend was Hemaprabha Basu, the sister of the renowned scientist Jagadish Chandra Basu (1858–1937), and later Professor of Bethune College. Sarala made friends with Shailabala, the daughter of the Brahmo leader Durgamohan Das (1841–97), and with Hemalata Sarkar (1868–1943), the daughter of Pandit Shivanath Shastri (1847–1919), later the founder Principal of Maharani Girls' School in Darjeeling. Among the senior students were Kumudini Khastagir (1865–?), Kamini Roy (1864–1933), and Abala Basu (1864–1951). As student leaders, Kamini and Abala aroused nationalist fervour among the girls in the school, wielding a distinct influence on Sarala. At the time of the Ilbert Agitation, under their leadership in school, Sarala had the first taste of agitational politics and wore a black ribbon on her wrist as a mark of protest.[20] Sarala was a first rate student, and highly popular with the staff and the students alike. Having passed the entrance examination, she joined Bethune College and in 1890 graduated from there with Honours in English. Women had just started to come out to pursue collegiate studies, the door having been opened only a few years earlier by Kadambini Ganguly and Chandramukhi Bose (1860–1944), who had graduated in 1883. By the end of the nineteenth century, only twenty-seven women had BA degrees.[21] Sarala was one of the foremost of these privileged women. She showed courage and individuality in her choice of subjects too, registering a protest against discrimination between boys and girls regarding the courses of study. Men were encouraged to take up science, women to opt for humanities. Sarala decided that she would read science. When, at her insistence, she was permitted to attend the evening lectures at Mahendranath Sarkar's Science Association, her two cousins escorted her on either side into the classroom, acting like bodyguards.[22]

## Paid employment

Sarala's background enabled her to pursue an unorthodox course. She took up a paid job in Maharani School in Mysore, to get a feel of gainful employment and to earn 'an independent livelihood', but she soon gave it up. During that short time, however, she courted criticism from the conservative press. *Bangabasi* asked, 'What was the need for women of such families to travel alone to distant places to take up a job? Surely, they are not wanting in food and comforts. Why create problems for oneself?'[23] Paid jobs for middle class women was not yet socially favoured. Sarala was content to make the experiment, and did not exhibit any concern for making the right to gainful employment a right to be fought for. She belonged to a class for the women of which paid employment was not a necessity. However, she valued the experience.

To know oneself one must be away from the cloying atmosphere of one's home. I came to realize this when I was away and living on my own in Mysore. My country, India, came alive to me, and I developed an understanding of Hindu religion and culture. No longer am I restless like a caged bird, for I have seen the outside world and come to understand myself.[24]

## Political involvement

Sarala was much more serious in her other commitment, that is, participating in the freedom struggle. Sarala's principal characteristic was patriotism. It may be safely concluded that she imbibed the spirit from her parents at home, from her uncles and aunts at Jorasanko, all ardent nationalists, and also from her friends and seniors in school. It was the time of the Swadeshi movement in Bengal against the British Raj.[25] The movement broke out in the open as a protest against Lord Curzon's partition of Bengal in 1905. Sarala was directly involved in it and became the foremost female political leader of her times; it may well be claimed that Sarala was the *first* Indian woman leader in our nationalist movement. Evidence of her fierce patriotism was manifest from her youth on many occasions. She had also a great pride in being a Bengali. As a child, she would opt to go to a Bengal circus rather than a European one, and in her entrance examination she wrote an essay arguing against the prescribed text, a piece by Macaulay condemning the Bengali character.[26]

Sarala's nationalism became accentuated with time. To begin with, its public demonstration took the form of music. She made her first political appearance during the Congress session in Calcutta. A national exhibition was inaugurated on 24 December 1901 by Maharaja Manindra Chandra Nandi, where Sarala led the chorus with the deeply stirring song composed by Atulprasad Sen, 'Utho Go Bharatalakshmi' (Arise, Mother India). Two days later, she sang at the inaugural Congress session. Sarala was exceptionally gifted musically, and composed and set to music a number of nationalistic songs.[27] She converted a few of Tagore's songs into Western pieces for the piano or for a band. Collecting songs with lyrics and tunes from various people like boatmen, *bauls*, and others was a passion with Sarala. She would take them to her uncle, who used them in his songs. Sarala claimed that 'Amar Sonar Bangla', now the national anthem of Bangladesh, was one such creation.[28] It is not generally known that while Rabindranath Tagore created the tune of the first two lines of Bankim Chandra Chattopadhyay's nationalist song 'Bande Mataram', the rest was set to music by Sarala Devi. She sang this inspiring song in the Banaras session of the Congress in 1905, and contributed in no small measure to its nationwide popularity and its later status as a national song.[29]

Sarala's signal contribution, however, lay in the encouragement of a martial, heroic culture in Bengal that would serve the nationalist cause. For this purpose she formed youth groups. She was aware of the prevailing views about the 'effeminate' and 'physically weak' Bengalis,[30] and felt shamed by the stigma of cowardice attached to the Bengali community: it was necessary to correct that. She believed that improvement in the health and physique of the youth was an essential step for the success of the freedom movement. Physical prowess had to be developed and mental strength simultaneously cultivated. Since 1895, through her writings in *Bharati*, she tried to inspire the Bengali youth with heroic ideas. Her essays like 'Byayamcharcha' (The Utility of Physical Exercise) and 'Bilati Ghusi Banam Deshi Kil' (The Conflict of Might Between the East and the West) were designed to attract young people to cultivate physical prowess. Through these essays she put forward three contentions. First, one must not be afraid to die, for this life was for courage, for adventure, and for service to others. Secondly, the most important component of a fearless, worthy life was a healthy and strong body. The mind and the body were closely connected. Regular exercise was, therefore, a necessity. Thirdly, if and when insulted by the British, one should take action oneself and immediately, without waiting to go to a court of law. Later, she formed an *akhra* (club) and a *byayam samiti* (gymnasium) which also served as linkages with *biplabi*s (revolutionaries). Her clubs were not secret organizations, but the members were asked not to talk about them, which in practical terms meant almost the same thing. She used to place a map of India before them and tied a *rakhi* (red thread symbolizing brotherhood) on their wrists, and made them promise that they would serve India with their entire body and mind.[31] She appointed Professor Murtaza, a Muslim *ustad* (master) to teach the boys of the club boxing, sword-fighting, games with knives and rods, in the backyard of her house.[32] Sarala herself used to be present and maintain an attendance register. Members from other clubs of Calcutta and from the Anushilan Samiti, a secret revolutionary organization of Dhaka, also came to the club and participated.

With a view to inspiring the youth of Bengal with ideals of heroism, Sarala Devi in 1902 inaugurated the Birashtami Utsav (Festival of Heroes) on the *ashtami* or the second day of the four-day celebration of Durga Puja (Worship of Durga). Along with members of her own akhra, she invited members of other clubs to observe the occasion with fitting homage to the country's past heroes. They were to gather around a sword and chant a poem composed by Ashutosh Ghosh which contained the names of a number of heroic men, starting with Krishna. As each name was pronounced, the participants were to shower the sword with flowers. After the ritual was over, there were demonstrations of various forms of physical training and competitive games. Interestingly, the prizes for the winners of these competitions were awarded by a Muslim woman, the wife of Sujatali Beg.[33] *New India* commented on 30 October 1902 that Birashtami, a movement started by Sarala Devi, would lead to the institution of a national sporting day. Such displays of prowess and skill were necessary. 'It is a peculiarity of the British character to respect only those who are able to beat them down in any fair competition.' The function attracted widespread attention. The *Bengalee* reported on 31 march 1903, 'Babu Baikantha Nath Sen of Berhampore has taken up Miss Sarala Ghosal's suggestion about the Olympic games and is organizing a display of national sports such as swordplay, *lathi khela* (playing with rods), wrestling, etc., in connection with the ensuing [Bengal Provincial] conference'. The games were actually conducted under the guidance of Murtaza, sent to Berhampore at Sarala Devi's instance.[34]

Happy with the success of this experiment, Sarala Devi planned to introduce celebrations in the memory of national heroes. Meantime, Sakharam Ganesh Deuskar had started in Calcutta the Shivaji Utsav (celebration for Shivaji) instituted by Tilak in Maharashtra. Sarala Devi followed the example and initiated Pratapaditya Utsav in May 1903. A number of young men from Bhowanipore, Kalighat, and Baghbazar participated in it. Sarala read an essay entitled 'Bangalir Pitridhan' (The Heritage of the Bengalees). She contended that while the Rajputs, the Marathas, and the Sikhs were recognized as the heroic people of India, Bengalis were denied the memory of their heritage, and consequently they lacked a sense of pride. Yet Bengal had produced brave heroes. Pratapaditya, the last independent Bengali Hindu zamindar of Jessore, had 'kept all the

Muslims of Bengal loyal to him', defeated the King of Orissa, ventured to resist Mughal arms, and met the challenge from the Portuguese pirates. The Bengalis neeeded to cherish this heritage and develop national pride and confidence.[35] Sarala's purpose clearly was to inspire the youth of Bengal with the legacy of the heroism of their own Bengali leader. The celebration had an immediate impact. In the popular theatre hall, The Star, the play entitled 'Banger Pratapaditya' was enacted amidst great public acclaim.

Aware of the popularity of such an initiative, Sarala Devi went on to invent another festival, Udayaditya Utsav, named after Udayaditya who, she maintained, had been 'the heroic son of Mother Bengal, but neglected in history'. A young prince of Jessore, he had repeatedly fought bravely against the Mughal army and died in the field of battle. In commemoration of him, Sarala wrote in *Bharati*, 'Please, Mother, we beg you, give us your milk mixed with blood to feed our valour. We need to grow up as a healthy, strong, well-developed nation'.[36] This was the keynote of Sarala's lifelong message. She advocated for her countrymen and women the cultivation of bravery, strength, and mental prowess. The *Bengalee* had published a notice about the Utsav on 20 September 1903: 'Udayaditya Utsav—to commemorate the death of Prince Udayaditya of Jessore, who at the age of nineteen died bravely fighting for his country, a meeting will be held at the Albert Hall today at 4:30 p.m. There will be songs and addresses'.[37] The weekly also published an English translation of Sarala Devi's article 'Kumar Udayaditya', which had appeared in *Bharati*,[38] indicating the paper's appreciation of Sarala's endeavours.

These celebrations, however, created something of a rift between Sarala and her uncle Rabindranath. Rabindranath refused to accept Pratapaditya as the model of a hero, as his virtues did not include a personal nobility. Tagore had portrayed him in a rather uncomplimentary role in his novel *Bauthakuranir Haat* (1882). Sarala contended that a political leader had to be judged politically. A man, who though a small zamindar, had the courage to defy the powerful Mughal Emperor Akbar and declare independence from him, was certainly worthy of being recognized as a heroic personality.[39] Be that as it may, a difference of opinion between an uncle and his niece was, after all, a family matter. Historically speaking, Sarala here made the same mistake as other Swadeshi leaders, who appealed only to Hindu heritage. Had she turned to Akbar, the greatest Mughal emperor, or Mir Qasim, the Bengali Muslim nawab who fought against the British East India Company, instead of making heroes of Pratapaditya or Udayaditya, she might have also succeeded in reaching out to the Muslim youth.[40] Sarala made no such effort, but continued to work with enormous courage and fortitude within a limited framework. It is interesting that at a time when women were fighting for the right to vote in free England, a woman in colonial Bengal was struggling to initiate the *men* of her country into an ideology of courage and prowess.

What was the significance of Sarala's projects? Two points need to be highlighted. First, by propagating Bengali heroes as role models for Bengali boys, she was promoting a special brand of nationalism: Bengali Hindu nationalism. Second, and more important, hers were no ordinary clubs of exercise or physical activities. Sarala was actually preparing the youth for an armed struggle with the colonial rulers. Unlike her parents, Sarala was not a supporter of the Congress variety of politics during the first part of her political life. For her, the organization lacked energy and initiative, and was unable to play a leadership role. In 1905, she wrote somewhat condescendingly,

All major movements are the outcome of the common people's efforts. Newspapers initiate intense debates about issues, and later only the pith of discussions that follow find a place in the official resolutions of the Congress. The Congress has never participated in any agitational programmes; this has been left entirely to the general public. The Congress has no record of leading any successful campaign where the efforts of common people had failed. This is but natural. The Congress has a session for a duration of three days only each year, and the deliberations during these three days to consider the year's activities are condensed into a resolution. The Congress comes alive only during these three days—like our Durga Puja in autumn![41]

Sarala's sympathy lay with the revolutionary philosophy. It would not be wrong to describe her as the first woman of Bengal to get involved in the *biplabi* (revolutionary) movement, for even before the emergence of the movement in Bengal, she took the initiative to prepare the stage. Her attempts to infuse the youth with courage and physical prowess, develop youth power and invent *utsav*s (festivals) were but part of her endeavour to contribute to the freedom of the country through armed revolt. Others followed the example of the club she had established at her residence, and soon many such clubs were founded in and around Calcutta. The revolutionary organizations formed in succeeding years originally developed in most cases out of these clubs for physical culture. For example, Pulin Das met Sarala Devi in connection with her centre for physical culture, and with her assistance and encouragement, started a similar centre in Dhaka from which developed the Dhaka Anushilan Samiti. Other clubs also received financial and material assistance from her. Early in 1902, when Jatindranath Banerjee came to Calcutta to establish secret societies in order to organize a revolutionary movement in Calcutta, he sought Sarala Devi's assistance. Sarala Devi helped him and both of them worked together till Jatindranath left politics in 1904.[42] She maintained a close link with the Suhrid Samiti, founded in 1900 at Mymensingh, a secret revolutionary society which drew much support from her even after her marriage.[43] Sarala was a leader; many a man followed her, but women did not join the *biplabi samiti*s at that time, although a few of them helped the cause by providing food and shelter to the revolutionaries who had gone underground.[44] To Sarala, the central issue of concern was anti-colonialism. She was also aware of international politics, and placed the whole question of colonialism in India against a larger canvas. She wrote:

> And then there is yet another issue which concerns not just India alone. We are not simply Indians, we are also 'natives'. The Japanese are also 'natives', the Chinese are 'natives', so are the Siamese, the Mongolians, the Turks, the Persians, the Afghans. Therefore, we Indians are a part of the pan-Asian community and are equally contemptible with all other Asians. The battle is not between India and her neighbours but between the so-called 'natives' and the community of Europeans, between the orient and the occident.[45]

It is important to note that Sarala never lost sight of this unequal battle. Her entire perception of social and political configurations as well as her understanding of gender were influenced by this philosophy.

## Marriage and politics after marriage

Sarala married late, in 1905, when she was 33. The spouse was a well-known nationalist in Punjab, Rambhuj Dutta Chaudhury, a lawyer-cum-journalist and a political activist who belonged to the Arya Samaj. Rambhuj had been married before to a north Indian woman who had died, leaving children. The marriage took place somewhat suddenly. Sarala had gone to visit Mayavati Ashram in the Himalaya when she was called back to visit her mother (who, she was told, was seriously ill) at a small town called Deoghar. She arrived only to find that her marriage had been arranged and all preparations for a wedding had been made. If she did attempt to resist parental pressure, she was unsuccessful. Her own choices for marriage had fallen through and the family, especially her mother, felt that it was high time for a Bengali woman to get married, and that the family honour was at stake.[46] This was perhaps not fair to Sarala. Sarala had often challenged traditional norms, but in this crucial area of her life, marriage, she had to bow to her parents' wishes. Her 'hands and feet were tied—there was no space for any movement'. She married Rambhuj and went with him to Punjab. Was it a happy union for Sarala, this marriage under family pressure to an elderly widower whom she had not known, and who took her away from Bengal? There is no evidence to indicate whether or not hers was a happy marriage. She ends her fascinating autobiography before relating the story of her life after marriage, which makes one feel that perhaps she did not wish to highlight it. However, she carried on political activities in the Punjab, in cooperation with her husband, and helped him in editing the powerful nationalist Urdu weekly newspaper, *Hindusthan*. Here, too, she displayed characteristic courage. When the colonial government decided to cancel the licence of the paper if Rambhuj remained the proprietor, Sarala stepped in and registered her name as the proprietor and editor. She published an English edition of the paper too.[47]

Sarala spent about eighteen years in the Punjab, participating in major anti-colonial programmes. When the Rowlatt Act was passed and nationwide agitation broke out against it, the government policy of repression reached its height in the Punjab leading to the Jallianwalla Bagh massacre. Sarala and her husband adopted a brave anti-British stand through their paper. Consequently, the government ordered the closure of both the Urdu and English editions of *Hindusthan*, and confiscated the press. Rambhuj was arrested. The arrest of Sarala too was planned, but discarded because the arrest of a woman might lead to fresh political complications. When Mahatma Gandhi came to Lahore after the Jallianwalla massacre, he was Sarala's house guest, and thus began a close friendship between them. In 1919, just before the Amritsar session of the Indian National Congress, Rambhuj was released. Sarala became a follower of Gandhi, and supported the non-cooperation movement, which caused a difference of political opinion with her husband who did not agree with the principle of non-violence. Thus a biplabi became a Gandhian and helped in the spread of Gandhi's *khadi* movement. Sarala's only son Dipak married Gandhi's granddaughter Radha.

*Literary activities*

Sarala wrote and spoke extensively. Her articles were published in *Suprabhat* (1907), *Banglar Katha* (1921), but most of all in *Bharati*. She wrote on a wide variety of issues, from politics to history, travel, international affairs, and music. The pieces are a testimony to her wide knowledge and keen intellect. She wrote her autobiography, *Jibaner Jharapata* (Fallen Leaves from the Tree of Life), which sheds light on her life as well as on contemporary society. Sarala took over the editorship of *Bharati* from her mother and edited it jointly with her sister for two years from 1302 BS to 1304 BS (1895–97). She also edited it alone from 1306 BS to 1314 BS (1899–1907) and finally from 1331 BS to 1333 BS (1924–26). Her purpose was to propagate nationalism as well as to elevate the literary standard of the journal.[48] As the editor of *Bharati*, Sarala was able to introduce a new strain to the journal: the spirit of nationalism. 'During the countrywide freedom movement, the rousing trumpet call in *Bharati*'s pages was as fiery as it was impassioned'.[49] In order to make it a journal representing the intelligentsia of Bengal, she decided not to confine it to the writers of the Tagore family only, and invited good contributions from outside. That is how 'Barodidi' (The Elder Sister), written by Sarat Chandra Chattopadhyay (1876–1938), was first published in *Bharati*.[50] She herself wrote numerous articles and contributed to the excellence of the journal. It was in the course of her editorship of *Bharati* that she came into contact with Swami Vivekananda (1863–1902) and Sister Nivedita (1867–1911). The translation of Nivedita's two essays on the duties and responsibilities of a good mother and of Ranade's piece on the Indian social system and Gandhi's article on South Africa enriched *Bharati*.

## Women's organization and women's education

Sarala Devi was a great leader of women. She had started the Lakshmir Bhandar (The Indian Store for Indian Women) on 7, Cornwallis Street with a view to popularizing indigenous goods, especially those made by women. The initial objective was to sell the handicrafts made at Bidhaba Shilpashram founded by her sister. Kedarnath Das Gupta (1878–1942) of Chittagong supervised the store for many years. The idea was that women would start using *swadeshi* products and introduce them to the family. Sarala herself used rough indigenous yellow paper for the jacket of *Bharati*. During the session of the Congress in Bombay, a national exhibition of swadeshi goods was organized to which Sarala sent some specimens from Lakshmir Bhandar, and won a medal. Sarala also worked for the spread of education among women and improvement of their condition. In Punjab, she established small centres for educating women and tried to persuade women to attend functions organized by the Arya Samaj. When back in Bengal, she established a girls' school called Siksha Sadan in 1930 in Calcutta. To Sarala belongs the credit of making what may be regarded as the earliest articulation of nascent feminist views in India. While working among women in the Punjab, she developed the idea of networking among women. In 1910, she founded the Bharat Stree Mahamandal (The Great Circle of Indian Women), the first ever all Indian women's organization born even before the inception of the All India Women's Conference in 1927.[51]

## Later life

Sarala returned to Bengal after the death of her husband in 1923, and devoted herself to the editorship of *Bharati* for the next three years, and to educational activities. She however retired from public life in 1935, and turned to religion. Although in her early life she had come into close contact with the Theosophical Society, and was later influenced by Vivekananda, she accepted Bijoykrishna Goswami as her guru and spent the last few years of her life in pursuit of religion. This confirms, and a number of her articles on the Himalaya and the Himalayan ashrams indicate,[52] that she had always had religious leanings, and had been drawn to Hindu religious discourse.

## Rokeya Sakhawat Hossain

### Family

Begum Rokeya had a totally different life from Sarala, not at all as glamorous, and not in the limelight before she started working for her school which brought her fully into the public arena. Like Sarala, she came from a well-to-do and well-known family, but there the similarity ends. Unlike Sarala, she had a stiflingly restrictive childhood.

Rokeya's father, Zahiruddin Muhammad Abu Ali Saber (?–1913), was

Rokeya Sakhawat Hossain

the landlord of Pairaband, a village in district Rangpur in northern Bengal, now in Bangladesh, and belonged to the upper caste Muslim Saber family. His ancestor, Babur Ali Abul Babur Saber Tiberji, had come to India in search of fortune from Tabriz in Iran. He had gone first to Bihar, and then settled in Pairaband in 1853. How the family acquired the zamindari is not known. Zahiruddin was the last one in the family to own land. He had inherited the huge property from his ancestors, but lost it because of his self-indulgence and profligacy, and indeed spent his last days in poverty. He had four wives, one of them a European. One of the wives was childless, the other three had between them nine sons and six daughters. Zahiruddin was a learned gentleman, at home in Arabic, Persian and Urdu as well as English, but was as superstitious as he was orthodox.[53]

Rokeya's mother, Rahatunnessa Sabera Chaudhurani, was the first wife of Zahiruddin Saber. She came from a distinguished family and was the daughter of Hossainuddin Chaudhury, a landlord in Dhaka. Unfortunately, nothing much is known about her. Even Shamsunnahar Mahmud (1908–64), and Motahar Hossain Sufi, the two most reputed biographers of Rokeya, omit her mother almost completely from their accounts.[54] She had two sons and three daughters of her own: each was highly talented. One can only conjecture that this woman, who gave birth to outstanding children, must have been in her quiet way quite out of the ordinary, although she left no tangible proof of this. In any case, she had no scope for exposure or expression or self-development, totally confined to the home as she was, and perhaps, one imagines, suppressed. Did Rokeya, too, think so? There is no way of telling, except that she dedicated her work *Abarodhbasini* (Women in Confinement) to her mother, an *abarodhbasini* herself.

The eldest of Rahatunnessa's children, Abul Asad Ibrahim Saber was, unlike his father, a 'progressive' man. He studied at St Xavier's College in Calcutta, and also came in touch with Dr K.D. Ghosh, the father of Aurobindo Ghosh (1872–1950), when he was posted as Civil Surgeon at Rangpur. Ibrahim Saber favoured the introduction and spread of English education among the Muslims and supported the pro-Western policy of Sir Syed Ahmed (1817–1898) and Syed Amir Ali (1849–1928), the two Muslim leaders who were pioneers in 'modernizing' Muslim education. Ibrahim believed that Muslim women needed to be educated, and taught both his sisters to read and write, a gift they gratefully acknowledged. Ibrahim joined the civil service under the British and became a Deputy Magistrate. Therefore, from the class of traditional zamindars, he joined the ranks of professionals and bureaucrats, the group that formed the backbone of the new middle class, both amongst Hindus and Muslims. Though not as famous as Amir Ali, Ibrahim had played an important role in the process of 'modernization' of the Muslim community in Bengal at a time when the community had chosen to remain aloof from the impact of 'modernization' through English education. Ibrahim's son, Iman Saber, died early and his daughter, Fatima, was married off. Fatima's son, Dr Ghulam Wahib Chaudhury, became a professor at Dhaka University. Ibrahim's younger brother, Khalilur Rahman Abu Jaigam Saber, was also educated at St Xavier's College, Calcutta, and was exposed to the influence of Western education. He became an Honorary Magistrate and lived in Dhaka.[55]

Rokeya's elder sister, Karimunnessa (1855–1926) was according to age-old custom, taught the Koran Sharif by rote like a parrot and nothing else. That was not however enough to quench her thirst for knowledge. Her younger brothers were tutored in the Persian language, and they repeated what they had learnt to their sister sitting at home. Young Karimunnessa avidly committed to memory what she heard. She picked up Bengali too by listening to her brothers doing their lessons. She learnt to write Bengali by scratching on the ground in the backyard of their house. When this offence of reading and writing was discovered, she was quickly married off in 1889 at the age of fourteen. Her husband, Abdul Hafiz Gazhnavi, belonged to the aristocratic zamindar family of Delduar in Mymensingh in eastern Bengal (now in Bangladesh). Karimunnessa continued her studies at home after marriage, and became proficient in Bengali and learned Arabic, Persian, and also some English. It was, however, Bengali she preferred over all other languages. Her incentive to learn Arabic, which she took up at the age of 67, emanated from the desire to understand the Koran. 'I am not satisfied to recite the Koran like a parrot,' she wrote to Rokeya, 'That is why I am learning Arabic'. A patron of learning, she offered generous financial assistance to Abdul Hamid Khan Yusufzai (1845–1910) to run the fortnightly journal *Ahmadi* (first published in 1886). This journal earned the reputation of being a secular publication, and aimed at fostering Hindu–Muslim unity. Karimunnessa herself wrote poems and essays. Rokeya, who was very close to her, and kept in touch with her through letters in Bengali, wrote a piece entitled 'Lukano Ratan' (The Hidden Jewel), in which she said that Karimunnessa composed many poems on domestic issues, but unfortunately none saw the light of day. 'Had her community not rigidly suppressed her talent, she could have shone as a bright star.'[56] Nine years after her marriage, Karimunnessa was widowed with two sons. She braved the criticism from the conservative section of society, and sent them to study at St Xavier's College in Calcutta. Her elder son, Abdul Karim Gazhnavi (1872–1938) went to England for higher studies. He was a highly respected man of his time and later became a member of the Legislative Assembly and of the Council of Ministers in Bengal. His younger brother, Abdul Halim Gazhnavi, was also a supporter of the new ideas emerging among the middle class Muslims.[57] Rokeya's younger sister, Homyera (?–1962), was married to the reputed writer and social worker, Amir Hossain Chaudhury. A patron of culture, he founded the International Nazrul Forum. Homyera dedicated much of her time to social work and to the school which Rokeya later founded. After Rokeya's death, she became the superintendent of the ladies' hostel of Lady Brabourne College. Her only son, Amir Hossain Chowdhury (1909–64) was an industrialist and a writer.[58]

It is significant that Rokeya's immediate family was educated in English, and that too in St Xavier's College, the premier English-medium institution in Bengal where British ideas and the influence of Western education predominated. All the important members of the family thus chose to be 'Westernized' to some extent, while retaining basic Muslim customs. This was Rokeya's familial background. She, too, was privileged in being born in a family where her siblings welcomed modernization and, despite the orthodoxy of their father, marched in advance of most people of their time.

### Childhood—the burden of abarodh

Rokeya's childhood was not as happy as it might have been. The family had a sprawling house. Says Rokeya, 'We were well-to-do. We used to eat well and dress well, decked up with ornaments. Our house, surrounded by deep woods had few equals. In the midst of three and a half *bigha*s of land stood only our huge house.'[59] It was not however for the likes of Rokeya, that is the women of the household, to enjoy the home and its surroundings. Zahiruddin Saber was a diehard conservative, and he imposed strict *abarodh* on the women of the family, believing this was in tune with their status. Not only were men not allowed free entry into the *andarmahal* (inner quarters of the house), but girls had to conceal themselves even from women. Rokeya recalls,

From the age of five, I had to observe purdah even before ladies who were not family members ... . If suddenly some ladies from the neighbourhood came calling, someone at home would give me a warning and I would run helter-skelter as if I was in mortal fear of my life. I would go and hide myself ... sometime in the kitchen behind a large wicker basket ... sometime inside a grass mat kept rolled up by a maidservant ... some other time under a bed.[60]

The village of Pairaband was a backward place and had little contact with Rangpur, the nearest town. The people in the locality, as Rokeya's memoirs indicate, were uneducated and superstitious, blindly following outdated customs. It may not be fair to conclude that every girl in a Muslim family suffered such a plight, although those who belonged to orthodox families were subjected to rigorous rules and customs. Rokeya recounts the stories of her childhood with great bitterness. She suffered as any child would have under the circumstances, but in her it created a resentment that lasted all her life and generated her most resolute opposition to the system. Rokeya tells us,

> Once while we were in residence in Calcutta and I was about five years of age, two maid servants came to visit my sister-in-law, wife of my second brother (stepbrother) from her home in Bihar. Those two maid-servants appeared to have unrestricted freedom to move at will anywhere and everywhere in our house. Poor me, I had to run away like a scared young fawn to hide myself from them—be it behind a door or under a table. There was an attic, hardly used, on the second floor of the house, and very early each morning I was taken there by my ayah, where I passed the whole day, often unfed and hungry. The maid-servants from Bihar, after thoroughly exploring the whole house, tumbled on to the existence of the attic. Halu, a nephew and almost of the same age as mine, rushed to tell me of this dreadful discovery. Fortunately there was a bed in that room, and I quickly slipped under it, scared even to breathe in case those heartless women suspiciously looked under the bed! There were a few empty steel trunks, wickerwork chairs and the like, which poor Halu, with all the strength of a six-year-old, tried to arrange around me. Hardly anyone bothered to ask if I had any food or drink. Occasionally when Halu arrived there during the course of his games, I would ask him to get me some food and drink. He would sometimes fetch me a glass of water, maybe some puffed rice, but very often he would forget. After all, he was just a child. I had to spend four days in that attic in such distressful condition.[61]

## Education

Rokeya, obviously, could not go to school. Her father was ambitious for his two sons and desired both of them to learn Arabic, Persian, Urdu, and English in order to get on in life. For his daughters his rules were radically different. They were not to have careers for themselves, but were to grow up as ideal women products of a highly élitist background. At home, as mentioned earlier, Karimunnessa learned from her brothers. Rokeya, too, was secretly taught by her brother, Ibrahim Saber, to whom in grateful remembrance she dedicated her novel, *Padmarag*.

> Ever since my childhood, I have been overwhelmed by your love and affection for me. It is you who moulded me singlehandedly. I have little or no idea how good a teacher one's parents or one's spiritual instructor can be, but for me, I know that you have been my only instructor.[62]

Other relatives who came to know about the efforts of the brother and sister taunted them, and tried to obstruct them, but neither she nor her brother paid any heed to them. Shamsunnahar Mahmud writes,

> Their father was utterly opposed to her learning Bengali or English. There was hardly any opportunity for her to study during the day. So the brother and the sister

would wait eagerly for nightfall. After dinner, when their father had gone to bed, the two of them would sit down with their books. In the depth of night, with the world plunged into darkness, a faint light would flicker in their room. The two of them would commence their lessons in candlelight in the silence of the night. The brother was the teacher, and his sister his earnest pupil, drinking deep at the fountain of knowledge.[63]

Ibrahim also taught Rokeya some English. He used to show her books with beautiful pictures and tell her, 'If you can learn English, the doors of the world will be wide open to you'.[64] Rokeya learnt some English, but concentrated on Bengali. She got assistance in her Bengali lessons from Karimunnessa before the latter's marriage, and later, letters to her sister kept her knowledge of Bengali alive. Rokeya, in grateful acknowledgment dedicated the second volume of her book *Motichoor* to her.

When I was very young, it was only because of your caring concern that I was introduced to *Varnaparichay* [a Bengali primer] so that I could learn to read and write the Bengali language. A large number of our relations was opposed to my learning Bengali, though they were not against Urdu or Persian. You were the only one who lent consistent support to my efforts to learn Bengali. In fact, I recall you were afraid that after my marriage I might totally forget my Bengali. I consider it a sign of your favour and grace that even after living in Bhagalpur for fourteen years after my marriage where I did not know a single soul with whom to speak in Bengali, my knowledge of Bengali did not rust.[65]

Of course, the relative most opposed to Rokeya's learning Bengali was her own father. His disapproval of Bengali has to be seen against the backdrop of contemporary Muslim élitism. Urdu had become the lingua franca of élite Muslims, and in Muslim-dominated schools the medium of instruction was mostly Urdu. Although in Bengal, the majority of the common Muslim population spoke Bengali, this was not considered appropriate for the culture of high Muslim society to which the Saber family belonged.

## Marriage

Unlike Sarala, Rokeya was married early, in 1896, to Syed Sakhawat Hossain (1858–1909), a civil servant from Bihar, a widower with a daughter. Ibrahim Saber, who knew Syed and judged that the man would appreciate his sister's talent, arranged the marriage. Sakhawat Hossain, a native of Bhagalpur in Bihar, was an educated man and a liberal in his views. He had for some years studied in Hooghly College in Bengal. A glimpse of his character is provided by one of his class mates. Sakhawat had told him:

I do not know anybody here. I am a poor Muslim from Bihar. Here the tuition fee for the college is only one rupee, while in Patna it is six rupees. So I have come here because I will be able to send the five extra rupees to my mother at home ... You should be able to speak Hindi. I also want to learn Bengali. I will feel ashamed if having come to Bengal, I do not learn to speak it. Perhaps I will not be able to read fluently, but through conversations with you I shall acquire some knowledge about Bengali literature.[66]

Sakhawat went to England with a government scholarship to study agriculture and joined the civil service. He had married the first time into a relation's family out of respect for his mother's wishes, but his wife had died leaving behind a daughter. Rokeya was his second wife. His family were Urdu speakers, but Sakhawat encouraged her to socialize with educated Hindu and Christian women in Bhagalpur. Rokeya taught him Bengali, which he had wanted to learn , and he taught her English on which Rokeya was keen. Sakhawat believed in the need for women's education and gave full support to Rokeya in her pursuit of learning as well as in her literary activities. Ghulam Murshid, in a recent book, says that Sakhawat had imbibed his ideas on women's liberation from the West, and that he had found in Rokeya an enthusiastic disciple and passed on his ideas of women's 'liberation' to her.[67] Perhaps Rokeya's indebtedness to Sakhawat has been exaggerated. Rokeya spoke about him respectfully, and named the school that she founded with her husband's money after his death Sakhawat Memorial School. However, she dedicated two of her works, *Motichoor* and *Padmarag*, to her brother and sister, clearly indicating where she thought her debts lay. She dedicated *Abarodhbasini* to her mother and hardly mentioned Sakhawat Hossain in her writings. Perhaps author Shamsul Alam is right in presuming that Rokeya avoided the subject deliberately and that her silence was a 'significant' indicator of 'her indifference'.[68] This is confirmed by one of her own letters:

As a child, I did not get affection from my father, as a wife I only nursed my husband during his illness, every day examined his urine, cooked his diet and reported to the physician. I became a mother twice, but could not fulfil my desire of parenting. One child died at the age of five months, the other at four months.[69]

Happiness to Rokeya hardly came from her family, apart from love of her siblings, and her work outside her home brought her only the prospect of struggle.

*Literary activities*

Rokeya's first publication, an article entitled 'Pipasha' (the thirst), appeared in 1902 in the journal *Nabaprabha* (first published 1901), edited by Gyanendralal Ray. Next appeared one of the most radical articles, 'Alankar na Badge of Slavery' (Jewellery, or Badge of Slavery?) in *Mahila* edited by Girish Chandra Sen, in 1903. This was followed by a number of articles in *Nabanoor* (first published in 1903), *Masik Mohammadi* (first published 1903), and *Saogat* (first published 1918). She mostly published in *Nabanoor*, a progressive paper, which urged men and women alike to contribute articles. It was during the early years of her marriage that she wrote an outstanding, almost revolutionary, piece, 'Sultana's Dream', in English (later translated by her into Bengali), which made its first appearance in the *Indian Ladies' Magazine* in 1905. This was a feminist utopian fantasy, and describes a society in an imaginary land, Ladyland, where women rule and men are kept at home. Women have brains, men do the menial work; women are free and roam about independently in the streets; men stay in the *mardana* (men's quarters) as opposed to *zenana*; women order, men obey. Under women, truth, love, compassion, and welfare are the guiding principles of governance. This remarkable piece, though written in the form of a satirical fantasy, gives us a clear indication of Rokeya's attitude towards patriarchy, her resentment against the many unfair restrictions on women, and her dream of transforming society into a more egalitarian order. She brought out several books: *Motichoor*, two volumes (1904 and 1922), *Sultana's Dream* (1908), *Padmarag* (1924), and *Abarodhbasini* (1931).[70]

The principal characteristic of Rokeya's compositions was sarcasm and her primary theme was protest against the degenerate anti-women customs of her community. She wrote in Bengali, and her writings aimed to articulate her views on the condition of Muslim women, and to make them aware of their life-situations. There was a literary flowering in Bengal at that time. Among the Muslim authors, Mir Musharraf Hossain (1847–1911), Ismail Hossain Shirazi (1880–1931), Kazi Imdadul Huq (1882–1926), Abdul Karim (1869–1953), Kaikobad (1858–1952), and Nausher Ali Khan Yusufzai (1864–1924) wrote regularly in well-known papers/journals, such as *Islam Pracharak* (first published 1900), *Mihir o Sudhakar* (first published 1889), *Nabanoor* and *Kohinoor* (first published 1898), and wrote a number of good books. Rokeya, too, received during her lifetime recognition as a leading author.[71] Her literary talent, her contributions to Bengali literature, her simple and penetrating style of writing have been discussed in recent researches, but they fall outside the scope of this work. The subject matter of her writings does however constitute one of the chief sources of our discourse.

*Political involvement*

Rokeya was not a political activist in the nationalist movement. To Rokeya, the politics of gender demanded greater attention than the politics of colonialism. To her, the battle against gender subjection was more crucial than that against colonial subjection; the former was far older and more deep-rooted than the latter, although the latter appeared to be the key issue before her contemporaries. To eradicate the former was her life's ambition, and she fought her battle, as we will see, through her books. Her books constituted her action, and in that sense she was a political activist.

Unlike Sarala, Rokeya played no active role in the Swadeshi movement, or the latter-day freedom movement. The nationalism that developed during the Swadeshi movement had strong Hindu overtones. The Hindu concept of motherland as the mother God was popularized, as the movement was spearheaded by the Hindu middle class, and naturally this failed to appeal to the Muslim community. The revolutionary clubs did not help to bridge the gap either. The biplabis were recruited exclusively from the Hindu middle class. Perhaps they saw that the British government 'was using the Muslims against India's political struggle and that the Muslims were playing the Government's game. The result was that the Hindus of Bengal began to feel that the Muslims as such were against political freedom and against the Hindu community.'[72] Under the circumstances, there grew a mutual distrust between the two communities. The Muslim League was born in 1907 and supported the partition of Bengal. In the field of literature too some animosity often surfaced. There were however other voices too. Both *Kohinoor* and *Nabanoor* advocated unity between the Hindus and the Muslims.[73] *Nabanoor* published several articles at the time of the partition of Bengal explaining the need for united Hindu-Muslim agitation against the British. During the Swadeshi movement Hedayatulla warned people against the British policy of 'divide and rule'. Rokeya subscribed to this form of thinking:[74] She did not accept the point of view of the Muslim League, which had already been established and advocated a separate electorate for Muslims. It is not wrong to conclude from this evidence, some direct, some indirect, that Rokeya was not affected by the growing Hindu–Muslim tension in the political arena being artificially whipped up by many Muslims and Hindus at that time.

When in 1907 the Congress session broke up amidst discord, Rokeya wrote 'Muktiphal' (The Fruit of Freedom). The gist of the story is that freedom was being delayed because of differences of opinion among brothers. It was women who could serve the motherland without quarrelling and bring her freedom.[75] Again, she wrote a poem entitled 'Nirupama Bir' (A Hero Without Peer), obviously written on the occasion of the death of Kanailal, a biplabi during the Swadeshi period. Kanai was hanged to death by the British in 1908 for killing Naren Goswami (who had turned an approver) inside Alipore jail. Men and women of Bengal showed overwhelming regard for him by assembling in large numbers to have a last look at his body as it was carried in a funeral procession. They chanted 'Blessed is Kanai, and blessed is Kanai's mother'.[76] Rokeya, empathizing with these sentiments, says in her poem that the whole of Bengal was indebted to Kanai, and his name would be for ever remembered in India.[77] Her sympathy with the cause of nationalism certainly continued. In a piece entitled 'Baligarta', published in *Masik Mohammadi* in 1928, she ridicules orthodoxy, which in her view was nothing but a perversion of genuine Islamic principles. The piece, declared to be 'an absolutely true story', however, begins with evident respect for one Kamala*didi* (elder sister Kamala), who was 'a Congress worker, with the motto of popularizing *charkha* (the spinning wheel promoted by Gandhi), and *khaddar*' (khadi, also popularized by Gandhi). Zaheda Bibi, a character in the 'true' story, is criticized by her relations for associating with Kamala Devi, being educated, and wearing khaddar.[78] It is clear from the way the story was written that Rokeya's empathy lay with Zaheda Bibi, as opposed to the Bibi's relations. She also penned one interesting satirical piece entitled 'Appeal' (published in 1922, written against the backdrop of the non-cooperation movement). Some *bhadralok* collaborators of the Raj are annoyed with the Indian nationalist upsurge and unhappy at the prospect of losing their titles (like Rai Bahadur) awarded by the British Government. Rokeya's poem, purporting to be an appeal from these gentlemen not to strip them of their 'honorific titles', ridicules these gentlemen. Freely translated, a stanza would read:

> The dumb and silent have no foes
> That's how the saying goes
> All of us with titled tails
> Keep so quiet telling no tales
> Then comes a bolt from the blue
> Passes belief, but it's true
> All of you who did not speak
> Will lose your tails fast and quick
> Come my friends and declare now
> In a loud and loyal vow
> Listen, ye world, we are not
> God's truth, a seditious lot.[79]

Rokeya wrote, but she went no further, and did not actively ally with anti-colonial political struggle. She did however take an active part in one political episode, the struggle for votes for women. The organized political movement by women in this arena was formally initiated when a franchise delegation led by Sarojini Naidu, and including Margaret Cousins, Annie

Besant, Abala Basu, Dorothy Jinarajadesa, Uma Nehru, and Ramabai Ranade met the Secretary of State, Edwin Montague, and demanded equal franchise for women with men. Not that much came of it, but the effort continued in Bengal under the leadership of the Bangiya Nari Samaj (Association of Women in Bengal). Encouraged by the right to vote in the Calcutta Municipal election in 1923, a women's delegation met the Viceroy, Lord Lytton, to seek support to the cause of women's right to vote in all elections. Begum Rokeya was a member of the delegation which was led by Kamini Roy.[80]

## Women's organization and women's education

Rokeya's married life was cut short by the untimely death of her husband in 1909. After her widowhood, she was much harassed by her husband's daughter by his first marriage, and had to leave Bihar in 1910. She had, however, started a girls' school in Bhagalpur in Bihar with the money given to her by Sakhawat Hossain, and moved it to Bengal along with her, re-establishing it in 1911. This was the celebrated Sakhawat Memorial Girls' School, which she struggled hard to preserve, and which survives to this day as a living memorial to her. She founded the Anjuman-i-Khawatin-i-Islam, an organization of Muslim women in 1914, four years after Sarala's Bharat Stree Mahamandal.

## Later life

Rokeya, unlike Sarala, did not retire from active life. She died on 9 December 1932 while still serving her school. Her death came perhaps a trifle suddenly; a moving description is to be found in a letter from her cousin who was present at the time of her death. (The letter has been published by Moshfeka Khatun.)[81]

## SUMMARY AND OBSERVATIONS

Sarala and Rokeya thus shared many similar experiences, though their stories also diverged at certain crucial points. Sarala belonged to the Brahmo-Hindu community and came from a privileged background. While the Tagore household was thoroughly patriarchal in structure, Sarala does not seem to have suffered from many of the disadvantages that most of other middle class girls had to face. She enjoyed the cooperation of the family in her educational, cultural, and literary activities. Indeed, she was able to get a BA degree, experience paid employment, and interact with the intellectual giants of the time. While all these formed her character, the most compelling force in her life was the nationalist movement. She imbibed her nationalism from her parents, from her Tagore relations who were staunch supporters of the nationalist upsurge, and from her friends in educational institutions.[82] It was this nationalism that shaped her perspectives on gender.

Rokeya, on the other hand, knew financial comfort, but was denied the opportunity of formal schooling, not to mention gainful employment. She was largely self-made. Her brother and sister assisted in her education and encouraged her literary talent. Her husband, proud of her, also helped. However, what seems to have had paramount influence in shaping her thoughts was abarodh. Its negative impact was transformed in her case into a potent positive influence. The deep resentment, the sense of deprivation and humiliation, steeled her into becoming a fierce fighter. The injustice she suffered opened her eyes to the oppressive system that kept Muslim women subjugated, even though true Islam had not ordained such subjugation. Gifted with a keen intellect, she perceived the deeply ingrained flaws in the social customs and restrictions prescribed for women, and strove hard against them.

Their families and the familial environment influenced both women deeply. One might ask: were the two families which produced these two remarkable women unusual for their time? Indeed, both families were somewhat out of the ordinary. Sarala's celebrated family played a pioneering role in the history and culture of Bengal in more senses than one. Rokeya's family seems to have been on the other side of the scale, more conservative than others in its milieu. Although almost all contemporary aristocratic Muslim families abided by the custom of strict purdah, there is no evidence that they enforced abarodh in the way that Rokeya's father did.

The passion and work of both women then arose within their families, in interaction with the tumultuous environments. Rokeya's experiences led her to fiercely resist women's oppression, while Sarala's led her to be part of the huge wave of nationalist activism. In the early part of her life, up to the first decade of the twentieth century, Sarala concentrated primarily on anti-colonialism. It was during the second decade of the century that she turned to the gender issues, while never losing sight of the freedom movement. For Rokeya, the centrality of gender issues transcended other concerns throughout her life. Yet, on the cause of women, the two firebrands of Bengal had a strong commonality. Both acutely felt that the position of women in Bengal, whether Hindu or Muslim, was intolerable. They also shared the view that the most effective recipe for improving women's lives was education and building women's organizations.

## 2. The Age and its Women

Why did Sarala and Rokeya ask the questions they did? What were the factors that prompted them to undertake the work to which they devoted so much of their energy and attention? What was the condition of women, Hindu and Muslim, at the time?

### Hindu Women

The majority of Hindu women lived in an unenviable position at the threshold of the nineteenth century.[1] Highly complex and manifold age-old social and religious customs prescribed differential power and status for men and women. Sons were integral parts of the patrilineal family system, while daughters were married off to another family and considered *parer dhan* (someone else's property). 'Why is a daughter so undesirable?' queried poet Kamini Roy, and answered herself, 'Because she is a liability to her parents. A son is likely to look after his parents in their advanced years. A married daughter is unable to do so. She belongs to another family, and all her time and energy is devoted to that family'.[2] Marriage for women was an obligation and their fulfilment was deemed to lie in giving birth to a son for the husband's family. They were married off very early, and after marriage, they customarily entered their husband's families, which usually followed the joint family system. Middle class upper caste Hindu women were generally not permitted to earn their living by gainful employment, nor were they normally entitled to inherit their fathers' or husbands' property. Worse still, an army of religious texts imposed on them an ideology of domesticity and *pativratya* (physical and mental chastity). They had forfeited the right to formal education in the distant past when they had lost the right to ritual initiation or *upanayan* without which there was no formal education.[3] There must have been some exceptions in some families where generous men taught their female relatives, and there was a wealth of orally transmitted knowledge, but generally women had no access to institutional education. With time, women lost their social freedom too; a sharp cleavage between *sadar* or the public and *andar* or private spheres restricted their movements within the confines of the home.

While ensuring that women had no education, no opportunity for self-sufficiency, or even awareness of the injustice of discrimination, Hindu society permitted various avenues for men's sexual satisfaction through polygamy, concubinage, and prostitution. There was thus from ancient times dual standards of morality: a differential code of behaviour ordained for men and women. There were regional variations, some caste and community modifications, certain familial innovations, and a number of permitted or tolerated customs or acts of departure. By and large, however, the observations of Kailasbasini Devi (1837–1900) in her book, *Hindumahilaganer Hinabastha* (The Degraded Condition of Hindu Women, 1863) depicted the situation:

The birth of a boy is heralded with music; offerings are made to Brahmins; the poor are fed; many rites and rituals are observed; gifts are widely distributed, all in the hope and prayer for the boy's long life .... No such celebrations mark the birth of a daughter; on the contrary, much is said and done lamenting her arrival. Dear God! Are women such inferior creatures that their birth and death are treated in the same mournful manner? Such is the contemptible custom of our country, a custom that bewitches and blinds our people. Alas! When will our Bengal become a land of joy and happiness? When, oh when, will this despicable discrimination be eliminated?[4]

Kailasbasini was the first woman in nineteenth century Bengal to make such a passionate plea through the medium of the pen. A few others soon followed, although the thought of women's organized resistance against such inequality was inconceivable to them. However, some improvement was made in women's life-situations, not by women, but by men in the mid-nineteenth century.

## Social Reform and Women

Changes became visible, though very gradually, from the mid-nineteenth century. The colonial connection, and the contact with Western ideas through Western education, provided the major motivation for reform, spearheaded by the middle class. After 1818, the previous British policy of tolerance and non-interference in India's society was swamped by an increasingly interventionist policy shared alike by the Utilitarians, the Liberals, and the Evangelicals. Unlike the Orientalists, who in the eighteenth century had sung the glory of Indian civilization, the Utilitarians and Evangelicals attacked contemporary Indian society. The condition of Indian women constituted an integral part of their civilizational critique. James Mill announced:

The condition of women is one of the most remarkable circumstances in the manners of nations .... The history of uncultivated nations uniformly represents the women as in a state of abject slavery, from which they slowly emerge as civilization advances .... A state of dependence more strict and humiliating than that which is ordained for the weaker sex among the Hindus cannot be easily conceived.[5]

The construction of the 'women's question' was doubtless a strategy that was political in nature. It became a crucial tool for colonial ideology to establish and assert the moral superiority of the colonial rulers over the colonized. The Western challengers were distinctly at an advantage in the given situation of Bengal. Politically dominated, economically exploited, Bengal was also culturally bankrupt. The Sanskrit tradition had long lost its creative power; Vedic studies were almost forgotten; Nadia, the classic centre of Sanskrit learning in Bengal, was in a pitiable state. Bengali, the regional language, needed refinement,[6] and the low position of women was a harsh reality.

Forced into a defensive position, and desperate to create a new self-image, the educated Hindu middle class sought to justify their culture by projecting a 'glorious' Indian past, when they claimed that the position of women had been high. In tune with this a strategic reconstruction of the 'glorious' women of this past was made, and the 'traditional' qualities—*selected* as traditional—of the women of a 'pristine' classical Hindu age were extolled. The brilliant past was construed as the age of the Aryans and the 'glorious' women were none other than the Aryan women of the upper castes.[7] There was also a second, if apparently contradictory, outcome. Responding to the civilizational critique of India, the English-educated middle class developed a strong desire for 'improvement', and 'modernization', and hence for the removal of some of the inhuman practices against women, which seemed to symbolize the degradation of the entire society. There followed what is described in history as the nineteenth century social reform movement. It had two strands. One strove to defend the indigenous Indian culture against the colonial onslaught by highlighting a past 'golden age', while the other attempted to 'modernize' society by importing ideas from the West. In order to comprehend the complexities of the class that supported the reform movement, one needs to examine a third dimension too. With the expansion and consolidation of British rule, the colonial power was seeking English-educated local men for recruitment to the bureaucracy at the lower level. In terms of career opportunities, the growth of the colonial urban sector had offered little to the educated middle class. They found employment only as petty clerks in administrative or commercial establishments, and eagerly sought opportunities for employment in higher posts. *Sambad Prabhakar*, the mouthpiece of the middle class, articulated their sentiments.

Our Government have made it a point of principle that no senior public positions will be open to our countrymen. Such privileges will be solely reserved for Europeans, as a result of which our own people are denied the opportunity of securing Government jobs and thereby improving their lot. The future prospects of Bengal will remain dim until and unless a positive decision is taken by our rulers to appoint suitably qualified persons of our country to responsible public posts.[8]

In the course of the nineteenth century, education became the chief marker of the middle class bhadralok. What did education imply for men? An analysis of the history of the times clearly indicates that the urban middle class was swiftly being drawn towards Western education. Hindu School (1817) was the centre of learning of the new élite. Love of scholarship was certainly a major motivation. One need only recall Michael Madhusudan Dutt's (1824–73) dream of becoming a Milton, or the study circles of Hindu School, for confirmation of this urge. However, to most members of the middle class, Western education offered promises of advancement in the career trajectory. Education to them came to mean learning English at a government or missionary-run school and college, followed by a Calcutta University (founded in 1857) degree, designed to serve as the mediating institution between them and the colonial Government.[9] The enthusiasm with which this cultural group accepted and promoted English education provided them with the lion's share of the new opportunities for professional, administrative, and clerical employment throughout British India.

The gradual growth of a bureaucratic class and the increase of geographical mobility among them led in actual practice to the loosening of strictly conventional behavioural-patterns, and the gradual weakening of joint family life whenever the women of the family went to Calcutta to live with their husbands. However, the Bengali 'bhadralok'—a term denoting primarily the upper-caste Hindu middle class gentry—did not sever their ties with the rural base, and sought to conform as much as possible to tradition. The role of tradition in moulding or neutralizing the forces of change must never be overlooked. This becomes more intelligible when we remember that there was a significant difference between the Bengali middle class and its Western counterpart. In Bengal, the nineteenth century middle class diligently cultivated the self-image of a class searching for its model in its European counterpart. Yet its own social roots lay not in industry or trade—as in the English case—but in government service or in the profession of law, education, and journalism. Whatever interest they had in technology or industry was not backed by capital, and so remained largely academic. On the other hand, there is considerable evidence to show that in keeping with such imperfect professionalization, they had persistent links with rural society.[10]

In the cultural and ideological encounter with the West, in order to situate women, the Bengali middle class imported the model of the 'modern' woman from Victorian England, but endowed it with 'traditional' feminine qualities. The colonial rulers had to be impressed, but indigenous Indianness was to be preserved. In the entire agenda, therefore, there was a hidden contradiction, and the re-ordering of women into new models was as much social as political.[11] While the intellectual ferment produced by the interaction with Western civilization through the medium of English education brought about a remarkable transformation in the socio-cultural arena, the challenge from Rammohan Roy (1772–1833), the founder of the Brahmo movement, indicated for the first time the difference between the new urban, Western-educated generation and the traditional Hindus. Rammohan was fortunate in being steeped in his indigenous tradition besides being well-read in the writings of Western liberal thinkers like Locke and Bentham. The Brahmo Samaj, founded in 1828, was based on the non-idolatrous scriptures of the Vedas and the Vedanta.[12] Its members were pioneers of the social reform movement in Bengal, and from the time of Rammohan their theoretical position was informed by a sympathetic understanding of the problems of women. According to Rammohan, men had unfairly deprived women of their right to independence and the right to freedom.

Women are in general inferior to men in bodily strength and energy; consequently the male part of the community, taking advantage of their corporeal weakness, have denied to them those excellent merits that they are entitled to by nature, and afterwards they are apt to say that women are naturally incapable of acquiring those merits.... As to their inferiority in point of understanding, when did you ever afford them a fair opportunity of exhibiting their natural capacity?[13]

Under Rammohan's leadership, moreover, the Brahmo Samaj's anti-Sati campaign furnished the first example of a systematic movement for the eradication of inhuman anti-women customs in the newly emerging milieu. Sati was abolished by Regulation XVII of 1829.[14] The historical importance of the Brahmo movement was that in a basically traditional society, where there had been little structural change, Brahmoism represented essentially the force of ideas—ideas born largely of the new urbanism that was influencing social and cultural practices.[15] Brahmos set up their own communities and worked together to advance the cause of female education, abolish certain irrational superstitions, eradicate caste distinctions, and propagate Brahmoism. The Brahmo women also played a part in the general social change. By the 1860s, some of them broke conventional customs in matters of education, dress, purdah, and most importantly, in the field of thought commensurate with alterations in religious beliefs. Gradually, the movement for reform came to be powerfully supported by some enlightened Hindus. Head and shoulders above all others was Iswar Chandra Vidyasagar (1820–91) who sought to introduce the practice of widow remarriage into Hindu society. Despite enormous opposition, widow remarriage was legalized in 1856.[16] The programme for women's education was inaugurated, and efforts continued towards various other social reforms.

Alongside such endeavours, an important religious movement founded by Ramakrishna (1836–86), and continued by his disciple Vivekananda, emerged as a strong force in the socio-religious life of Bengal. Ramakrishna, the rustic priest of Dakshineswar, developed a unique religious philosophy which was as flexible as it was humanitarian. Construction of womanhood provides the key to an understanding of the movement, for gender was a recurrent theme in its thought. Much of the nineteenth century bhadralok discourses persistently problematized conjugality, constructing the woman— usually the wife—either as a degraded human being in need of male reformist endeavours, or as the last depository of indigenous virtues in a world otherwise lost to foreign domination. Ramakrishna, who saw all women as mothers, contributed to a decisive shift in the direction of identifying ideal womanhood with an iconic mother-figure. This new and enormously valorized relationship soon assumed patriotic overtones.[17]

Vivekananda gave further orientation to the movement. He inspired at the heart of what had begun as inward-looking *bhakti*, a tradition of activism. The spirit of selfless social service became very important to him, and with him. The catholicity of Ramakrishna, modulated by the constitution of a crystallized 'Hindu' identity, became for Vivekananda grounds for a claim to superior worth, which he advocated in his tours abroad and across India. Although a missionary anxious to avoid political involvement, he was certainly, if indirectly, political, as he was asserting the cultural supremacy of India before the Western world. His patriotism was as virile, as aggressive, and as uncompromising as his championing of Hinduism: one reason why the middle class intelligentsia gathered around him. Moreover, his discourses, as revealed from his letters and works, repeatedly describe caste oppression and degradation of women as the two central evils of Hindu society. To him, the lack of education among women was the cause of their social devaluation. Like Ramakrishna, he too believed that the highest ideal of womanhood in India was motherhood. This was in tune with the nationalist discourse on women, as we shall see, and contributed to the popularity of his teachings. His messages also had an enormous appeal for biplabis.[18] Sarala, it may be noted, was greatly influenced by his ideas. Vivekananda had an energetic and remarkable woman activist as his disciple, Sister Nivedita, who continued to propagate his ideas after his death. Nivedita dedicated herself to the cause of women's education, and became a supporter of the political revolutionary ideology of the biplabi or secret revolutionary anti-colonial societies emerging in Bengal. This provided a common meeting point between Sarala and Nivedita.

## Education of Women

By the time the ideas of Ramakrishna and Vivekananda had made their presence felt, women's education had begun to make some headway in Bengal. Here Christian missionaries had taken the initiative, but their schools did not find favour with the bhadralok because of their proselytizing zeal. However, the bhadralok themselves felt the need for women's education: it was the obvious answer to the lowly position of women and for the improvement of the society at large. The dichotomy between an educated manhood and an uneducated womanhood was seen as one of the principal obstacles to progress. It was responsible for the debased nature of the husband–wife relationship, and the communication gap between them. There was a growing appreciation of the British ideal that a wife was the intellectual companion of the husband, offering him sympathy, advice, encouragement, and relaxation . An emblematic letter appeared in *Samachar Darpan,* 'Bengali men are receiving education and consequently their minds are being enlightened. Under these circumstances, how can they get along with their uneducated wives?'[19] No wonder then that the bhadralok were seeking female company outside the home, and visiting mistresses had become a commonplace phenomenon. Most wives, aware of their limitations and the educational superiority of men, meekly reconciled themselves to such nocturnal expeditions by their husbands.[20] Recognition of this reality and its adverse effects on conjugal relations and family life set social thinkers questing for a means to the advancement of women. Education came to be seen as an essential first step for resolving the acute problems of conjugal adjustment.

There was another reason too. Desperate to climb the social ladder under the colonial government, middle class men wanted women to lend support to their arrival in society. A woman needed to be educated in order to match her husband and to be able to perform her domestic role effectively in the 'modern' context. Contemporary didactic literature was replete with the view—of which Bhudev Mukhopadhyay was the chief exponent—that women should aim to be competent housewives, intelligent companions to their husbands, and good mothers to their sons.[21] Education for women came to be regarded as a component of good management of all these domestic functions. This attitude was clearly expressed by Pyarichand Mitra (1814–83), one of the leading intellectuals of the time.

A home where women do not have *suvivechana* [the power of good judgment] becomes a ruined home ... . It is not easy to acquire a good power of judgment . It is not as simple as merely plucking a fruit from a tree. One has to earn it, and the process of earning is called education.[22]

For a majority of girls, however, the custom of early marriage was a formidable obstacle to formal education in schools. To counteract these, the scheme of zenana education was launched. Suitable female teachers were employed to teach the women at home. Syllabi were formulated, and examinations conducted for zenana education. *Bamabodhini Patrika*, launched in 1863 by the Brahmos and the leading journal for women, published the syllabi for the information of its readers.[23] In some families women took lessons from the *vaisnavi*s, that is, women from a religious sect which did not prohibit education for women, while in many other families women were taught by their male relations, principally the father, brother, husband, or even brother-in-law. Swarnakumari Devi, for example, was taught at home by her father. Brahmamoyee Devi (1845–76), was educated under her husband's guidance. These private efforts were socially more acceptable than school education. They were at once 'progressive' and 'traditional', aimed at giving some necessary basic education to women while keeping them within the parameters of the home. Women themselves were being drawn to learning. An interesting example is that of Rasasundari Devi (b. 1810). To her, the ability to read was a tool for access to religious texts. In her autobiography, *Amar Jiban* (My Life, 1876), she narrates how in order to be able to access *Chaitanya Charitamrita* (The Life and Works of Chaitanya), a sacred text for the Hindus, she taught herself to read.[24] Writing was taught to her by her son. Similarly, Bamasundari Devi (1838–1888) was also self-educated. Many women, unable to get assistance from their male relations, persisted on their own until some other assistance became available. Shivanath Shastri, the Brahmo reformer, writes that his father, whenever he came home from Calcutta, used to teach his wife, and bring books for her. She used to read them all as far as possible without help, and in the event of experiencing problems, sought help in her husband's absence from younger boys in the family.[25]

Progress, however, was not easy. Inevitably, resistance came from a powerful section of traditional men who feared change resulting in a loss of social control. They argued that education was inherently de-feminizing or

Westernizing. It would foster in women a distaste for domestic duties, a love of luxury, selfishness, and disrespect for traditional culture. It would also give them greater facility to engage in unfaithful liaisons because of their ability to write letters, a husband's control over his educated wife would be less secure, and she would certainly want to live away from the joint family.[26] In any case, while men's education had economic value, female education had no such function. As a result of such social thinking, an educated woman became a figure of fun. Iswar Chandra Gupta (1812–59), a popular contemporary poet, composed a satire that gained wide circulation. Freely translated, it reads:

> In my grandmother's days girls were so pure !
> They lived by the code and the rituals to be sure.
> And then came Bethune and anon
> All these feminine virtues have gone.
> And gone with the wind is the woman demure.
> And jettisoning those old world charms
> These modern girls with books in their arms
> Must learn their As, Bs, and Cs
> To speak like the Feringhees,
> And drive their own four-in-hand
> To visit the Maidan, and listen to the Band,
> Sooner or later, boots will adorn their figures
> And who knows, they may even take to cigars.[27]

Opposition also came from the older generation of women who were not educated themselves and feared the intrusion of unfamiliar and unconventional elements as a threat to their control over domestic affairs and as an invasion of Western culture into the sanctity of the home. Shivanath Shastri writes how, when his father used to teach his mother at home, he was criticized by his relations. 'My aunt (father's elder sister ) used to scold him and women of neighbouring families used to tease my mother day and night'.[28] Undaunted by such opposition, female education continued to make headway in Bengal. Indigenous leadership was provided by the Brahmos and enlightened Hindu reformers like Iswarchandra Vidyasagar and Madanmohan Tarkalankar (1817–58), and also by some orthodox Hindus like Radhakanta Deb (1783–1867). Madanmohan Tarkalankar wrote an outstanding essay in *Sarbasubhankari Patrika* in support of women's education, Vidyasagar penned a number of books for new learners, and Radhakanta Deb started a school in his own residence.[29]

The milestone in the field of women's education was the establishment of Bethune School in 1849 under the patronage of Drinkwater Bethune and with the support of men like Dakshinaranjan Mukherjee (1814–78),

Madanmohan Tarkalankar, and others. Vidyasagar himself was the Secretary of the school for twelve long years. Bethune School was soon followed by other girls' schools in different parts of the country, like Victoria Institution (1882) and Brahmo Balika Vidyalaya (1890).[30] There developed, however, a difference of opinion in the eighteen-seventies among the supporters of women's education about the curriculum as well as the extent of that education. To one group, comprising Keshab Chandra Sen (1838–84), Pratap Chandra Majumdar (1840–1905), and Mahendranath Basu (1838–1915), women should be educated, but the aim should be to instil in them knowledge wedded to spiritualism, and to enable them to play their rightful role in society as well as to develop their 'feminine' characteristics. According to the more 'progressive' group to which Shivanath Shastri, Durgamohan Das, Anandamohan Bose (1874–1906), and Dwarakanath Ganguly (1844–98) belonged, women should have equal rights to education as men, and there must not be any bar to their university or medical education. They should have equal access not only to literature and philosophy, but also to history, science, and medicine. The fight was bitter, but the 'progressive' party had a lead, especially in urban Bengal.

Slowly, the government, too, lent some support. The Indian Education Commission of 1882, recommended improvement of zenana teaching, and financial grants for girls' schools. In 1883, Kadambini Ganguly and Chandramukhi Bose (1856–1944) graduated from Bethune College, obtaining BA degrees, and making history. Chandramukhi went on to pursue her Master's, while Kadambini opted to study medicine and was allowed to join Calcutta Medical College. In 1885, the National Association for Supplying Female Medical Aid was set up for the teaching of women to qualify as doctors and nurses. By 1890, the number of girls attending schools rose to 78,865, and by the end of the century, Bengal had three colleges for women and thirteen schools for girls.[31] It needs to be mentioned here that although men like Rammohan Roy, Vidyasagar, and Vivekananda dedicated themselves to the cause of educating women and upgrading their life-situations out of genuine concern and idealism, the middle class was with them from a desire to make their private life conform to their public and professional life. As Ghulam Murshid puts it, the middle class spearheaded the movement for women's education 'as a part of modernizing their own world'.[32] The aim of the reform movement was not to make women independent or equal partners of men in the family or public life. Rather it was to make them better equipped to fulfil their conventional roles as wives and mothers in the colonial setting. The reformist literature tirelessly dwelt on this theme;[33] any contemporary discourse on women's education and development for their own sake was conspicuous by its absence.

## The Nationalist Movement and Discourse on Women

By the turn of the nineteenth century, the anti-colonial nationalist movement was emerging in Bengal.[34] The moment of political confrontation came when Curzon announced in 1905 the possible partition of Bengal. It sparked the fire of protest throughout Bengal which is historically known as the Swadeshi movement. The menfolk of Bengal wanted women to participate in the struggle. For centuries, women had been denied any public space. Why then the sudden call to them to get involved in the hitherto exclusively male sphere of politics? The explanation must lie in the numbers game. It was simple logic, later developed with greater finesse by Gandhi, that the support of half of the population would give the movement a greater mass base. There was another reason too. As has been said earlier, men had initiated the nineteenth century reforms; they had felt a need for the partnership and companionship of women in their lives and activities. The Swadeshi movement would be best fought with the participation, direct or indirect, of women.

Most importantly, the nationalist leaders subtly converted their socio-economic struggle against the British into a worship of the motherland. The motherland became Mother Goddess, and *Bande Mataram* (salutation to the motherland) the new *mantra*.[35] The intellectuals helped the politicians to achieve this transformation in the domain of culture. Rabindranath Tagore composed a song portraying Bengal as Goddess Durga, Abanindranath Tagore painted India as *Bharatamata* (Mother Goddess India), and Ramendrasundar Trivedi created a text of rituals, *Bangalakshmir Bratakatha* (Book of Prayer for Goddess Bengal, Calcutta, 1905). As the distaff side had been traditionally responsible for maintaining religious faith and rituals, the conversion of politics into religion created a political space for them, and made their participation easy and natural. A small number of women took part in the Swadeshi movement, but participated in larger numbers in the latter-day Gandhian movement.[36]

Simultaneously, another significant development was occurring while Sarala was growing up. The nationalist construct of women was being shaped. It was based on the social reformers' discourse on the model woman. Through a number of 'contradictory and heterogeneous moves' the bhadralok were reconstituting their women and their culture. Concepts originating in mid-nineteenth century reform and the nationalist requirement moulded the normative model of womanhood. How were the 'women' constructed? What were the expectations from them? At one level, the British employment structure reshaped Indian people's lives by implicitly demanding hard work, punctuality, and efficiency from all those who served under them. As the institution of the family was itself entangled in wider social relations, the organization of life in the home had to be reoriented, and new norms for family life and the conduct of women had to be reformulated to cope with the changes in the public world. In the civilizing-cum-nationalist body of thought around the second half of the nineteenth century, the internal discipline of the European home was seen 'as a key to European prosperity and political power'. Therefore, the Victorian fetishes of 'discipline', 'routine' and 'order' gained popularity in Bengali didactic writings on domesticity, personal conduct, and 'domestic science'.[37]

At another level, the crucial requirement was to retain the basic values of the traditional domestic system and the 'inner spirituality' of indigenous social/familial life.[38] The social or political changes, surprisingly, did not fuel a total revolution in family values; on the other hand, the old norms showed a remarkable capacity for survival, and also for adjustment and reinterpretation. The home came to be considered the principal site for the expression and retention of the spiritual quality of national culture. It was emphasized that women, the traditional repositories of spiritual values, must take the responsibility for protecting and nurturing the spiritual quality of the nation. The essential distinction between the social roles of men and women in terms of material and spiritual virtues, respectively, was highlighted. Men might be Westernized or stray away from ethical moorings or change under the pressure of new occupational roles; women symbolized the Indianness of their husbands and represented the 'real' essence of the home. In the material world western civilization might be superior, but in the spiritual domain the East outshone the West. On women was incumbent the task of preserving spirituality, of nurturing *dharma* (prescribed righteous conduct) and regenerating men from the ignominy of political subjection and/ or moral bankruptcy. The *griha* (home) was thus conceived more in terms of an emotional and moral rather than a physical construct,[39] and women were valorized as Lakshmis, or the presiding deities of the homes. The new model of *grihalakshmi* (goddess of the home) was developed in a mixture of the old and the new to suit men intellectually colonized, but emotionally rooted to the Indian tradition.[40] Listen to this: 'Women are the Lakshmis of the community. If they undertake to improve themselves in the sphere of dharma and knowledge ... there will be an automatic improvement in the quality of life.' And this: 'A woman who like Goddess Lakshmi worships her husband, as if worshipping Hari [Lord Krishna, husband of Goddess Lakshmi], will after death enjoy the company of her husband in heaven, just as Lakshmi does with Hari.'[41]

In constructing the image of the 'ideal' woman, the reformists and the nationalists continually reverted to 'classical' Hindu tradition, to the days when women had been educated, and even had composed hymns and participated in learned debates. As Partha Chatterjee points out, the image thus constructed was quite the reverse of that of traditional, indigenous common women who were always portrayed as typically coarse, vulgar, and quarrelsome. The new woman was accorded a status of cultural superiority in comparison to her counterpart in the West because she was the repository of dharma, of spiritual force and moral power. The nationalist iconography of womanhood/femininity, therefore, became the most important ideological site for questioning as well as appropriating the superiority of the West. Some virtues in the English home were extolled only to be adapted to create an indigenous nationalist philosophy of domesticity, whose built-in spiritualism was used as a tool of resisting the materialism of the West.[42]

In this newly defined role, *pativratya* (devoted wife) was important, running an 'orderly' home was necessary, but motherhood became central, especially as and when the nationalist movement and nationalist ideology began to take shape.[43] Women were assigned a specific and crucial role in rearing a special breed of men, patriotic, brave and nationalistic. The emphasis on enlightened motherhood for the training of a race of intelligent, vigorous, and patriotic children was a direct fallout of the nationalist movement. The nation needed strong sons to fight against the colonial rulers; the nation needed brilliant sons to restore its lost glory, and to infuse self-respect in the body politic. And the nation needed daughters to lend support to their nationalistic men and mother nationalistic heroes. There was gradually a subtle change in emphasis. Wives' help was sought for supporting the freedom movement. The more noble duty however was to produce good children, especially sons. The bearing and rearing of sons, traditionally regarded as a woman's primary obligation to the family, now acquired an added significance. The child came to occupy centre-stage in a family. Tracts and manuals as well as articles in journals began to appear on how to look after the health and well-being of children. An analysis of the extant literature indicates that the trend was set in motion in the nineteenth century, but in the twentieth it became almost an obsession with doctors and social scientists alike. In the West, the nineteenth century had seen the redefinition of motherhood as a full time occupation for middle class mothers (who had hardly any economic function), and as a symbol of family solidarity. That philosophy suited the Indian intelligentsia, especially because it fitted with the traditional Hindu religious concept of the Divine Mother.

The ideal woman with her newly added social responsibilities was a recurrent theme in many genres of nationalist literature. If in the earlier period the cultural encounter with the West provided the motivation, in the latter it was the demands of nationalism that set the agenda. While the early to mid-nineteenth century reformers extolled motherhood for the nurturing of 'good' sons, the burgeoning nationalism of the last quarter of the nineteenth and the first quarter of the twentieth century captured the image of the mother as representing the nation's aspirations. The worldly mother under the Divine Mother was to play a pivotal role in the production of a powerful nation. Thus womanhood came to acquire several accretions of political as well as social meaning. If we collect together the nationalist thoughts of various people articulated through various media, a fascinating image emerges. The new woman was to be an educated and brave wife as an appropriate partner of an English-educated nationalist man, able to run an 'efficient' and 'orderly home' like her Western counterpart, be high-minded and spiritual like the women of the 'golden' age, become 'grihalakshmis' like the Divine Lakshmi and fulfil her primary role as courageous mother producing heroic children for the service of the nation. If the model was absurd, or inimitable, and indeed full of contradictions, no one was bothered. That was the new woman the nation needed, and it was women's *duty* to live up to it.

It is important to ask to what extent women's own perceptions and world-view were influenced by the valorization of motherhood and the changes in the construction of womanhood since the days of the social reform movement. When caught up in the mainstream of change and conflict, how did they respond to the new expectations from them? Did they accept the male-defined new ethics or did they question it? Significantly, as women became educated, they began to write. As early as the mid-nineteenth century Rasasundari Devi, Kailasbasini Devi, Swarnakumari Devi, and a few others had taken up the pen. A good number of them began contributing to journals, especially women's journals. It seems that initially the large majority of educated women, at the receiving end of male patronage, internalized male concepts of the new womanhood and made little attempt to assert their special interests, at least in the nineteenth century. Women's journals, echoing men's views, repeatedly emphasized the nurturing role of women, their spiritual potentials, the emotional support provided by a woman to her husband, and the basic difference between men's and women's natures and roles. Their writings reveal their keenness to cultivate the tastes which their husbands appreciated, and to become their 'worthy' companions and 'worthy' mothers of 'good' sons. In *Bamabodhini Patrika*, educated Brahmo women declared almost unanimously that women should be able to read and write Bengali, and preferably some English (presumably to communicate with the ruling class), learn household skills, and aspire to become *sugrihini* (a competent housewife), *pativrata* (a devoted wife), and *sumata* (a good mother). Leading women like Swarnaprabha Basu aired the view that excellence in family life was the handiwork of women, and hence the responsibility of educated women. They should run the household and bring up children with dharma.[44] An article contributed by Charumati Devi, a housewife, in *Bamabodhini Patrika*, encapsulated this ideology:

It is our belief that women are the real source of instilling the concept of righteous conduct in their children. Just study the lives of great men, and you will find at once that their sterling character could not have been formed but for the inspiration of their mothers. Mothers helped in developing their spiritual ideas and thoughts until these took deep roots in their minds. This world of ours still does not appreciate the influence and contribution of a mother in forming the character of a child.

Charumati Devi further averred in a prize-winning essay that in order to reduce the high rate of infant mortality, the overall hygiene of the home had to be improved, and that it devolved on the mother to keep a healthy home.[45] Even *Bharatamahila* (Women of India, first published 1905), edited by the fiery Sarajubala Dutta (1880–1963), carried similar articles. Hemalata Sarkar felt that a woman must concentrate on running an ideal home, and learn how to bring up children properly. Shatadalbasini Biswas who, almost like a latter-day feminist, often questioned gender asymmetry in society, readily accepted the newly idealized concept of motherhood.[46] In sum, most of the compositions by women restated the home-oriented stereotypes in more 'educated' and 'patriotic' forms. However, some resistant voices appeared, especially in women's journals.[47] In her study of a number of personal narratives, Malavika Karlekar also finds 'a subtle resistance' growing within a few homes. 'This resistance, which was much more the exception than the rule, did not develop into a movement, nor was it always explicit'. Often it was a mere regret or a wish, but sometimes it was a 'well-articulated resentment against those in positions of authority.'[48] A few women started asking questions challenging male-oriented values. Men had constructed women, it now remained for women to reconstruct themselves.

## Muslim Women

For a historian, studying Muslim women along with contemporary Hindu women of the nineteenth century makes for a fascinating exercise. One becomes aware of how very similar the conditions of the Muslim women were to that of their Hindu counterparts, how akin the attitudes of men of both the communities were to the distaff side, and how alike their ideological concerns regarding women and reform under colonial rule.

In moral terms, Islam places the two sexes in a position of equality before God, although in social terms, women are subordinate to men. The Koran emphasizes the just treatment of women, prohibits female infanticide, and provides legal protection for women in matters like inheritance and divorce. In the context of seventh-century Arabia, the Koranic injunctions regarding women constituted a progressive force but the scriptural norms gradually merged with social practices current among non-Arab civilizations, like the Greek or Iranian culture, with which early Muslims came into contact. This included the complete seclusion of women from men, which had long been a mark of privilege in upper class Byzantine and Sassanian society. By the second half of the eighth century, the seclusion of women and the wearing of the veil had become official policy at the Abbasid court in Baghdad. Soon urban Muslims of all social classes followed the court's example, with the result that by the fourteenth century, women had effectively disappeared from public life throughout the Arab Muslim world.[49]

M. Eaton in his history of the rise of Islam in Bengal maintains that this was not the case in Bengal. As late as 1595, Abul Fazl recorded that in Chittagong, when a chief held court, the wives of the military would be present, the men themselves not attending to make their obeisance. In the Bengal countryside, neither the veiling nor the seclusion of women had yet taken hold. Gradually however the normative vision of a segregated society that formed part of scriptural Islam and fostered gendered division of labour and female seclusion, sank roots in Bengali culture. Clearly, among communities that had become Muslim from the sixteenth century on, there was a time lag between the appearance of the normative vision and its eventual realization.[50] With time, the control over women's lives and behavioural-patterns was enforced with much greater rigidity in the aristocratic households. Then, when Bengal came under colonial rule, in the fluid and uncertain atmosphere of the new setting, the position and seclusion of women were additional means of determining social status. Under strictest purdah, upper class women belonging to the *sharif* (aristocratic) families, were confined to the *andarmahal* (inner quarters) or subjected to the greater form of seclusion—abarodh (literally, confinement), that secluded them from men and women alike.[51]

The women of the upper and middle class families received some traditional education that consisted primarily of knowledge of the Koran and a few religious texts. Education was usually imparted from the age of four or five, and the girls in about two years learned to read the Koran in Arabic, without any comprehension. In some families they were taught some Urdu too. Sometimes, passages from didactic literature, like Thanavi's *Behesti Zevar*, Keramat Ali's *Muftahul Jinnat* and *Rahenazat*, were read out to them.[52] These upheld the ideology of domesticity, seclusion, and 'a structural hierarchy of authority connecting Allah, men and women'.[53] Norms of a woman's role and duties, and concepts of womanhood—'women in her wanton and chaste aspect, one juxtaposed to the other'—are specified in didactic literature and orthodox discourse.[54] The thoroughness of socialization at home by orthodox elderly women and the lack of exposure must have been factors contributing to women's acceptance of their prescribed roles, as indeed was the case with their Hindu sisters.

## Reform and Change

Bengali society witnessed the emergence of a new type of Muslim men and women towards the end of the nineteenth century. Sonia Amin has used the term bhadralok and bhadramahila respectively for them, though the terms were used by the Brahmos and Hindus to mean themselves. Amin argues that actually there was not much difference between them and the corresponding Muslim gentry, that is the enlightened emergent Western-educated Muslim urban middle class. 'This claim is based on a similarity of certain core class, cultural and educational traits, shared by the middle class professional gentry of both communities.'[55] According to Amin, the same logic may be applied to justify the term bhadramahila meant for the Brahmo and Hindu women who had come out of the *antahpur* to denote Muslim women of the andarmahal who were participating in the process of 'modernization'.

One has to agree with Amin that the term bhadramahila can be applied with equal ease to the educated Brahmo, Hindu, and Muslim middle class women. Indeed, author Mankumari Basu (1863-1943), a Hindu, Sarala Devi and Kadambini Ganguly, both Brahmo, and Begum Rokeya and Shamsunnahar Mahmud, both Muslim, had much in common. Their husbands/fathers or brothers were in some form of professional service mostly under the British, they dressed in similar style, they were educated (though, Rokeya had no formal education), they wrote and published, held many aspirations in common, and 'shared' many similar values.[56] Amin probably stretches the similarities, but her basic formulation is far from wrong. The principal reason for the similarity was that the class character of these women was comparable, the colonial rule that they were subjected to was common, the educated middle class concern about the women and the home affected them alike, and consequently the nature of their response to many events and issues was similar. Sangari and Vaid argue in the context of the Brahmo-led social reform movement of the nineteenth century, 'Middle class reforms undertaken on behalf of women are tied up with the self-definition of the class, with a new division of the public from the private sphere, and of course with a cultural nationalism'.[57] The same observation holds good for Muslim women of the time.[58] Maleka Begum dates Muslim women's *jagaran* (a term often used by Muslim writers, literally meaning awakening, actually denoting revival or regeneration) from the late nineteenth century and the birth of the Muslim women's movement from the early twentieth century.[59] The changes amongst Muslim women must be seen as a part of late nineteenth century Muslim nationalism.

## Muslim Nationalism

One must pause here and take a quick look back at the second half of the eighteenth and early nineteenth century. One must recall that while changes in ideas and perceptions as well as in life-situations were taking place among the Hindu middle class by the early nineteenth century as a result of the contact with Western ideas, the Muslims remained unaffected. They were late in accepting Western exposure; contemporary movements among them were primarily religious in character, focusing on the original and pristine Islamic heritage and having an anti-British slant.[60] One reason must have been the loss of power to the British, the Muslims having been the ruling class before their coming. British rule totally derailed the Muslim ruling class,[61] and the initial shock changed their living patterns as well as avocations. Wakil Ahmed analyses:

After Muslims lost their authority to rule the country, many who were engaged in State employment or otherwise, found it humiliating to serve under the Christian masters, and preferred instead to go in for agriculture. Until then, the most honourable avocations for the upper class Muslims had been the army, serving as bureaucrats, or life as landed gentry. Any other occupation, such as keeping shops or running a business was considered damaging to their status. Most of them had come from outside Bengal. They did not consider tilling with their own hands prestigious, but after being deprived of power, they had no alternative but to turn to agriculture and land. This class preferred to settle in the villages rather than in towns.[62]

The second reason was the late emergence of the Muslim middle class. The earlier Bengali middle class was Hindu-dominated, the Hindus advancing more than the Muslims in urbanization, in trade and commerce, and professional services under the British. Under the British the aristocratic Muslim families were deprived of their earlier privileged position—military posts, revenue offices and judicial and administrative appointments, all at the highest level[63]—and were also denied the earlier court patronage; many even left Bengal.

The upper strata of the Muslim community in the pre-British period were, on the whole, divorced from medieval trade or moneylending and were mainly engaged in military and administrative careers. Further, they predominantly resided in Northern India which came under British rule much later. The vast Muslim population of Bengal mainly belonged to the poorer classes. Hence a modern intelligentsia, a modern educated middle class and a bourgeoisie, on a substantial scale, sprang from within the Muslim community later than that from within the Hindu community.[64]

Or, as Wakil Ahmed says,

The Hindus and the Muslims took two different routes when the British rule was established. The Hindus took full advantage of the opportunities offered by the British Government. Opting early for English education, the Hindus prospered with access to government and other employment. On the other hand, the Muslims were indifferent to British rule and turned their face against English education. Inability to secure gainful employment coupled with reluctance to engage in trade and commerce led to the decline in the circumstances of the Muslim community. The unequal development of the Hindu and the Muslim communities, especially of their middle classes, was a great tragedy in the social history of Bengal.[65]

In any case, during the post-1857 period the Muslim community was keen to preserve and advance their culture. In AD 1780 the Madrassah was established in Calcutta to promote the study of Arabic and Persian. It was only in 1829 that for the first time English was introduced there. The Muslims had no access to Hindu College. As late as 1836, in the English Department of Hooghly College, there were only 31 Muslim students out of a total of 948.[66] The Muslims were unwilling to send their wards to Christian missionary institutions for fear of possible conversion. Anisuzzaman writes that it was around the eighteen-seventies that the Bengali Muslim became aware of 'modern' times, and the need of 'modernization'.[67] The rising of 1857 had been suppressed, the Wahabi movement had ended in 1872. 'There was no alternative for the Muslims but to cooperate with the British'.[68] The leadership, therefore, began to think along new lines. Indeed, after the rising of 1857, there was a move at the all-India level to persuade the Muslims to accept the need for modernization and also to reconcile them to British rule. It appears that the Muslims made a two-pronged advance in the same direction—establishing links with the process of 'modernization' in the cultural arena and amity with the British in the political field.[69]

The leaders of the new movement were Sir Syed Ahmed in North India and Nawab Abdul Latif (1828–93) in Bengal. Sir Syed was the first to start a reform movement, the keynote of which was to promote exposure to Western ideas and entry in the administrative infrastructure through active cooperation with the British. He made no bones about declaring that without English education, the Muslims will lag behind 'in the race for position' not only in India, but 'among the magnates of the world'. He established the Translation Society in 1865 and founded the Anglo–Oriental College at Aligarh to spearhead the spread of his ideas. Later known as Aligarh College, it helped to establish a link between the Muslims and English education.[70] Like Sir Syed, Nawab Abdul Latif, too, had twin aims, that is, to introduce the Muslims to the world of Western science and to forge a friendship with the British. The question of Muslim education was his greatest concern. He firmly believed in the efficacy of English education for the advancement of Muslims. In 1866 he established the Muhammedan Literary Society in Calcutta with a view to spreading Western ideas amongst the Muslim youth through discussion and debate, and establishing a rapport between the Muslims and the British administration. The Lieutenant Governor of Bengal was the patron, and men like the Duke of Edinburgh, the Prince of Wales, Lord Mayo, and Sir Cecil Beadon attended its functions.[71]

Another leader in Bengal, Syed Amir Ali, established the National Muhammedan Association in 1877, which came to be known as Central Muhammedan Association.[72] He wrote an article in 1880 on Bengali Muslims' education, which was widely discussed in various circles. Men like Abdul Hamid Khan Yusufzai, the editor of the journal *Ahmadi*, lamented, 'My community, the Muslim community, is extremely backward in terms of education'. Mir Musharraf Hossain, a reputed author, recalled the pattern of education in his childhood. In the villages, the Arabic language and the Koran Sharif were routinely taught, but the system of' instruction 'was very odd indeed. As soon as one had mastered the alphabets, it was obligatory to study the Koran Sharif. But this was such a pointless exercise, no more than just a mechanical reading of the text without any comprehension of what the Koran Sharif was about.'[73]

Education was thus the first requisite, and it was English education that was the need of the hour. Consequent upon the slow and steady growth of the Muslim middle class there thus arose a demand within the Muslim community for such education. A section of Muslims had come to terms with the realities of colonial rule, and gradually evolved into a professional and bureaucratic middle class. These men were largely engaged in some form of government employment, had broken away from the old way of life and the familial structure of the landed gentry.[74] Their urge for English education was all the more pronounced because they had a late start and had to catch up with the upwardly mobile Hindu middle class in the professions and administration. Moreover, in the eighteen-eighties there developed an international demand for jute. Muslim-dominated eastern Bengal met the demand, and consequently, the cultivators in the region became quite prosperous. With cash in their hands, they wanted to educate their children and get them employed in government jobs. The government response proved positive. Madrassahs were established in Dhaka, Chittagong, and Rajshahi where English was taught. While in 1871 only 14.7 per cent of the Muslim population went to school, a decade later, in 1881, the percentage rose to 23.8.[75]

## Bengali–Muslim Nationalism

The movement led by Sir Syed Ahmed at Aligarh and Nawab Abdul Latif and Syed Amir Ali in Bengal deeply affected the 'mentality' of the Bengali Muslims. Like their Hindu and Brahmo counterparts, the new generation of Western-educated Muslim men also turned their thoughts to social reform. There followed a two-pronged development. On the one hand, attention was directed to the evils in the existing social system, and on the other, a movement started for the revival of the Islamic heritage in its pristine form. Those concerned with the community and society were unanimous about the all-round decline that had set in. For example, Syed Emdad Ali summed it up in one sentence, 'Lethargy has taken deep roots in our national life'. Kazi Imdadul Huq deplored in the pages of *Bharati* that the Muslims comprised the poorest section among the people of Bengal, but they were too lethargic and ignorant to wake up to the reality of the situation.[76] The immediate tasks were to identify the causes of this unfortunate regression, and find the steps imperative to reverse the process.

Anisuzzaman considers the eighteen-seventies as a watershed between medieval and modern Muslim literature. Through literature was articulated an inspired redefinition of Islamic history, Islamic culture, and social policy.[77] A number of journals/newspapers such as *Nabanoor, Masik Mohammadi, Saugat, Islam Pracharak, Sudhakar* (1889), *Kohinoor* (1898), *Basana* (1908), *Bangiya Musalman Sahitya Patrika* (1918), *Sikha* (1927), *Dhumketu* (1922), and *Bulbul* (1935) were published.[78] This gave a new dimension to the perception of the needed reforms of the accepted faith as well as of the current social conditions, bolstered by the resurgent awareness of the Islamic culture. Islam formed the keynote of all the writings of the time. Like the Hindu–Brahmo reformers, the Muslim intellectuals of this generation also turned to a 'glorious' age of the 'glorious' past, the pristine days of early Islam.[79] Articles were published on the various aspects of the current decadence and on ways regenerating Islam. Attention was almost inevitably focused on the degraded condition of women. The customs of child marriage, polygamy, and *talak* came in for severe criticism. Reform was urgently called for.

The new consciousness amongst Muslims about their own society prepared the stage for epochal changes in their thoughts. The quest for Muslim identity was one component of this process.[80] However, the quest, like all such quests, was partly social and partly political. Abdul Latif and Amir Ali took the lead in the task; they were joined by a galaxy of brilliant men, such as, Mir Musharraf Hossain, Abdul Hamid Khan Yusufzahi, Syed Emdad Ali, Syed Shamsul Huda (1862–1922), Abdur Rahim (1867–1952), Abdul Karim (1863–1943), Nausher Ali Khan Yusufzai (1864–1924), Mirza Sujat Ali, Yakub Ali Chowdhury (1887–1940), Syed Nawab Ali Chowdhury (1863–1929). They wrote profusely, conducted research, sponsored publications of authoritative books and new textbooks to enunciate Islamic heritage and culture. Of these path-finders, Abdul Latif advocated English education, Amir Ali harped on political consciousness, Mirza Sujat Ali and Syed Shamsul Huda favoured vocational education, Nawab Ali Chowdhury and Mir Musharraf Hossain argued for the promotion of the Bengali language, Muhammad Riyazuddin Ahmed (1862–1933) and Syed Ismail Hussain Shirazi (1880–1931)concentrated on the revival of Islam, and Dilwar Hossain Ahmed (1840–1912) and Kazi Imdadul Huq made social reform the priority agenda. There were thus different strands in the movement, but the single-minded aim of all of them was to liberate people from the baneful effects of poverty, illiteracy, and indignity, and to direct them towards the path of progress. The important point to note is that in this historical exercise, the first two leaders, Abdul Latif and Amir Ali, were not concerned with a Bengali identity[81] but the new generation of educated men was. They articulated through Bengali literature and the media the urge for an Islamic revival and the quest for a Muslim identity. Wakil Ahmed says, 'This sowed the seeds of Muslim nationalism'.[82]

It may be convincingly argued, however, that this sowed the seeds of Bengali–Muslim nationalism. Indeed, if one analyses contemporary journals and newspapers, one would find that two themes dominated the discussions: one, the issue of language, the other Islam. Muslims in Bengal were not only being made aware of their Muslim identity but were also being made to regard themselves as a Bengali-speaking people. They had to distinguish themselves from the Urdu-speaking Muslims of north India and to resolve how much they should imbibe from the Islamic culture and heritage beyond India.[83] This perhaps was where the deepest roots of the modern state of Bangladesh lay. Here are some contemporary pronouncements: 'What can be the language of the Bengalis except Bengali? Those who want to give Urdu the status of the mother-tongue of the Bengali Muslims only are trying to achieve the impossible', warned *Nabanoor* (1310 BS). *Kohinoor* asserted, 'The mother tongue of Bengali Muslims is Bengali. This is as clear as daylight.' (1322 BS).[84] The *Masik Mohammadi, Al-Islam*

(1915), *Bangiya Musalman Sahitya Patrika* (1918), *Sudhakar, Saogat,* and *Sikha,* that is, the new genre of publications, voiced the same note.[85]

In 1893, Dilwar Hossain, Nawab Shamsul Huda, and Syed Wajed Hossain founded Calcutta Muhammedan Union, followed by Bengal Provincial Muslim Education Society (1903). The aim was to situate the Bengali language as the mother tongue and spread education amongst the masses through the medium of Bengali. Thus the struggle to assert Bengali–Muslim identity was already underway by the 1880s. Syed Mannan is absolutely correct in saying:

> This *jagaran* was not static; it was dynamic, moving. The language movement of 1952 soon after the Partition of the country was not just an isolated explosion of protest. It was on the other hand a pregnant outcome of a long enduring undercurrent of anguished consciousness. And this exhilarating vernal atmosphere found expression in the music of Abbasuddin (1901–59), in the paintings of Jainul Abedin (1917–76), and in the choreography of Bulbul Chowdhury (1919–54).[86]

## The Education of Women

The new breed of Muslim reformers, once again like their Hindu–Brahmo counterparts, devoted themselves to the 'women's question'. Faisal F. Devji argues that the movement for women's reform in Muslim India during the period under discussion was an attempt initiated by the emerging new service gentry with a view to the Islamization of women. The new woman, chaste, rational, pious, was placed on a pedestal and extolled as a 'heavenly gem'.

> From the wreckage of their dissolved empire, the new urban middle class elite tried to reconstitute their own polity. The private terrain had come to be seen as a sort of fortress in a sea of hostility, but its old pagan denizens came to present a formidable problem. This threat was neutralized by incorporating the *andarmahal* into the new polity by education and Islamization.[87]

Faisal Devji's analysis draws attention once again to the similarity of the attitude of men—both Hindu and Muslim—towards women's issues and roles. One cannot but wonder why in times of crisis the responsibility of being 'good' and of giving 'moral' support to men rests primarily on women, be they Hindu or Muslim, or conforming to any other religion. Why should the private terrain be a sort of fortress/resort/defence wall when it proved difficult for men to maintain control of the public terrain?

Be that as it may, in north India the movement for women's advancement started earlier than in Bengal. The Aligarh College founded by Sir Syed Ahmed and the Deoband School, founded in 1867 by the reformist ulama, represented the two strands of the movement, one comprising the

Western-educated Muslims, the other appealing to the reformist ulama. The two had their conflicting views and perceptions, but both wanted some reform for women, and both articulated in their own fashion what it meant to be an ideal Muslim woman in the India of the time. Interestingly, in their advocacy of reform, they appealed to the glorious days of pristine Islam, just as their Brahmo–Hindu counterparts had referred to the golden Vedic age. Women's education, women's responsibilities, condition in general, women's duties, and the purdah system which was the chief obstacle to women's progress, were increasingly being discussed by many north Indian Muslim men. There emerged a voice amongst some of them for advancement of the women's cause and rights based on a reinterpreted, reformist Islam. For example, Nazir Ahmad (1833–1912), in his writings, articulated his belief in the equality of men and women; Altaf Husain Hali (1837–1914) in his novels pleaded for women's education and rights.[88] A new didactic literature for women was being written, and a number of books appeared as guides for women's household duties. Maulana Ashraf Ali Thanavi (1864–1943) was perhaps the foremost among them to write on the duties and behaviour of women, with emphasis on the equality of men and women before God. Sayyid Mumtaz Ali (1860–1935) through his journalism, especially for women, fearlessly advocated the erosion of purdah and the reinstatement of rights granted to women in Islam that were denied to them in practice. Of course, even within the purdah there were a few women, like Azizunnissa Begum (1780–1857), Sir Syed Ahmed's mother, who had the distinction of acquiring a basic literary and religious education and Ashrafunnissa Begum (1840–1903), who like Rasasundari Devi, taught herself to read by sheer determination. They were before long followed by a number of educated, publicly active women.[89]

Returning to Bengal, we see that here, too, when Muslim reformers initiated the process of change among women, the first arena was predictably that contentious subject: education. What was the state of the education of Muslim women in Bengal? While men were being educated and turning to writing as well as to other professions, most élite women even in the early twentieth century were behind purdah. In aristocratic families, as has been mentioned earlier, women received some elementary education at home—in contrast to most Hindu women before the inception of social reforms—but the nature of this education was primarily religious: how to read the Koran, and household-oriented: how to keep an account of the family expenses; perhaps some basic Urdu. Reading and writing Bengali were discouraged, because Urdu was the language of the Muslim élites in north India. The education imparted was not worth the name; those who received it merely gained the ability to recognize the alphabets and read but did not understand what was read. In short, they were hardly better off than those who did not have this rudimentary education.

Under the circumstances, the two key questions were: one, whether women were to be educated at all and, second, if so, to what extent and in which direction and whether at home or in a school: exactly the same questions that had dominated the debates on education of Hindu women. On the first question there was some (although not absolute) consensus. The Muslim reformers, coming from comparable social groups, wanted education for women almost for similar reasons as their Brahmo–Hindu counterparts. Indeed, Muslim educated men increasingly desired educated wives for almost the same motive that had actuated their Brahmo–Hindu counterparts. Education would make women better companions to their husbands, better mothers to their children, and better homemakers, in short, expressed in Brahmo terms, *sakhi, sumata,* and *sugrihini*. There was however an additional dimension too. The Muslims were searching for identity, and creating Muslim nationalism on a somewhat different plane than the nationalism of the anti-colonial character that emerged during the freedom movement. Here the need was not so much for a son, strong and courageous, who would brave the British, but for sons who would restore the pristine glory of Islam. Women, when educated, would become better Muslims, learn to appreciate the message of Islam and, consequently, be better equipped to bring up their children in the true spirit of Islam. To quote a contemporary exposition:

Continuing corrupt indoctrination has poisoned our society to its foundation. Women, as mothers, can be the source of both progress as well as of harm to society. Attitudes and dispositions of mothers leave indelible imprint on the minds of innocent children. Children are born with the infirmities of their mothers, mothers, who are illiterate, who suffer from ignorance, and who are steeped in superstitions. Until and unless we are able to invest our women with appropriate education, there will be little hope of any betterment in our circumstances.[90]

Imdadul Huq advocated the cause of education with eloquence, and appealed to the Muslim youth, as his Brahmo–Hindu counterparts had done, to take up the cause.

We now realize that the key to prosperity is the extensive spread of education, and more particularly, education of women. My appeal to young men of our Muslim community is that they should devote all their energy to ensure wide dissemination of education and that our women are not deprived of the opportunity of a good education.[91]

It was with regard to the second issue, the extent and the site of education, where opinions differed. To send girls out of the home to formal schools was not accepted by many who otherwise agreed on the need for their education. For instance, in 1867, the issue of educating Muslim girls was raised at an assembly of the Bengal Social Science Association. While discussing a paper by Abdul Latif on Muslim education, Pyarichand Mitra asked whether steps had been taken for the education of Muslim women as for Muslim men. Abdul Latif did not respond. During the past forty years whatever he had done for the advancement of education had targeted only men. The response came from Maulvi Abdul Hakim of the Calcutta Madrassah. He dismissed the idea, maintaining that the education provided to girls at home was adequate for them. He asserted that Islam had given importance to the education of both men and women, and that Muslims were aware that an educated mother would raise an educated son. They could not however send their daughters to school as they observed purdah.[92] Thus a powerful section of the community was opposed to school-education for women and preferred zenana education or education at home.

In 1883, in Dhaka, a group of young 'progressive' men, mostly students of Dhaka College, founded the Muslim Suhrid Sammelani (also known as Anjuman-i-Ahbabiya-i-Islam) with the aim of regenerating Muslim society. It also decided as a priority area the spread and development of female education. Bearing in mind the community's extreme regard for purdah, it drew up a scheme whereby the girls could study the courses for classes 1–5 sitting at home, and take the examination with the help of their guardians. The successful candidates were given certificates and awards. Teaching was imparted through either the Urdu or Bengali medium. To meet the demand for home-education for women, a class of female tutors emerged, some of whom went from house to house teaching young girls Arabic, Persian, and Urdu, and, in some cases, also English.[93]

Unlike Abdul Latif, Syed Amir Ali proved to be supportive of women's entry into formal institutions. He stated at an important gathering, the All India Muslim Educational Conference in 1891, that female education should advance at the same pace as male education. If their advancement was asymmetrical, the balance of society would be upset. However, he too was unable to do anything concrete for women's formal education. Of the schools for girls, at the end of the nineteenth century, only isolated accounts are available. A few girls studied in the schools conducted by the Ladies' Association, a missionary enterprise. A Muslim lady, Latifunnessa, passed the final examination of Campbell Medical School in 1896, making history. In 1896, a few distinguished Muslim citizens of Calcutta met at the residence of Barrister E. A. Khondkar with a view to starting a school for Muslim girls. As a result, the Muslim Balika Madrassah was established in 1897 with 25 students. This was the first school in Calcutta initiated by

Muslims.[94] Up to the late nineteenth century, there were no serious efforts made by men to send girls to formal schools, though a number of girls in Dhaka, Barisal, Mymensingh, and Calcutta had started to take advantages of the limited opening, and become educated. Of this first generation of educated women, many were tutored at home, some were to a great extent self-taught, and just a few attended formal educational institutions at the lowest level.

It is a great tribute to Muslim women that they were no passive recipients. Many of them took active parts in the process of change, and actually came forward to help other women, and they have left written records for us. As early as 1822 a Muslim lady in Calcutta had helped establish schools for Muslim girls. Some schools were established in Calcutta, but they did not last. In 1897, the Calcutta Girls' Madrassah was set up with the patronage of Murshidabad's Nawab Firdaus Mahal, a lady who donated a large amount of money for the purpose. The credit for being the real pioneer of formal education for girls in Bengal goes to Nawab Faizunnessa Chaudhurani (1834–1903) of Comilla who, although a woman, was granted the title of Nawab. In the post-1857 period when Muslims had turned their back on Western education, she felt that an exposure to modern education was necessary to keep pace with the modern times. Although born in an aristocratic family and forced to live in purdah, she founded in Comilla a free madrassah for girls, which later became the reputed Faizunnessa Degree College. She also set up primary schools at each of the administrative centres in her estate, and went on to establish an English medium school for girls in 1873, known as the Faizunnessa Girls' Pilot High School, designed for *pardanashin* girls, that is, girls who had to observe purdah. She was liberal enough to take the help of the Brahmo leader of Comilla, Kalicharan De.[95] The initial response from the Muslim community was naturally lukewarm, but later many eminent women studied there.

Meanwhile in Dhaka, Eden School for girls, modelled on the Bethune School, was founded in around 1878.[96] *Bamabodhini Patrika* reported in *Baishakh* 1296 BS (1879) that there were 87 students in the school, though none had yet passed the entrance examination. In 1880, out of 153 students at Eden only one was a Muslim. According to the *Report on Female Education in Bengal*, 1881–2, out of 184 students in the High English School classes, there was not a single Muslim woman, and at the Middle English School level out of 340 students, only four were Muslim. Nonetheless, a beginning had been made, and the way prepared for the arrival of someone like Rokeya. By the early twentieth century, a host of newspapers and periodicals edited by Muslims, like the *Mussalman, Nabanoor, Sadhana,*

*Bulbul,* and *Saugat,* adopted a supportive stand on the question of women's education.[97] Syed Emdad Ali, a distinguished poet and the editor of *Nabanoor,* was a champion of the women's cause. In his poem entitled 'Bibi Fatema Zohra', he proclaimed that if men could uplift women they would in turn be lifted high by women. In another poem he urged Muslim women to inspire men and contribute to their awakening; his *Tapasi Rabeya* (1917) bears testimony to his regard for women. He was joined by a number of other 'progressive' writers, such as Syed Ismail Hossain Shirazi and Kazi Imdadul Huq. The education of women was becoming a prime concern of men, though the majority was still opposed to higher education for women. The journal, *Mihir o Sudhakar,* pithily articulated the majority sentiment:

> Education for women is desirable, certainly, but it needs to be kept within certain prescribed norms. For example, women must be able to read the Koran Sharif, and they should also be familiar with the Urdu and the Bengali languages. Knowledge of Urdu will make it possible for them to study the essential religious texts to assimilate the teachings of Islam, and also to be able to follow faithfully the dictates of the Shariat. On the other hand, certain selected Bengali books, like Lalana Suhrid, will tell them how to run a well-regulated family, of the need for the care of health, of how to bring up children as well as of their obligations to their elders. That is about all that women need to learn. We do not favour higher education for women.[98]

Whatever might have been the calculations of men, many women, when they became educated, started writing and expressing their own sentiments and views, a trait they shared with their Hindu–Brahmo sisters. One Taherunnessa contributed an essay to *Bamabodhini Patrika,* Latifunnessa sent a poem to the same journal addressing it to Muslim women;[99] Nawab Faizunnessa wrote *Rupjalal* (1876), a very interesting literary composition written as a long poem with occasional prose passages. Azizunnessa was one of the earliest women to have published an article in a Muslim periodical, *Islam Pracharak.* Khairunnessa (1870–1912) too, contributed essays to *Nabanoor,* a reputed journal. In 1904, she published an essay entitled 'Amader Shikshar Antarai' (The Impediments to Our Education) and in 1905 in a piece called 'Swadesh Anurag' (Love for the Country), she appealed to women to boycott foreign goods in the context of the Swadeshi movement. She was perhaps the first of the women writers to formulate clear ideas on social as well as political issues. In her *Satir Patibhakti* (The Devotion of a Chaste Wife to Her Husband), she listed the duties of a good wife, an important contribution to the didactic discourse aimed at women of contemporary times.[100] By and large, therefore, newly educated Muslim women, like their Hindu counterparts, were echoing men's views. Dissident notes were not yet audible.

## Summary and Observations

The Hindu and Muslim communities in Bengal transformed themselves politically and socially from the mid-nineteenth to the mid-twentieth century. These changes started earlier among the Hindus, but the pattern was in many respects similar among both: the growth of an urban middle class, social reforms, emergence of nationalism, and the construction of new roles for women. Women were to be educated and become partners of their husbands and mothers of sons suitable to the needs of the time. Among the Hindus, social reforms accompanied religious reforms, a new 'Hindu identity' was fashioned, and womanhood was redefined. Nationalism gave a further fillip to it by endowing motherhood with new roles and political responsibilities. Among the Muslims, there was growing awareness: a need to question existing social evils and at the same time revive the valuable Islamic heritage. Again, what followed were modern reforms, the efflorescence of a new genre of literature, the reformulation of the duties of a good Muslim woman, and the emergence of a strong, new force—Bengali–Muslim nationalism.

Both Sarala and Rokeya were certainly aware of what was going on in Bengal and in the larger canvas of India. They were both products and parts of contemporary developments. Both devoted their time and thought to issues that concerned women. They had however to contend with different social realities which influenced the ways in which they reacted and expressed themselves. Sarala conformed to the emerging ideology in the community and went ahead to strengthen it with energy and leadership. Rokeya rebelled: rebelled against her society's existing customs, conformed to certain aspects of the new thought, and raised some difficult questions.

## 3. Sarala and Rokeya: Women's Issues

Both Sarala Devi Chaudhurani and Begum Rokeya Sakhawat Hossain were deeply concerned with the abject position of women in society and the means of alleviating it. However, both looked at the issue from their own points of view that were shaped by their respective social and familial backgrounds and other historical circumstances that they encountered. I will first investigate how they looked at the degenerate position of women in society and what their prescriptions for improvement were.

### PERSPECTIVES

#### Sarala Devi

Sarala was primarily a political person. It was her resentment against British political domination that preceded her awareness of male domination, but she was not anti-male. She did not blame men for the degradation of women, as Rokeya did. Sarala repeatedly recalled the contributions of 'progressive' men like Rammohan Roy, Iswar Chandra Vidyasagar, Dayanand Saraswati, Ranade, and many others without whose committed endeavours women of the twentieth century would have still lived in medieval darkness. A key statement of hers was, 'In India more than anywhere else the women's cause is the men's cause'.[1] Sarala's central thesis was that women were the real source of power in society, and it was necessary only to bring them out of the temporary decline that had currently set in. With her the central task was to make women conscious of their latent power, and rekindle it. The analysis of the decline was not the key issue; to remove it, was.

One has to recall here Sarala's religious convictions. That self-knowledge is crucial for self-confidence and that it is a cornerstone of power is ingrained in Hindu Upanishadic philosophy, and Brahmoism, to which Sarala subscribed, was based on the Upanishads. Hindu scriptures recognize woman-power as *adyashakti* (primordial force), and acknowledge women's creative, protective, and destructive power. In Hinduism Goddess Durga, the embodiment of *shakti*, defeats Mahishasur, the embodiment of evil and the enemy of the gods, when all male gods fail. Sarala was influenced by this heritage.[2] She once said, 'Ours is the country where, since time immemorial, Chandi (another name for Durga), the Goddess incarnate of power, has been venerated. Each Bengali home ritually pays homage to this deity of power.'[3] Interestingly, Anushilan Samiti, the secret revolutionary organization with which Sarala was associated, worshipped Durga to derive inspiration and strength in its fight against the superior British might. Sarala also admired the concept of Kali, a primordial version of Durga, and the embodiment of Divine woman power. She had a Japanese artist draw a Kali portrait which adorned the wall of the front room of her home.[4]

For Sarala woman-power was real. In an article entitled 'Ramanir Karya' (The Duties of Women), published in the journal *Suprabhat*, edited by Kumudini Mitra, she argued that women were the driving force in society, men merely the machine. Women's authority actually extended through the home to the entire society. Women can make the home a heaven or a hell. They are the real Lakshmis. If women remembered their twin qualities of *shree* (grace/beauty born out of serenity) and *kalyan* (benevolence), they would be able to rule the society and turn it into a peaceful place.[5] *Suprabhat* was a pro-nationalist journal propagating the current version of nationalism, and Kumudini, daughter of Lilabati and Sanjay Kumar Mitra, the celebrated nationalist couple, was herself a staunch nationalist. Through her journal Sarala was thus communicating to women readers the nationalist discourse on women. The Lakshmis must be convinced of their power and make every home in the nation a veritable centre of orderliness, competence, and support. At the core of the article underlay two messages to women: an expectation that they would perform their traditional domestic role, and a demand that they should master a whole new set of household abilities. One must recall here the nationalist normative model of womanhood. Women, the grihalakshmis, were to manage the household with the Indian shree and Western 'efficiency' for the benefit of the nation.

Why were women not able to meet these rising expectations from them and satisfy the demands of the nation, queried Sarala. Why had they sunk so low? To Sarala, the prime responsibility for women's degraded condition lay primarily with women themselves. She wrote, 'In the context of our retrogradation, not only men named us *abala* [weak], women also treasure this untrue epithet. It is alright to cultivate bashfulness, but it is a sin to lack self-confidence and insult one's own self.'[6]

But then, Sarala conceded, for centuries the women of India had been made to think of themselves as inferior, incapable and weak. This belief had taken firm root in their minds through innumerable incidents and in untold ways. From birth they had suffered discrimination vis-à-vis the other sex, and had been made to internalize a sense of inferiority both within the family and outside. Unfortunately, the elder women of the family had a major role to play in this process of socialization. The rejoicings that greeted the arrival of a male child were not even fractionally evident in the birth of a female child.

Instead there is an all round embarrassment in even recognizing the female child's existence! And when this child grows into a woman, she does so without any conception of her dignity. She grows up with a sense of inferiority, and accepts that she has no right to any authority, or any useful role in life. 'I am an ignorant and insignificant person', is what she comes to believe, 'and so I have nothing to offer to society'. This continuous attrition in their own self-assessment leads to inferiority that naturally hinders the governance of the family, society and the nation.[7]

It was Sarala's mission to assist women to become aware of their potential and be confident of their power. In order to do so, she turned to history. It was necessary to inspire men and women alike with the traditions of the past. Sarala, in tune with current nationalist thought, valorized select qualities of select women of the past, and believed that women should emulate the lofty spirit and the worthy moral qualities of their predecessors. Repeatedly, she told Indian women that they were Sita and Kaushalya reborn.

When I look at women I am reminded of many legendary women of our country— Kaushalya, Sumitra, Kunti, Satyavati and Gandhari. These names are well-known to everyone, but have you, women of my country, ever pondered to realize that you yourselves are all incarnations of these very celebrated women?[8]

It may be recalled here that the nationalist discourse harked back to the heritage of women of ancient and Puranic India, and urged contemporary women to emulate the qualities of those 'glorious' women. None did it better yet simpler than Vivekananda.

So shall we bring to the need of India great fearless women—women worthy to continue the traditions of Sanghamitra, Lila, Ahalyabai and Mirabai—women fit to be mothers of heroes ... It is only in the homes of educated and pious mothers that great men are born.[9]

Sarala sincerely believed in this theory, and with characteristic energy proceeded to communicate the message to women in inspiring and convincing terms.

The mighty Ganges which flows from the mountains north of Hardwar, and comes down to Calcutta, its each ripple travelling all this long distance, and then it runs past Calcutta and meets the sea. In a similar fashion the stream of time has carried all of us from the distant past to our present days.

Indian women needed to be educated and, once they were conscious of their innate power, they would produce brave sons like 'Bhisma, Arjuna, Lakshmana and Bharata', and thereby continue the past heritage.[10]

## Begum Rokeya

Rokeya was far sharper in her views regarding women's backwardness vis-à-vis men. She had two principal premises for her thesis. One was that women were used by men and were willing collaborators in their own oppression. The second was that men and women constituted two equal parts of society. Hence, if one was weak the other could not thrive. On these two premises her perception and actions rested. She believed that progress in society depended on the joint contribution of men and women alike, not only on those of men. Women constituted half the population; if they were left behind, how could society progress? In a satirical description to drive home the point, she wrote,

> Imagine you are standing in front of a full view mirror reflecting your image from your head down to your feet. The right half of your body is that of a man and the left of a woman. Your right arm is about thirty inches long and muscular, your left arm just twenty-four inches long and slender. Your right foot measures twelve inches, your left foot dainty and small. Your right hand shoulder is five feet in height, and the left only four feet, so you cannot stand straight and your head inclines to the left. Your right ear is as large as that of an elephant and your left ear is long like a donkey's. Now watch, watch carefully! If you do not like your image, then let us have a look at the two-wheeled cart. If one wheel of the cart is larger (the husband) than the other (the wife), then the cart can hardly move forward. It will go round and round at the same spot. This is precisely the condition of us Indians; we are hardly able to press forward.[11]

Why were women in India so degraded? How could the process be reversed? Rokeya's point, unlike Sarala's, was that if one had to start working for the unnati of women, one had to identify the factors responsible for the degradation. She identified two: (i) selfishness of men and (ii) mental slavery of women. With characteristic vigour, she took up the cause and in her book *Motichoor* (1905), she presented her diagnosis in extremely daring terms by the standards of the time. Her basic statement was—and the idea occurred repeatedly in her writings—that women had become slaves of men. 'In this twentieth century what are we? Female slaves. They say that slavery has been abolished in the world. But have we been freed from our slavery? Why are we slaves? There are reasons.'[12] While investigating the causes for this degeneration, Rokeya was indeed bitingly sharp towards members of her own sex. She agreed with Sarala that the most deplorable fact was the loss of women's *atmaadar* or self-respect. Women had ceased to feel ashamed of behaving as the 'weaker sex' and accepting men's help in everything. Over a long period of servitude women had come to accept slavery as a matter of course. In this process, through continuous neglect their mental faculties, such as, self-reliance and courage, had been dulled. Physical faculties were also conspicuous by their absence for the lack of cultivation. 'A woman's body was as much a piece of stagnation as her mind'.

But then, whose fault was it that women had reached this state? Showing acute analytical perception comparable to modern-day feminism, Rokeya pinpointed 'the lack of opportunity' as the key cause of women's slavish condition.[13] Women had been denied equal opportunities with men by the male-imposed social system. To give but one example among many of the unfairness of the system, the women-turned-slaves were without any proper homes. They merely resided in the homes of their masters, their male relations, and were subservient to them. These homes were for them more like walled prisons.

In this wide world, we have no place. Regardless of the state of our finances, we always live under someone's custody, always in the custodian's homes, not ours .... When the reeds covering our fragile cottages wear thin (that is, when we are poor), ... when rain water leaks on our heads, even then we live in the houses of our custodians ... If perchance, we are daughters or daughters-in-law of a king and live in a palace, we are still inmates of the homes of our lords and masters .... Or, as daughters or daughters-in-law of an ordinary householder, wherever we are, we live under the subordination of our masters .... We women cannot claim even a humble cottage as our home. No living creatures are as helpless as we, because they all have a home.[14]

Two points must be made clear here. First, in this essay entitled 'Griha' (The Home) Rokeya's view was opposed to Sarala's. While Sarala tried to impress upon her female audience that they were the mistresses of their homes, Rokeya reminded her readers that in India a majority of women did not possess a home which they might call their own. In other words, Sarala was pressing for rights in the home, Rokeya was urging for a right to a home; the former wanted to develop skills, expertise, and a whole set of domestic abilities and responsibilities, while the latter decided to prioritize a sense of deprivation before a sense of duties. Secondly, these strong words do not mean that Rokeya was anti-Islam or was condemning Islamic law. Quite the contrary; she was proud of Islamic religion and law, and forcefully argued that under Islamic law, women were entitled to inherit their father's property, including house property—(Hindu women did not enjoy the right at that time)—but the rule was never observed. Men denied women their rights, while most women were unaware of their rights, nor could they exercise those, even if they were aware. The necessary social support and access to tools for implementation were both lacking.

Rokeya was perhaps at her bitterest when describing the condition of women living under abarodh (literally confinement). Rokeya attacked abarodh mercilessly, but in some of her writings and speeches, she made a concession for purdah and distinguished it from abarodh. Her approach was pragmatic, and she needed to formulate a workable solution by rejecting the worst form of suppression, but accommodating what could not be done away with. Hence, in her article entitled 'Burqa', she stated that the custom was acceptable so far as modesty of women was concerned; but to the extreme use of the purdah she was totally opposed. Confinement to a room or to the interior of the house was injurious to health; it denied women access to formal education and social interaction. That dulled their brains, and made them adhere to worthless behavioural patterns. She asked the orthodox opposition: 'Purdah does not mean deprivation of all rights and confinement within four walls. Have you read at all the Koran Sharif? Or, do you just hang it around your neck?'[15] She prefaced her book entitled *Abarodhbasini*, where she cited with merciless sarcasm the pitiful condition of women in abarodh, with the words:

When visiting Kurseong and Madhupur, I picked up beautiful attractive stones. From the sea-beaches of Madras and Orissa, I gathered sea shells of many colours and shapes. And during my twenty years of service to the society, I collected only curses from our die-hard Mullas ... . Every part of my body oozes sin, so I make no apology for any fault in this book.[16]

Rokeya's courage of conviction was transparent in every part of her work. She made no secret of the fact that she considered men primarily responsible for the abject subjection of women. In a truly startling piece entitled *Sultana's Dream* (1908), an extremely courageous, if bitterly satirical composition, she drew an imaginary picture of an ideal land, Ladyland, where women ruled; and laws and customs applicable to men and women in our society were inversely applied to them. The work portrays her as travelling to the strange land in a dream and having conversations with one of the citizens, Sister Sara. To quote from the text written by her in English in the original version (later translated by her into Bengali):

I became very curious to know where the men were. I met more than a hundred women while walking there, but not a single man.
  'Where are the men?', I asked her.
  'In their proper places, where they ought to be.'

> 'Pray let me know what you mean by their proper places'.
> 'O, I see my mistake, you cannot know our customs, as you were never here before. We shut our men indoors.'
> 'Just as we are kept in the zenana?'
> 'Exactly so.'

In this work Rokeya openly asserted her grievances against the man-made social system as well as her condemnation of women for letting themselves be taken for a ride.

> 'We have no hand or voice in the management of our social affairs. In India man is lord and master. He has taken to himself all powers and privileges and shut up the women in the zenana.'
> 'Why do you allow yourself to be shut up?'
> 'Because it cannot be helped as they are stronger than women.'
> 'A lion is stronger than a man, but it does not enable him to dominate the human race. You have neglected the duty you have to yourselves and you have lost your natural rights by shutting your eyes to your own interests.'[17]

Even more daring than this imaginary piece was an essay which had first appeared in the Brahmo journal *Mahila*, edited by Girish Sen, in 1310 BS (1903) entitled, 'Alankar Na Badge of Slavery' (Jewellery, Or Badges of Slavery). It was published again in the journal *Nabanoor* in 1904 and was entitled 'Streejatir Abanati' (Degradation of Women). As a result of a storm of protest, when the article was re-published under a slightly altered title, 'Amader Abanati' (Our Degradation) in *Motichoor* in 1908 the following portion was expunged:

Whenever a woman has tried to raise her head, she has been brought down to her knees on the grounds of either religious impiety or scriptural taboo. Of course, it cannot be ascertained with certainty, but this appears to have been the case. What we could not accept as correct, we had to concede later in the belief that it had the authority of a religious dictum .... Men have always propagated such religious texts as edicts of God to keep us women in the dark. It is not my intention to open a debate on the mysteries and spiritual aspects of any particular religion. I will merely restrict myself to discussing the social laws and regulations enshrined in the religious texts. Our righteous friends may, therefore, rest assured ... You can clearly understand that the scriptures are nothing but a set of regulating systems prescribed by men. You hear that the prescriptions were laid down by saints. If a woman could have become a saint, perhaps she would have prescribed opposite regulations .... We must not allow ourselves to bow down to the undue authority exercised by men in the name of religion. It has been seen time and again that the stricter the religious restrictions, the more severe is the women's victimization .... Some may ask me, 'Why do you bring in religion when you are only discussing social conditions?' To which my reply is, 'Restrictions imposed by religion are responsible for tightening the chains of our slavery. Men are ruling over women under the pretext of laws prescribed by religion. That is why I am obliged to bring in the question of religion in my discussion, for which my apologies to righteous gentlemen'.[18]

Rokeya's words reflect not just courage but also a mind that was far ahead of its time. Her women contemporaries were not ready to appreciate or indeed understand her views.[19] Rokeya knew that the primary barrier was lack of education. Women would have to be educated before they could realize the impact of her ideas and strive to change their situation.

## THE ISSUE OF WOMEN'S EDUCATION

### Sarala Devi

Among the Hindus, especially the Brahmos, women's education, as mentioned earlier, was progressing, but slowly. One of the periodicals that took up the cause was *Bharati*, which published a fair number of articles on the subject. For Sarala, the education of women was essential for the elevation of all in society. It had a higher purpose than the enlightenment of an individual; it was necessary for the enlightenment of the entire nation. Without an educated womanhood, it was pointless to dream of a reformed India. The point is then hammered home: 'Of the parents, the mother is the real teacher of the society. If she herself is uneducated, how will she inspire her children to serve the national cause? ... . Educate the women in your homes quickly, free them from fear, they will give you courage.'[20] Obviously, women's education was not envisaged only for the liberation of women but for their service to the larger society. In a lecture delivered in Bombay at a conference of women at Arya Samaj Hall in 1907, Sarala asserted that women must be permitted to work with men in the anti-colonial political struggle outside the home. The nationalists, she argued, must lay equal emphasis on the education of men and women. If women were educated, they would appreciate the implication of freedom and encourage their husbands to fight for it. She stated, 'The leaders of the political movement must know for certain that as long their wives do not join them and work together with them there is no hope of success of their endeavour'.[21]

To Sarala, however, women's education did not mean a renunciation of their domestic role. She was steeped in the contemporary ideology of the nationalist construction of Indian womanhood. While believing in women's power to enforce righteous conduct at home, she was clear in her ideas about what women should do. The chief duty of a woman, she stated, was to inspire her husband to follow the path of dharma. An uneducated woman was incapable of performing this task. If a wife was to shape herself as a true friend, confidante, and guide of her husband, her expertise in culinary art alone was by itself insufficient. She had to be knowledgeable on many other subjects. It was the ignorance and illiteracy of women that was responsible for the debasement of the husband–wife relationship. Education was the only tool that could bridge the gap. Sarala did not blame men for women's lack of education as sharply and categorically as Rokeya did. In one of her articles in *Bharati*, however, she did mention men's culpability for women's current unenviable position, urged men to treat women with honour and dignity and take every possible step to open up educational opportunities to them.

In ancient India when the Aryans were at the peak of their civilization, women were at par with the men in acquiring knowledge and education. In the process, they were able to earn the respect of their men. Today, unfortunately, because of the appalling way they are treated, the women of the same country are producing only imbecile, cowardly, disloyal and self-seeking children. But look after them properly, open the doors of knowledge and education to them, encourage their hopes and aspirations, you will see that once again they will become mothers of characters like Rama, Bharata, Yudhisthira and Krishna ... Hindu saints have said that knowledge destroys fear. So educate your women, make them fearless, and you will see that they will be able to invest you with resolution.[22]

Sarala held that women's responsibility as mother was crucial in shaping the destiny of the nation. Women were entrusted with the task of rearing children. If children were not properly guided in the early stages of life, they could never grow up into physically and mentally healthy adults. If the mother was not educated, how was she to educate her children? A teacher, Sarala argued, could teach the pupils only on the basis of his own knowledge and thoughts. If women were given the torch of truth and knowledge, they would direct their children on the path of 'progress'. When she did not possess the light herself, her children's lives were bound to be devoid of light. Why was India as a nation in such a pitiable condition? asked Sarala. According to her,

It is because one-half of our people, namely the women, have remained so neglected. The root of our nationwide corruption and decadence lies in the lack of education in our women .... It is only the parents who can impart sound education to their children and inculcate in them a sense of human values. In reality, it is the mother who is the principal educator, but if the mothers themselves are totally uneducated, how can they be expected to teach their children to grow up as worthy persons to help the country?[23]

Thus Sarala's prescription for women's education was mediated by nationalist consciousness. She had internalized the nationalist discourse about mothers being the educators and rearers of martial, heroic sons.[24] Women should be educated, otherwise how can they contribute properly to the freedom movement or the rearing of worthy children? But then, to Sarala, a woman was the mistress of the home—the real power and maker of the family and the home in the widest sense of the term. In her article 'Ramanir Karya' (The Duties of Women), she said,

> Women can turn their homes into heaven or hell, because they are the presiding deities in their homes .... It is women who can create a beautiful home, keep it clean and run it in an orderly manner. It is women again whose negligence can turn a home into an ugly and foul place, where one can only expect to see dirt and filth.[25]

It is easy to see that Sarala was adhering here to the male reformers' construction of the 'new' women, or grihalakshmi. It was women's duty to turn the home into a heaven. A man was not able to create a real home. Only a woman could create a home. In order to be able to do so, however, a woman had to be properly educated. An educated woman could do housework more skillfully and systematically than an uneducated one. In Sarala's perception, the concept of the home was inseparably intertwined with the concept of womanhood and, therefore, a good home implied stewardship by an educated woman, who would know how to manage it. But what constituted the ideal home, which the educated woman was to nurture? Said Sarala,

> A clean and healthy environment, a decent husband, a loyal and companionable wife, and obedient children make a good home. If one has to keep a healthy home, one has to be aware of the rules of hygiene and run the household in accordance with those rules. It is necessary to be educated, to be disciplined and punctual in routine work, and to be orderly in order to make the home an abode of restfulness and comfort. The home is not a temporary inn, it is a resort for life.[26]

We must recall here that the nationalist discourse constructed the home as the site for spiritual qualities, and women were to nurture the site. Who but the educated women could comprehend the high ethical and spiritual traits of the nation, and uphold them through everyday homely life? It is significant that Sarala also treasured the traditional Hindu routines of the home. She once visited a Bengali home when, as the evening was approaching, she heard the lady next door calling out to her daughter-in-law, 'Daughter, go and get the lamp for the evening ceremony'. At this command, 'a young girl, her face covered in veil, came out with a lighted lamp and went through all the dark rooms to mark the evening hour. Auspicious sound of conchshells greeted the eventide. What a lovely ritual!'[27]

The ritual that so impressed Sarala was but an everyday occurrence in a traditional Hindu household. The 'lovely' ceremony had religious overtones; the celebrant was bringing light into darkness and welcoming the Goddess Lakshmi to the household. It was a woman's task to perform this. That women had within them the power to bring happiness into the family was only one part of the statement; that they had also the responsibility of doing do so was the other and more important message. Sarala would not, however, limit educated women solely to domestic duties. She pressed for extension of the scope of the power and duties of women. They were not to remain confined to their own homes, but to take on the responsibility of bettering their neighbourhood and society, because they constituted the constructive as well as destructive forces in society. What a woman could accomplish, a man could not.

If our women can keep in view the concept of 'grace and beauty', then surely they can help in keeping our streets and neighbourhoods clean and sparkling. And if motivated by the other aspect of Lakshmi, namely, benevolence, then we shall be able to keep our home and neighbourhood free from unseemly disagreement and improper activities.[28]

One must point out here that Sarala subjected women to the old patriarchic order in a new form. Giving them full responsibility for the home would hold them there for much of their time, while a comparable responsibility for the neighbourhood would demand similar commitment outside the home. Here Sarala redefined the duties, the responsibilities, as well as the concept of womanhood. It had already become a part of the nationalist discourse that women had a key role in nation-building. They had the charge of the future of the entire nation. Motherhood was extolled for tending the next generation, a generation of heroic, patriotic men. 'What can women do for the country?' was the question that Sarala asked, and she answered it herself. A nation was but a conglomeration of people, and women were mothers of people. Therefore, women were the teachers of the entire nation. The educating role was important in view of the need to create a people strong enough to assert independence from foreign rule, and also make a place for themselves in the community of nations. It was possible for women to serve, and indeed it should be the aim of their lives to serve, the whole of human society by virtue of love, compassion and the spirit of benevolence,[29] as they were able to influence the higher instincts of human beings. Thus Sarala emphasized the power of women, and also asserted that women's field of activities was not confined to the household; it should extend to 'an unlimited sphere'. If this realization of a 'high and noble aim of life' gave them confidence in themselves, they needed to organize themselves as a body to concretize their potential. A true education, in Sarala's view, must equip women with the necessary tools to achieve all this and follow the right path.

What did she think of education for men? Did she visualize an education for men that would be somewhat different from that of women? As she was concerned with the nation as a whole comprising both men and women, she was concerned with men's education too. It was necessary to inspire young men and women with patriotism, with pride in the heritage of the past, and with lessons from history. Her advice to the young generation was:

> Get to know about the achievements of your ancestors. Develop respect for their noble deeds. Try to fix in your mind that these achievers were no more than flesh-and-blood people like yourselves and, therefore, you ought also to be able to emulate their feats. ... In the first instance, study the areas where their attainments have their imprints. Delve deeply into your country's history with assiduous research. And convert that past glory into present reality.[30] What is the point of a university which only produces bookworms, which does not build characters of enterprise and energy, a university which does not equip one with broad vision to go out in the world, but merely offers you a degree and keep at home? I certainly cannot call that an institution of learning; it is in reality a den of darkness and ignorance.[31] Do you wish to remain just bookworms, preoccupied only with passing examinations, and then secure a clerkship as your meal ticket? Do you accept this as the typical Bengali character? As human beings, are you or are you not motivated by any sense of aspirations and spirit of enterprise, or dream the impossible dreams? Go out and let the world know that Bengalis are men of worth.[32]

Here Sarala's pride as a Bengali comes out loud and clear. She was perhaps as much concerned about her community in Bengal as Rokeya was about her community in the state. In a sense, therefore, both Sarala and Rokeya were proponents of a form of Bengali nationalism. Sarala wanted to see Bengali men as nationalist heroes and Bengali women as homemakers and moral power generators in nationalist homes. Education was to equip them with the requisite tools, refined and modernized.

The number of girls going to school was increasing. In order to carry out her ideas regarding women's education, Sarala founded a school for girls on 1 June 1930 at Bhowanipore. It was named Siksha Sadan, and was set up by the Bharat Stree Mahamandal. Here, girls were coached to appear at the Entrance (Matriculation) Examination. Later, the school was transferred to Albert Hall in College Square. It attracted a substantial number of students, and soon a girls' hostel was also set up. Gradually the responsibility for running the school was devolved on a body of teachers, educationists, and social workers.[33]

## Begum Rokeya

If Rokeya had a somewhat different perspective on education, it was defined by her position and the conditions prevalent in her community. For Rokeya, the education of women was an all-important issue. It held the key to Muslim women's emergence from social bondage. Muslim women had not yet begun venturing out of their homes; the question of their participating in political movements did not arise. The primary obstacles to their living as complete human beings was the absence of education; it was the principal cause of women's backwardness.

Like our bedrooms which shut out sunlight, our intellect is denied the fruits of enlightenment because there are no adequate schools and institutions of learning available to women. A man can go on learning, but will ever access to education be fully open to women? If one single liberal man attempts to assist us a thousand men put up obstacles.[34]

Most people had a mental block against women's education. Society was prepared to ignore many failings in an uneducated woman. If however a woman with a modicum of education made a small error, everyone would ascribe it to the 'pernicious' effect of their education. Education for men was considered important because it was a passport to gainful employment. Women were not allowed even to go out, and so the question of their gainful employment did not arise at all. Even those men who favoured some education for women were opposed to their taking to higher education. According to most of them, a woman should be able to cook, should know how to sew, should be hard-working in order to run the household, and might be allowed to read a book or two; that was more than enough. Rokeya herself was not against cooking or needlework for women. 'Food and clothes being the basic essentials of life, acquisition of skills in these fields is certainly necessary, but that does not mean that we confine our life to the kitchen only.'[35] In reality, the existing practice of keeping women illiterate was doing incalculable harm to Muslim society. Not only had it impeded the overall development of the Muslim community, but was injurious to family life. Lack of education had created a mental schism between educated husbands and their uneducated wives. What mental affinity could there be between them to make partnership in married life fruitful?

There were two special impediments to the education of Muslim women. The first was the custom of strict purdah. Abarodh especially deprived women of access to education. 'Removal of that artificial restriction keeping women confined to homes will lead to unrestricted spread of education among women,' she said. 'And it will then be impossible to arrest the progress of such education.'[36] The second impediment to women's education was the custom of early marriage for girls. In Rokeya's dreamland, Ladyland, education was spread far and wide among women. Early marriage had been stopped. No woman was allowed to marry before the age of twenty-one. Purdah had vanished. In real life India, however, daughters were married off early, and most Muslim fathers discriminated between their sons and daughters. A father who appointed four tutors for his sons did not bother to appoint even one for his daughter's education. Sons were encouraged to go through the university system, while daughters were not even permitted to finish school even by those who agreed to let them go to schools. The curriculum for girls was faulty too. They were to learn the Arabic alphabets, then the Koran without understanding the meaning of any of the verses, argued Rokeya. They just memorized and repeated the verses like parrots. There were no suitable books on Persian and Urdu, while Bengali girls were not taught Bengali. For this sorry state of affairs, Rokeya squarely blamed men. 'Because men have deprived us of the right type of education, we have become useless.' She went on to sum up the situation in her characteristic way. 'In their selfish interest men have denied us education.'[37] In a tone of sharp ridicule, she continued, 'Men believe that riding on a few universities like the Aligarh, and a few other Islamic colleges, they would comfortably cross the spiritual bridge to the other world, carrying their wives and daughters in a handbag!'[38]

To mend matters, men should now come forward to help the cause of women's education. Let fathers spend money on daughters' schools rather than on their ornaments. Ornaments were no substitute for learning. They decorated the body, not the mind. It was high time to change priorities and educate daughters.[39] To Rokeya, education had a wide connotation. Blind imitation of any particular country or community or memorizing a book was not its aim. 'We are born with certain natural faculties, gifted by God, and to hone these faculties through rigorous training is real education.' One must aim at both physical and mental efflorescence, and learn how to put to effective use all the organs gifted by God. One had to develop one's hands and legs, observe carefully with one's eyes, listen attentively with one's ears, and think intelligently with one's brain.[40]

Rokeya placed particular emphasis on women's physical strength, and believed that true education must include physical training. Although Rokeya and Sarala both valued courage and sturdiness, there was some difference in their approach. Sarala, in tune with the revolutionaries of the time, passionately believed in physical prowess and wanted Bengali youth to be strong and sturdy in order to be able to fight against the British in a possible war of independence. Rokeya thought only of women and desired them to become healthy and tough in order to live life with dignity. While Sarala promoted gymnasia for young men, Rokeya advised parents and teachers to give physical training to girls both at home and at school. She advocated teaching girls how to play with swords and rods, and how to grind corn in indigenous machines known as *janta* (which would develop arm muscles).

I ask for that kind of education that will equip *women to acquire their rights as citizens,* the kind of education which will mould them into model daughters, model wives and model mothers. Education must be for both physical and mental advancement. Women must know that they were not born into this world merely to be decorative pieces in fine dresses and expensive jewelleries. On the contrary, they are born as women to achieve certain particular objectives. Their life is not to be dedicated for the sole purpose of pleasing their husbands; let them not be dependent on others for their upkeep.[41]

Rokeya did not believe that women's education should avoid having an economic function; one of her principal arguments was the need for economic independence for women. Educated women should join the labour force. Why must parents of young girls bemoan the birth of their daughters, just because it was difficult to find suitable matches? 'Educate the daughters properly and let them go out and fend for themselves', she advised, questioning the orthodox view.

Why should we not have access to gainful employment? What do we lack? Are we not able-bodied, and endowed with intelligence? In fact, why should we not employ the labour and energy that we expend on domestic chores in our husbands' homes to run our own enterprises?[42]

Rokeya here displayed a radical streak. At a time when Muslim women were under purdah, and 'progressive' Brahmo women like Swarnaprabha Basu and Hemantakumari Chaudhuri defined educated women's dutiful role at home,[43] Rokeya talked of the right to employment. In 1905, when Rokeya advocated this point of view some women had already taken up paid jobs, like Kamini Roy and Kadambini Ganguli, but from them, too, no ideological assertion had come, nor had society accepted gainful employment for women as desirable.[44] Rokeya, almost alone, dared to say that marriage was not the ultimate goal, family was not the ultimate end. From here it was only one step to argue that girls might choose not to marry at all or marry the man of their choice even across community lines. Rokeya did not spell out any approval of marriage outside the community, and indeed seems not to have approved of it. As one of her essays, 'Dhangsher Pathe Muslim Samaj' (Muslim Society on the Road to Destruction) would indicate and her novel *Nurse Nelly* would confirm. Nonetheless, she was clear in her views about the dispensability of marriage/married life for a woman. In her novel, *Padmarag*, the two principal characters, Siddika and Latif, were according to Muslim custom *akd*, technically husband and wife, although they had not met. When they met, still unaware of their mutual relationship, they fell in love. Once the relationship became known, Latif repeatedly begged Siddika to come back to him. Siddika refused. Although fond of him, having once been rejected by his family, and consequently by him, she decided not to ignore the insult and return as an obedient wife. She would set an example for other girls. She explained her stand to her colleagues at Tarini Bhavan,

Are we no more than just clay dolls that men can either accept us or reject us at will? I wish to tell men that opportunity knocks only once, and no more. We no longer live in the times when you could kick us and we licked your boots. I have taken the vow to dedicate my life to work for Tarini Bhavan in order to serve the cause of women, and in the process kill the purdah system, roots and branches.[45]

It was not necessary for a woman to perform wifely duties under any circumstance, to put up with insult, oblivious of *atmaadar* (self-respect). Through the parting conversation between Latif and Siddika, Rokeya's own view about women's independence is revealed,

Latif: 'Tell me clearly, Siddika, will you not come home as my wife?'
Siddika: 'No, I shall not. You go your way, and I shall take my own road.'[46]

One other character in the novel, Sakina, says:

I wish to demonstrate that there are recourses other than just living in the husband's home. To care for one's husband and his home is not the be-all and end-all of a woman's life. God has given us a very precious life—not to be misspent in cooking and domestic chores and to moan over destiny. We must declare our war against this unfair society.[47]

Obviously, Rokeya constructed a thesis stating that for women marriage and maintaining the home were not as crucial as society made those out to be. What was important for them was the ability to 'fend for themselves' and live with dignity. Education was the only tool which could impart that ability. Clearly for Rokeya, marriage, and consequently good wifehood, was not the real goal of education. What was it then? Service to society, as Sarala would argue? That was an important aim for Rokeya, but the most crucial objective for a woman at that point of time was social equality and independence.

The key question is how to get about regaining our lost position. What must we do to stand up and be counted as worthy daughters of our country? To start with, we need to take a firm resolve that in our daily life we shall be on an equal footing with men, and that we must have intense self-confidence not to feel a burden to any man. We will do whatever we have to do to gain equality with men. If the means to our attaining independence is through our ability to earn our living, then we must do so. From office workers to lawyers, and magistrates, even judges—we shall get entry to all jobs and professions, presently the privileged precincts of men. Perhaps fifty years down the road we may see a woman installed as Viceroy, thus elevating the status of all women.[48]

So for Rokeya, the ultimate goal of a woman's life and education was to rise above existing degradation, be able to hold her head high and tread the men's world as an equal. She tried to implement some of these ideas through a school she established first in Patna and later transferred to Calcutta: the Sakhawat Memorial Girls' School, which became the centre of her life from its inception.[49] The school was an Urdu-medium one, but Rokeya tried to set up a Bengali-medium section.[50] She started her school without any personal experience of the system of school education, but she gathered knowledge by borrowing ideas from the Brahmos, the vanguards of women's education, a pointer to Rokeya's liberal approach. She visited Brahmo Samaj and well-known girls' schools in Calcutta, observed their techniques, and imitated as well as modified them. Within a mere five years, the number of students, initially eight, increased tenfold, and together with Muslims, a few Hindu and Parsi students also joined. At the annual assembly in 1914, Rokeya read her annual report in English. She mentioned that the two major problems the school faced were getting adequate transport for the students, and finding suitable and qualified teachers for teaching.[51] It may be recalled that Bethune School had faced the same problems when it started, although under full government patronage. There was a dearth of teachers, a dearth of students (who initially had to be persuaded to attend), and ridicule greeted those who went to school in carriages. The bus (when the school acquired one) that Sakhawat School used to bring girls from different parts of the city was so closed to maintain purdah, that it was described by some as 'a large almirah on wheels', and a 'moving black hole'. Rokeya describes it: 'There is a strip of narrow wire netting on the back door of the bus, and a similar narrow strip in the front. But for this 18 inches by 3 inches strips of netting the bus would have been totally air-tight.'[52] As girls fainted due to the lack of ventilation the net was replaced by curtains, and then, says Rokeya,

I received four letters by the evening post—none with the sender's address. One letter, written in English was signed just 'Brothers-in-Islam'. The other three were written in Urdu, two unsigned and the third carrying five signatures. The theme of the letters was identical. After conveying their good wishes for the school, the writers complained about the unsatisfactory purdah arrangements for the school bus. The screens covering the sides of the bus get wind-blown, thus exposing the interior of the bus. If this was not rectified by the following day, the writers warned that they would all be perforce obliged to write to the many Urdu daily newspapers denouncing the school, and also see to it that no girls ever used this purdah-less bus service.[53]

The bus that brought girls to Bethune School was also ridiculed. In the words of a contemporary educationist, Sivanath Shastri:

'Treat daughters with affection and educate them with utmost care' was the legend—taken from an ancient Buddhist text—inscribed on the carriage employed by the just-established school for girls. Whenever this carriage was out on the road, people would gape at it and talk. Rude remarks were passed at the cost of the little innocent schoolgirls. Comments, such as, 'If things could get worse in this present dark age of *Koli*, then they have already done so,' were frequently heard.[54]

The history of women's education in India, among both the Hindu and the Muslim communities, reads alike in broad outline; both faced the same problems, the same debates, the same hurdles.

The curriculum at Sakhawat School in its early years included Arabic, Persian, Urdu, Bengali, and English, as well as mathematics and needlework. By 1930 the school had become a high school with a secondary school curriculum. It also emphasized basic household skills: cooking, sewing, childcare, and gardening. Furthermore, physical education and some vocational skills like nursing and handicrafts, were also taught. It is interesting that a few years after the establishment of the school, in an ardent appeal for the support of all Muslims for its maintenance and development as a model school, Rokeya said in 1931 that it had not been set up to improve her own image or to keep alive the memory of her husband, but because she wanted to do something for 'the social welfare of the Bengali Muslim community'. Muslim women in Bengal were in a deplorably illiterate state as their Hindu sisters had been, but while the Hindu and Brahmo social reformers had founded institutions for the education of their women, the Muslim community had continued to be indifferent. Muslim girls also needed formal educational institutions to equip themselves with knowledge and become model Muslim women. Moreover, Muslim men desired educated wives, and as educated Muslim brides were not available, they were ready to marry Hindu, Brahmo or Christian girls. That was not right for the Muslim community:

The only remedy to remove such disabilities is to found a model school for Muslim girls, where our girls can be educated at par with girls of other communities and other states of our present world. Girls from advanced communities and, in fact, Muslim girls from other states of India have qualified as physicians, lawyers, have been appointed councillors and as members of the Round Table Conference. What are the faults of the Muslim girls of Bengal that they should be denied such opportunities? Model girls' schools for Muslims will build model Muslim girls, whose children will be future Hazrat Omar Farooques, Hazrat Fatema Zohras. And for this it is vital that the teachings of the Koran Sharif is expansively propagated and modern Bengali language translations of the Koran Sharif be available on a large scale.[55]

In 1931, in an article entitled ' Educational Ideals for the Modern Indian Girl', published in *The Mussalman,* she seems to have adopted a more moderate and traditional approach.

We must seek the elements of value in our ancient heritage. We must assimilate the old while holding to the new .... The future of India lies in its girls .... In short, our girls should not only obtain university degrees, but must be ideal daughters, wives and mothers—or I may say, obedient daughters, loving sisters, dutiful wives and instructive mothers.[56]

One can almost hear Swarnaprabha Basu and other Brahmo women educationists speaking in the same vein. The old Rokeya touch is conspicuous by its absence. Twenty-five years had elapsed since *Motichoor* had startled the community. Perhaps time mellowed her, or the need to placate the conservative section of the community in the interests of her school made her alter her approach somewhat. As she said, she did not want the school to die with her and yet until the end Rokeya in her heart of hearts cherished the concept of man–woman equality. In her last incomplete essay entitled 'Narir Adhikar' (The Rights of Women), she wrote,

Marriages in our community are contracted with the consent of both the bride and the bridegroom as laid down by the tenets of our religion. That being so, God forbid, if there has to be a divorce, then surely this must also be with the mutual consent of both the husband and the wife. But in reality that is not so; it is entirely a one-sided affair, only the husbands being allowed to divorce. I have known many instances of marriage break-ups amongst middle class families of North Bengal, and it is always the husbands separating from their wives on the flimsiest of grounds.[57]

This concept was with her from the outset of her writing career. In a masterly sentence she had asserted as early as 1905 that a husband should be called not *swami* (meaning master), but *ardhanga* (meaning the other half of the same body).[58] This must be regarded as a manifesto of early feminist thought.

## SUMMARY AND OBSERVATIONS

Fundamental differences emerged in Sarala's and Rokeya's apportionment of blame for the oppressive ignorance under which both believed women lived. Sarala held women primarily responsible for their backwardness, and chastized them for their inertia and lack of awareness. She showed no particular ire against men, and did not roundly accuse them of oppressing women deliberately to serve their own selfish interests. Rokeya also strongly criticized women for their debased condition, and for 'shutting their eyes to their own interests', but to her, men were the real culprits. Not only had they planned the strategies and systematically transformed those into social rules for dominating women, but had also punished any woman who had tried to resist. The reason for this difference of opinion between Sarala and Rokeya may be attributed partly to the difference in their early experiences. Sarala enjoyed greater privileges than were allowed to women of her generation and therefore did not share Rokeya's bitterness. Besides, liberal men in Bengal and the male-dominated liberal press stood by her in her many enterprises, nor did Sarala suffer the humiliation that Rokeya had to undergo when she was compelled to leave Patna for Calcutta after her husband's death. Deprivation and ignominy added an edge to Rokeya's feelings. Perhaps the extent of the oppression that Rokeya suffered opened up for her a more comprehensive and systematic critique. Rokeya's perception of social evils went deeper than Sarala's and to her the roots lay in patriarchal society.

One expression of the differences between Sarala and Rokeya may be seen in their use of the Bengali language. Rokeya's language was simple and laced with bitterness. 'I almost die of shame every time I think of the pathetic cowardice of women', said Rokeya, and asked, 'What must we do to stand up and be counted as worthy daughters of our country?'[59] On the other hand, Sarala's language was sophisticated and chaste. 'Looking at these women reminds me of the many legendary women of our country,' she said. 'Have you my countrywomen ever pondered the fact that you yourselves are all incarnations of the celebrated women of the past?'[60] The similes Sarala and Rokeya often adopted were also reflective of their perceptions. Sarala compared women with lionesses: 'The new thing that has appeared in Bengal is that the lioness [women] is waking up.'[61] Rokeya conjured up images of slavery when describing women's love of ornaments. 'Our jewelleries—what are these if not the symbols of our bondage? Handcuffs for prisoners are made of steel; ours are made of gold and silver and we call them bangles. Perhaps in imitation of dog collars we have fashioned our neckbands, strung with jewels. Horses and elephants are tethered with iron chains and we happily put gold chains round our necks'.[62] Rokeya's writings had an anguish that was voiced through biting sarcasm. Her essays portrayed women's devalued situation. Sarala's writings emphasized woman-power. Sarala projected the past into the future, Rokeya intently gazed at the present. Sarala hoped and inspired, Rokeya raged and rebelled.

Both Sarala and Rokeya believed that to effect sustainable change, the problem of education needed to be addressed immediately. Yet here too their approaches differed. Sarala wanted to make educated women capable homemakers and ardent nationalists, while Rokeya's emphasis was on making women self-respecting individuals at home and ideal Muslims in society. If Sarala upheld the home as a central place for educated woman, Rokeya devalued it. Rokeya did say that education would make women ideal sisters, wives, and mothers. In her essay, 'Sugrihini' (The Efficient Housewife) in *Motichoor*, she outlined the duties of a good housewife, but her primary motive was to convey to women the centrality of education in their lives—even in the discharge their daily responsibilities.[63] The difference in the two arguments was that Sarala projected education as the tool for becoming a good homemaker and, in the process, of serving the nation. To Rokeya, household duties were secondary; education for self-development was an end in itself. Further, education could lead to opportunities for employment and thus economic independence of women. Finally, Rokeya dared to claim women's equality with men, the ultimate goal of women's education. Ghulam Murshid is right when he comments that no other contemporary woman, whether Hindu or Muslim, had staked a claim to equality.[64] Gyanadanandini, Kamini Roy, Krishnabhabini Das, and even Sarala, while condemning the injustice done to women and trying to redress the situation, had not asked for gender equality. Rokeya occupies a unique place in this arena.

## 4. Organizing Women

The formation of women's associations had started in the mid-nineteenth century since the Brahmos took charge of women's education in Bengal. Several such associations worked for women's education and income-generation of indigent women. Tattwabodhini Sabha of Debendranath Tagore (1839) inaugurated a new era by advocating for women's rights. Samajonnati Bidhayini Suhrid Samiti (Society for Social Reform) followed in 1854 and aimed at the abolition of polygamy and child marriage. Bamabodhini Sabha (1863) started *Bamabodhini Patrika* (Journal for the Enlightenment of Women) for women's education, and Uttarpara Hitakari Sabha (1864) established several girls' schools. The Barisal Female Improvement Association (1871) and Vikrampur Sammilani (1879) were associations in the district towns of Bengal and were committed to women's welfare alone. Although the target of all these organizations was women's welfare, it was men who spearheaded them. Somewhat different from these were Bama Hitaishini Sabha (1871), Arya Nari Samaj (1879) and Banga Mahila Samaj (1879) which were women's associations and that aimed 'to effect the improvement of Bengali women socially, morally, mentally and spiritually'.[1] Nonetheless, these were also founded by men and were, expectedly, flavoured with both patriarchy and patronage. Swarnakumari Devi was the first woman to have formed a women's samiti. Structured on the ruins of the women's branch of the Theosophical Society, the Sakhi Samiti was, however, small and short-lived. It was left to her daughter, Sarala, to lay the foundation of an all India women's organization, formed by women, for women, of women, and led by women.

### Sarala Devi

Sarala's central focus was on woman-power. Being a political person, she was used to thinking in terms of the entire nation and its political regeneration. For this, the generation of women's power was essential. Said Sarala:

Sarala Devi with colleagues

Women's power is a source of enormous strength in any country, and no nation can progress by ignoring this strength. If the energy of women is allowed to be dormant, how can a nation then be inspired to achieve its potentials? Therefore, to stir and stimulate women into action is a priority.[2]

In a stimulating article, she wrote,

You are endowed with intellect; you are bright as a beam of light; down the ages poets have sung hymns of praise to you. Yet, why are you so spiritless now, so different, inert like a wet rag? You are regarded as a hindrance to the manly development of your husbands and sons; an impediment to their success; in fact, you are accused of being the root cause of your country's pitiful condition! But this is all wrong. All these allegations are baseless. You are not at fault at all. On the other hand you are part of *Shakti*, the Goddess of strength and power; you are Mahadevi, you are Shivani.[3]

Sarala repeatedly endeavoured to make women feel that they were embodiments of the Goddess of power, and urged them to realize the potential within them. 'Women of India! Wake up. Let the world know you for your true identity, in the image of Durga, wielder of power and authority. Find yourself. Know yourself.'[4] The influence of the ancient Hindu belief-system is clear. Women are the source of power, thus the Shastras ruled, and the Upanishads had said, 'Know thyself'. Knowledge of oneself was, according to the Upanishads, the keystone of self-development. There may be truth in the Upanishadic dictum, but the Shastric proclamation of women as goddesses was confined to the verses in the scriptures. Did women receive their due homage as goddesses and were they in a position to exercise their inherent authority? Why, if they were goddesses, were they ignored in society or ill-treated at home? These questions were not seriously raised in early twentieth century India. Sarala also did not attempt to resolve the contradiction in theory and practice, between myth and reality.

It is also evident that underlying all the talk was an extremely negative image of women. They were uneducated, ignorant, and superstitious; the country had no future in their hands, unless they elevated themselves and aroused themselves from the disastrous stupor. According to Sarala, potential power to arise and act was already within women; they only needed to be confident of it and exert it. She therefore announced to women, 'At the very beginning we must fully convince ourselves that I am the reigning queen of my home, and that I have an existence. And then we must also assume that we are the ruling force behind our societies and families.'[5] She did believe herself, and wanted other women to believe, that men were vehicles for the performance of certain duties; and that moving force behind them was women. 'Women', she proclaimed, 'are the instruments who create, who preserve and who also destroy. Not men.'[6] In order to develop self-respect, self-confidence, and self-reliance, women must continuously recite to themselves the magic words, 'I exist', 'We exist.'[7] The query that then automatically arises is, exist for whom or what? Sarala was ready with an answer.

As we grow in the intensity of appreciating our existence, the questions that will automatically follow are, why do we exist? What is the point and purpose of my personal life as a woman? What is the significance of being a woman? How can I serve India, the great country of my birth? How indeed can I help in achieving the glory and status of other women of this world?[8]

It was Sarala's prescription for the women of India that they should first try to develop their own selves, then attempt to improve their own society and turn to the larger world. To reach this destination obviously a united effort was necessary. With a view to translating her ideas into action, Sarala formed the Bharat Stree Mahamandal (literally, The Great Circle of Indian Women) or the All India Women's Association in 1910. She has given an account of the formation of this body in an article published in *Modern Review* edited by Ramananda Chattopadhayay. The idea of founding an organization for the amelioration of the condition of Indian women had been discussed for some time. Women's meetings had been organized by men in conjunction with the sessions of the Indian National Social Conference held at the time of the annual session of the Indian National Congress. Sarala had suggested on one such occasion that a permanent association of Indian women be formed with an annual calendar of programmes, rather than meet just once a year at the time of a big conference. The proposal received support from the men and women present. Finally, in November 1910 in Lahore, the nucleus of the Circle was formed at a private meeting of Indian women under the presidency of Mrs B.N. Sen. Sarala Devi Chaudhurani was appointed the General Secretary 'with powers to take all necessary steps for the establishment of the Society on a permanent footing, to extend and enlarge it, to give it a formal shape by the drafting of objects, rules and a constitution'.[9] It was decided that the inaugural meeting would be held in Allahabad in December when many women from different parts of India would assemble there.

Sarala herself provides a description of what followed. When she started preparing for the meeting, she faced opposition from 'a phalanx of mere men' despite the fact that her proposal had been accepted at an earlier conference. Possibly some of the men had not realized that women would be able to get organized so soon. It was acceptable for men to organize women's meetings, but women organizing themselves was an altogether a different proposition. 'Woe to the women if they venture to act for themselves'. A bull was actually issued from Bombay discouraging the attempt and insisting on 'a man-manipulated meeting of women just as usual'. Writes Sarala sarcastically,

Surely traditions die hard—even among social reformers of India. So they are not to blame if the shade of Manu still haunts them and actuates them in their want of faith in the capacities of Indian women and prompts them to follow the usage long established of keeping them under thraldom at every stage of their growth.[10]

However, with the support of some liberal men, the conference was held as planned. Nevertheless, there were two women's conferences in Allahabad, one organized by a section of men, the other by women, clearly demonstrating a division among the women. A salient feature of the inaugural session of the Mahamandal was that it was presided over by Her Highness the Begum Saheba of Janjira, a Muslim woman, and was graced by the presence of Her Highness the Nawab Begum Saheba of Bhopal, the only ruling princess of India, also a Muslim woman. It was a good beginning for the Indian women's movement that Hindu, Muslim, and Christian women joined hands together to give it solidarity. Sarala was appointed the General Secretary and authorized to work on the lines resolved at the conference.[11]

The objectives of the Mahamandal were clearly stated . The chief aim was the advancement of Indian women. For this, it was necessary to unite the intellectuals with the activists.[12]

The object of the Bharat Stree Mahamandal is the creation of an organization by means of which women of every race, creed, class and party in India may be brought together on the basis of their common interest in the moral and material progress of the women of India; and in and through which organization they may work in association and in a spirit of mutual helpfulness for the progress of humanity through that of their own sex.[13]

In order to achieve this general objective a plan of action was drawn up. It was decided that:

(i) It would set up branches in the all important cities of India under a central body at Lahore.

(ii) In view of the very small percentage of school-going girls on account of early marriage and persisting purdah, the Mahamandal would start a system of home-education for married girls in a manner suitable for Indian conditions in different areas of the country.

(iii) Literary committees would be appointed at different centres to encourage the growth and spread of Indian vernacular literature in order to make modern thought accessible to literate Indian women in a convenient form.

(iv) Depots would be set up and other facilities provided at each centre for bringing the handicrafts of Indian women into the market and to encourage indigent women to engage in productive work to be able to earn some money for themselves.

(v) It would start an inquiry into available medical aid for women, and devise means of inducing them to take advantage of existing institutions.

(vi) It would affiliate to itself any other women's association having similar aims, and, importantly, would open bureaus of information regarding women's societies, women's work, and women's progress in the country.[14]

Obviously, to the members of the Mahamandal the chief problems for women were lack of education, absence of medical facilities, lack of information and communication, and poverty. In their recognition of women's issues they came close to modern thinking, although the method chosen were extremely limited, and the endeavour was confined to a small section of women. After the inaugural session, Sarala went to Calcutta, met with a number of ladies, held a few public meetings of women, and established a branch of the Mahamandal under the secretaryship of Krishnabhabini Das (1864–1919), also a remarkable woman on many counts.[15] This was the first branch, to be followed soon by branches in the Punjab and the United Provinces (of Oudh and Agra). Membership was open to any woman of any creed or nationality on the payment of an entrance fee of one rupee. The annual subscription was also fixed at one rupee.

The branch at Calcutta under two distinguished women, Swarnakumari Devi as the President, and Krishnabhabini Das as the Secretary, commenced zenana education from April 1911. By June, nine teachers were instructing forty-four women in twenty-six families. One problem that the association faced was that even women who had discarded purdah were unwilling to walk on the public roads, and therefore the teachers had to be sent to the homes of their students in carriages, which proved expensive and a constraint on the expansion of the Mahamandal activities. In Allahabad, the President was Mrs Sunderlal, and the Secretary Mrs Lalitmohan Banerji. The Branch started their scheme of education in May. It decided to adopt four methods of zenana education: by sending teachers from home to home, by opening classes in various different localities, by framing a curriculum and holding examinations at various centres, and by persuading zenana women to take the vow of the 'gift of knowledge'. The last method, it was hoped, would involve an obligation on the learners to disseminate knowledge among other women, and enthuse them to learn. Of these methods, the first and the last were put into immediate effect. Soon they decided to select special textbooks for the various stages of instruction. By June, three teachers were teaching thirty-four women in twenty-five families. In Lahore, free primary classes were started at a place outside the city to educate zenana women three times a week for two hours. Six women rendered voluntary service as teachers to those who wished to learn English, Sanskrit, Hindi, Urdu, arithmetic, needlework, painting, and music. In addition, housewives from middle class families, and a number of teachers from some of the existing schools also came to attend these classes in order to become better qualified. The one condition was that the beneficiaries would in turn provide free education to women in their respective areas. By June the numbers of students was thirty-two. Besides this school running outside the city, the Lahore branch set up several schools in the city for married women. Sarala Devi herself went on periodic visits to women in various families to persuade them to devote some time every day to learning and spreading the message of education. Moreover, attempts were made to provide facilities for the sale of women's handiwork under the name Nari Nirvaha Bhandar (The Women's Mart). The proceeds of the sales went to the indigent women workers. The Mahamandal also undertook the work of translating the *Mahabharata* in lucid and simple Urdu, Hindi, and Punjabi. A book of the scores of Indian songs and translations of *Miss Edgeworth's Moral Tales* in Bengali and Hindi were under preparation.[16]

It is true that the Association brought no spectacular changes in women's conditions, nor could it last long, surviving only for a few years. There was no attempt made to evolve links with any grassroots organization at any level. The programme of action was such as suited its middle class members. The upper middle class character of the organization also becomes clear from the social background of the leadership, and the fact that Ranis and Begums were to preside over the annual meetings and that 'ladies of rank, position and distinction' were to become vice-presidents. In a sense, one could even describe the organization as designed for social work by well-to-do ladies. Yet by the standards of the time it was a significant step. It marked the beginning of the women's movement in India under women's leadership, and it proclaimed itself as such, announcing clearly its distinction from the men-led women's organizations of the nineteenth century for the 'uplift' of women. Another equally important feature of the organization was its secular character. It was not conceived as a limited organization for Hindu women alone. Sarala said that the organization must include women of all creeds, 'Indo–Aryan, Indo–Semitic, Indo–Mongolian, and Anglo–Indian', and would have to adopt a liberal view towards all religions. The Hindus should not think of themselves as the only exceptional people in the world, she felt. They needed to acknowledge that all the communities in the world had their good points, and only a combination of all communities could best serve the interests of humanity.[17] Thirdly, the organization aimed at a pan-Indian unity of women and conceived of alliances with other similar organizations. 'To join the parts, to bring the several fragments together into one moral unity, to deepen the sense of sisterhood and common humanity of the women of all the races and parts of India is one of the main features of the Bharat Stree Mahamandal.'[18]

On returning to Calcutta from Lahore, Sarala took up the work of the Mahamandal from Priyambada Devi (1871–1930) who had been looking after the Bengal branch. The Mahamandal concentrated on zenana education; about three thousand women were being taught at home. As the number of girls going to school was rapidly increasing in the country, Sarala decided to start a formal educational institution. On 1 June 1930, the Mahamandal founded Sikshasadan (school) at Bhowanipore.

What was the actual contribution of the Mahamandal? Sarala answered the question in an article in *Bharati*. Taking a bird's-eye view of fifteen years' work, she restated the objectives of the organization and the strategies it adopted for realizing them. The central aim remained unchanged, i.e. the improvement of the position of women with sustained spiritual and material benefits. The modus operandi was

(i)  to hold periodic meetings to bring together women members from all the provinces of India,
(ii) to arrange for teaching elderly women in their homes,

(iii) to encourage enrichment and propagation of Indian languages so that women could be exposed to modern thought and knowledge through the medium of their own language (and for this, efforts should be made to make good books available easily and at low cost),
(iv) to maintain contact with associations catering to the needs of working women, such as, nursing sisters, and if necessary, to establish suitable institutions for them,
(v) to open outlets to market handicrafts made by women (this would help many poor and indigent families),
(vi) to launch branch offices of the organization in all provinces and important towns throughout India with a view to ensuring that the action-programmes of the Mahamandal were implemented in a systematic and co-ordinated way,
(vii) to cooperate and link up with similar associations in the country.[19]

Three important points need to be emphasized once again. First, the importance of networking with various women's organizations was well understood by Sarala. She missed no opportunity to exhort the members of the Mahamandal to attempt to work in collaboration with women who were working for the cause of women. Through its programme of activities, Sarala hoped, the organization would serve as a cementing force among women otherwise unknown to one another. 'It is only through work for themselves that the women of India can come together; there is no other alternative. Bharat Stree Mahamandal will serve as a link,' she said.[20] Second, Sarala was opposed to caste and community hierarchies. The door of the Mahamandal was equally open to all. This is in tune with her earlier assertions against the use of the caste platform for national political purposes. Third, Sarala had grown sensitive to the needs of women for gainful employment, and to the requirements of working women. Although she had given up the experiment to earn her living, she came to appreciate the situation of those who needed to do so. Through the organized and united resources of the organization, she planned to expand the opportunities for other women.

Sarala also planned to enlist the help of menfolk in her struggle to improve the position of women in the country. She asked every patriotic man to inspire and induce the women of his family to join the Mahamandal and to encourage friends to enroll female relatives as members. They were to take the initiative to send names and other particulars along with due subscriptions to the offices of the Mahamandal. Sarala believed that it was with the combined effort of both men and women that society could march ahead. Although Sarala was intent in advancing women's cause, she had no real grievance against men and did not believe in a confrontational stance.

In the history of the women's movement in India, Bharat Stree Mahamandal has a special significance. It marked the beginning of women's organizations by women leaders and set the trend for many later organizations. The Bengal Women's Education League formed in 1928 pushed for educational reform for women. Sarala Devi was an enthusiastic member along with Kumudini Bose, Mrinalini Sen (1879–1972), Abala Basu, and Sarala Ray (1879–1972). The body suggested the adoption of a reformed syllabus for girls, the introduction of free compulsory primary education, and the inclusion of female representation on educational administrative bodies at all levels, from the rural to the university stage. The Rural Primary Education Act of 1929 did not accept any of these suggestions, and the League was not much of a success. It was nonetheless another landmark in women's organizational activities.[21] At the district level in Bengal, too, women's own organizations began to emerge—the most important among them being the Dipali Sangha of Dhaka. Its journal *Jayasree* used to supply detailed information on such associations in different parts of Bengal. At a wider level, the Mahamandal was followed by the Women's India Association of Madras (1917), and then the All India Women's Conference (1927).

The basic limitation of these early twentieth century women's organizations, including the Mahamandal, was their middle class character and their inability to involve the majority of Indian women living in rural Bengal. All their aims and endeavours were clearly oriented towards the fulfilment of middle class urban aspirations, their piecemeal schemes of uplifting the rural or urban poor notwithstanding. Yet, viewed in perspective, these women's organizations can claim a twofold importance in women's history. First, they signified the transfer of leadership in women's movements from men to women. Issues and questions were raised from the women's perspective rather than that which men thought was appropriate for women. Equally, they provided a platform for women and generated a belief that the responsibility of regenerating women belonged to women themselves. This comprehension is the genesis of bonding among women and of the emergence of feminism in an embryonic form.

Second, the example of the Mahamandal reveals an interesting dimension of the women's movement in India. Contrary to the popular belief that the movement took its cue from Western feminism, there was a connection between it and the anti-British nationalist movement. Sarala, like a few other women leaders of the time, played a dual role. Women political activists, whether or not informed with a conscious feminist ideology, became intimately associated with women's organizations, thereby establishing a link between the freedom struggle and the women's movement. To name a few: Sarojini Naidu (1879–1949), Hemaprabha Majumdar (1888–1962), Basanti Devi (1880–1974), Urmila Devi (1883–1956), Ashalata Sen (1894–1986), all belonged to this group, probably becoming aware of gender subjection through their resentment at political subjection. Indeed, an important part of the socio-political scenario in Bengal was that women were organizing themselves at the district level in line with the women in the metropolis, both on the political and social fronts. For instance, Bankura Zilla Mahila Sammelan (Women's Confederation of Bankura District) and the Chittagong Divisional Mahila Sammelan (Women's Confederation of Chittagong) were both playing the dual role of promoting Swadeshi goods at the political level and generating self-reliance among women at the social/individual level. Ashalata Sen founded the Gandaria Mahila Samiti to promote Swadeshi products and established Shilpashram (Institute for Teaching Crafts) in Dhaka.[22] Dipali Sangha founded by Lila Nag (1900–70) in Dhaka was the most effective of such organizations, propagating biplabi ideology and carrying out a vitrutal crusade against the institutionalized oppression of women.[23] Women's experiences in the Swadeshi movement, and later in the political campaigns of the nineteen twenties and thirties had given them a taste of agitational politics and the self-confidence to champion their own cause. Sarala Devi was the foremost of this generation of women, a political activist becoming an activist for the women's cause.

## BEGUM ROKEYA

It was another story for Rokeya. Contemporary men might or might not be caring or understanding—a few were, the majority were not—but circumstances made it difficult for Rokeya to believe that men were by and large supportive of the women's cause; certainly they had not been in the past. Women had to assess their own situation and take up the cudgels for themselves. It would not be easy. Muslim India would condemn their women to a 'death-sentence', and Hindu women would be consigned to a 'slow death by fire'.[24] Rokeya however believed that every noble work would have to encounter social or familial opposition. It was courage that was wanted. The first step would be to get every woman to believe that women did not belong to the class of slaves, and the ultimate goal was gaining equality with men. Rokeya gave a clarion call to all women.

My sisters! Rub your eyes and wake up—march forward. Mothers, please declare that you are no more animals. Sisters, please deny that you are inanimate objects like furniture. And daughters, please aver that you are not decorative pieces to be conserved with jewellery and preserved in a safe. And together shout: we are human beings. And demonstrate through your work that we women are half of the best of the world. In truth, we are the begetters of the world.[25]

Here Rokeya was putting forth the same arguments as Sarala, trying to convince women that they were the real creators—the mothers—of society, although with less fervour and passion than Sarala. Her emphasis clearly was on infusing rebellion against existing social conditions, and on awakening Muslim women from their 'stupor'. To drive home the point, she appealed to their religious sentiments. In a fine comparison with Islamic practices and in tune with them, she placed her contention before Muslim women in inspiring religious terms. Muslim women of other countries were marching forward. Allah willed it. His emissaries were passing on the call; would the Muslim women of Bengal lag behind other Muslim sisters?

Mothers, sisters, daughters! Come, get up, leave your comfortable beds; go forward. The muazzin calls, can you not hear him, the summons from Allah? Do not laze in your beds, the night is over, it is now dawn, the muazzin is calling to the Faithful for prayers. Elsewhere in the world women have woken up, they are protesting against all social evils. Women have risen to become Education Ministers; there are now women doctors, philosophers, scientists, ministers of wars, generals of the army, writers, poets, etc. And we, women of Bengal, are in deep slumber in a dark and damp room, and dying in thousands by consumption.[26]

It was time to wake up. It was time for women to organize themselves. Men had so far taken charge of women in the name of protecting them, but why should they? In characteristic fashion, Rokeya ridiculed members of her own sex:

For sometime now our masters have been regarding us as if we are their valuable ornaments. Perhaps that is why so many 'Societies for the Protection of Women' are being founded. Truly, since we are nothing but live luggage pieces, alert watchmen are needed to keep an eye on us lest we get stolen! My hapless sisters! Does not this invoke a sense of humiliation in you? If it does, then why do you suffer silently such indignities?[27]

To be equal with men, women had to come out of men's shadows, and build their own power-base. 'You all club together and form various associations to protect your rights and demands.'[28]

The thought was beautifully portrayed in her novel *Padmarag*. The central question that was asked through the novel was: what should be the remedy for the oppression of women who had to abide by unfair social customs? A wife could be abandoned at will by her husband, or was compelled to live with a mad man or with co-wives. Was there no way out for women? In *Padmarag*, Tarini Bhavan (literally meaning an abode for protection) was a place where distressed women found a shelter and a happy place to live in. It had different departments, one of which was the Society for protection from cruelty to women. In answer to the question whether there was any panacea for women, Saudamini, one of the characters in the novel, asserts,

Yes, there is. And that protection will come from this Society for Protection from Cruelty to Women of Tarini Bhavan. Come, come to us; all you neglected, abandoned and helpless women. Then we shall declare war against this unfair social condition and Tarini Bhavan will be our fortress.[29]

It is widely acknowledged that authors often speak through the characters they create. Following the argument, it may fairly be said that Rokeya, through Saudamini, was sending messages to all women to form their own associations and centres (like Tarini Bhavan) for the protection of women suffering from unfair social customs. By the time *Padmarag* was published (although written much earlier), women's organizations by women had already begun to appear in India. Sarala's Bharat Stree Mahamandal, the Women's India Association, and the All India Women's Conference were women's organizations set up not by those whom Rokeya described as 'our masters', but created by women themselves. The AIWC claimed to represent all Indian women regardless of religion or class, and many Muslim women had joined it, but they also built up an organization that addressed issues specially affecting them. This was the Anjuman-i-Khawatin-i-Islam (All India Muslim Ladies' Conference), which claimed to speak for all Muslim women in India. But then, just like the AIWC, the Anjuman was also basically a middle class women's organization primarily concerned with middle class Muslim women's issues. The national AKI was founded in February 1914 as part of the colourful ceremony inaugurating the new residence hall at Aligarh Girls' School. Shaikh Abdulla and Wahid Jahan Begum had invited prominent Muslim women from all over India, and the Begum of Bhopal was to preside. Following the ceremony, the women reassembled to found the AKI, dedicated to the advancement of education and rights for Muslim women. The Begum in her presidential address reiterated the need for education without which Muslim women would not know the rights granted to them under Islamic law. The meeting chose the Begum as the President of AKI, and Nafis Dulhan Sherwani as the Secretary. The headquarters of the organization was at Aligarh, the officers were mostly from Aligarh, and obviously control lay in the same place. Nafis Dulhan was the wife of Habibur Rahman Khan Sherwani, a trustee of the Aligarh College and almost all the other women in the Working Committee were related to one or the other of the local trustees who controlled the Aligarh College and the All India Muslim Educational Conference. The plans of the AKI were also Aligarh-centric. Its principal objective was to encourage the growth of schools for Muslim girls, and to contribute to the progress of Aligarh Girls' School. It had broader aims too: to work for unity among Muslim women, spread women's education, promote both religious education and practical training among women and make them ideal homemakers. A very important plank of its programmes was to oppose marriage before the age of sixteen for Muslim girls, since early marriage stood in the way of education. Its annual resolutions advocated more schools for women and abolition of purdah restrictions. The members, however, all drawn from upper middle class, ardently supported purdah, both as a symbol of religious identity and as a mark of high social status. It is on this score that a disagreement arose between the Aligarh group and Begum Rokeya.[30]

Rokeya founded the Calcutta branch of the AKI in 1916. In the formative days of this association, Rokeya faced much derision when she canvassed from door to door to interest people in her project. No one could conceive of Muslim women leaving their homes and coming out to attend the meetings of an association. Many women, used to staying at home, would have liked to respond, but courage failed them in the face of the strong antagonism of the family. Rokeya encouraged such women to come out on the plea of visiting relations, and then go and attend meetings. Many of these women had little or no conception of what an association was supposed to do or what a meeting was. Shamsunnahar Mahmud recalls an amusing incident recounted by Rokeya. Apparently, after much persuasion, a lady of an educated Muslim family had agreed to attend a meeting of the Anjuman. When the meeting was over and the assembled women were on their way out, this new entrant, much puzzled, asked where the association and the meeting she was supposed to attend was located. It took some time to convince her that she had just attended it and that now it was over. Rokeya also found that after each meeting the walls of the room were splashed with red *paan* (chewed betel) juice, needing frequent whitewashing jobs. And very few of the women had any appreciation that they ought to sit quietly in their own places when a meeting was on. The way meetings were held those days would be inconceivable today.[31]

According to the brochure of the AKI,

To ensure all comprehensive development of Muslim women is the principal objective of the Anjuman-i-Khawateen. By repudiating the long endured superstitious beliefs, Muslim women should be able to establish themselves in every field—

in education, in their own families, in the larger society. They will become good mothers, good wives, good citizens; they will find their own distinctive niche in life; and that is the sole aim of this Association.[32]

The programme of activities of the Anjuman was to cover convening meetings of members, fostering amity amongst them, initiating discussions on issues related to women, disseminating knowledge pertaining to health care and childcare, providing aid to the poor, and arranging for vocational training to make women self-reliant. Vocational training and elementary education were accorded high priority in the programme. It was decided that so long as the Association was not be able to establish suitable schools to provide vocational training to women, either due to paucity of funds or other difficulties, efforts would be made to set up training centres at various localities. These centres were to offer training for gainful occupations, such as garment making, wickerwork, and the like, and would also run courses in the art of making various types of preserves and condiments including lessons in basic cooking. Informative programmes on healthcare and childcare were to be conducted. Primary level education was also to be provided in Urdu or Bengali.

Any Muslim woman was eligible to be a member of the Association. Each member had to pay a minimum subscription of three rupees a year. A working committee of twelve members was constituted, and it was to be responsible for the management of the affairs of the Association. There was to be a President, four Vice-Presidents, and a Secretary. It was mandatory for at least one of these office-bearers to have knowledge of the English language. Branches of the association could be established anywhere, and these were to follow the programmes and guidelines laid down by the principal association.[33] Rokeya was made the first Secretary of the association. While she was building it up, in 1918 the national AKI had a very successful conference at Lahore where it took a resolution against polygamy: a daring step in the context of the time. The following year Rokeya invited the committee to hold its annual meeting in Calcutta, and there problems arose, apparently on the choice of the site, but perhaps due to an underlying tension over control. Should the Aligarh group dominate wherever the conference was held, or should local branches enjoy some decision-making power?

In 1919, the Calcutta Anjuman hosted the all-India meeting of the Anjuman-i-Khawatin-i-Islam, and Tayyiba Begam Khediv Jung came from Hyderabad to preside. Rokeya's local committee had arranged a venue for the meeting on a large property in Ripon Street, but the purdah arrangements were deemed inadequate by Nafis Dulhan, leading the Aligarh and

Hyderabad based officers to move the meeting elsewhere. Rokeya and her local organization were slighted in the process, and Tayyiba Begum did nothing to curtail the authority of the Aligarh group. For a person of Rokeya's stature and personality, this was very annoying. First, a last minute change of venue was likely to reduce attendance, which it did. Second, the question of organizational method was involved. If the central committee did not have confidence in the local committee and could disregard its decisions without much ado, the organization would be too centralized and its branches weak. Third, the tricky question of purdah further complicated the situation. The members of the AKI, as has been mentioned earlier, maintained that they were in favour of purdah, but preferred a less restrictive system than that in vogue. In Calcutta, however, they proved that the veil was in reality essential to women as a mark of identity, and so had to be very carefully and punctiliously observed. Rokeya's attitude towards the observance of purdah was somewhat different to that of her colleagues. She had penned many a satirical piece on the galling constraints of purdah and the way women perpetuated their own humiliation and subordination. She put up with it to just the degree it was essential, since discarding it would reduce her support from the Muslim community, both men and women. In short, to Aligarh women purdah was a useful social marker, to Rokeya, it was an unavoidable necessity. The entire incident revealed Rokeya's lack of success in getting along with the more dominant Aligarh group. The all India AKI almost disappeared after 1932.[34]

Not that the national AKI, during its brief spell of existence, could or did represent all Indian Muslim women, or formulate an effective programme for their development at the all-India level. But then neither could Rokeya. Her efforts remained confined to Bengal. Her AKI, known as AKI Bangla, or Nikhil Banga Muslim Mahila Samiti, was a Bengal-based organization, with little linkages with other parts of India. Although Rokeya chose primarily to address women through her writings and advance women's cause through the medium of her school, she did devote considerable time to the Anjuman too. Under her leadership, the Anjuman attempted to raise among Muslim women a sense of awareness about the various issues that concerned them, like marriage and divorce and income generation. It tried to instil in them a cognizance of their rights, explaining to them how helpless they had become in a male dominated social order. They were told that without education they would never be able to claim their rightful dues. Islam as a religion had given them many advantages but, living in a world of ignorance and hidebound by superstitious beliefs, they did not have a clue as to what these benefits were. Meetings were frequently held to propagate amongst women this message of resurgence.[35] Rokeya often told her colleagues that the Anjuman constituted an important part of her life's work. However, the task was so difficult that any tangible result could not be achieved by the efforts of a few. It would need generations of women to change women's life-situations.

There is one more interesting point about the AKI in Calcutta. Under Rokeya's leadership, it sympathized with the freedom movement as well as the Khilafat movement. True, members of this association could not come out openly to participate actively in the freedom movement, but the association did take major steps to inspire patriotic sentiments amongst Muslim women. The *charkha* or the spinning wheel campaign was at its height, and women members of the Anjuman produced a vast quantity of yarn by plying the charkha to be woven into khadi. They also played a positive role in boycotting foreign goods.[36] This is evidence, if evidence was needed, of Rokeya's support to the nationalist movement.

## Summary and Observations

Sarala's and Rokeya's organizational strategies were shaped by significant differences in philosophy and perspectives towards women. First, to Sarala, women's advancement was a means to an end: the general improvement of the nation. For Rokeya, the goal was emancipation from men's control: freedom for its own sake. Second, Sarala did not have a concept of gender interests separate from other political or social factors. To Sarala, the entire country was in a state of decline, and both men and women had to be inspired with the example of past glory to recreate it: women more than men because they were in reality the more powerful sex. On the other hand, Rokeya's focus was clearly gender. She believed that women were in a particularly abject condition and that this suited men's interests. Third, precisely because of her overwhelming critique of men's power and women's powerlessness, Rokeya did not take women's agency into account. She did not recognize women as knowledgeable actors who could make strategic use of the means and resources available, however limited these might be. She did not see that mothers could have a strong influence over sons, or that wives could prevail upon the decision-making of their husbands and that sisters might have a persuasive hold on brothers through bonds of affection. Rokeya saw nothing but humiliation in a Muslim woman's position in the family and in the larger society. Her strength therefore was not in promoting bonds between women but on analysis of subordination. Indeed, her Anjuman was more of a welfare organization than an instrument to empower women. She once said:

I have already said that gangreous sores need surgery. Let no one please get the idea that we are proposing ourselves as the healers of diseases. All we are doing is to point out what the diseases are, and it is up to our social reformers to assume the role of the physicians to provide treatment.[37]

Sarala, on the other hand, emphasized the power of women, and urged them to harness it for themselves and for all women. She saw contemporary women as natural successors of the women of ancient India: strong and capable.[38] Her organization tried to develop women's networking at the all-India level, and to increase women's active role in public life. Sarala had a profound belief in women as social actors and her central focus was on marshalling and developing the conscious use of their own power.

Sarala and Rokeya both raised key issues that feminists in India are still grappling with. Let me touch upon two. The first is the issue of violence, one of the forces behind the contemporary phase of the women's movement. Rokeya was concerned with violence, but did not probe into the reasons for men's violence against women, nor did she try to fight against it through the Anjuman. Rather she suggested a remedy for ensuring women's freedom from fear, possible only in a utopia: Ladyland, portrayed in *Sultana's Dream*. There she imagined a world in which men were confined to the four walls of the home in order to make the outside world safe for women to roam around.[39] While this was not a feasible solution for the real women, it does cleverly question the logic of keeping women confined to the home for fear of men's violence. Sarala, too, gave some thought to the issue of violence. There were four ways, according to her, by which violence against women could be prevented. They were as follows:

(i) To establish societies for protection of women, as well as institutions to deter misconduct and abuse by men,
(ii) to inflict exemplary punishment on men found guilty of mistreating women, and to ostracize such men from all social dealings,
(iii) to accept back in the society innocent, tormented, and untainted women and to establish organizations to reform wayward women,
iv) to instil a sense of freedom from fear in women, and to train them in some form of martial arts for their self-defence.[40]

Sarala did not elaborate on these points, each of which could be a subject for intense debate and penetrating investigation. For instance, how would institutions deter men's misconduct? Or, what would be the form of punishment to the guilty men? How far was society prepared to accept tormented or raped women? And who were 'wayward' women? Whose fault was it that they were wayward, if indeed they were? The modern women's movements are scrutinizing different aspects of these and similar other questions. Sarala's Mahamandal left them untouched. One wonders why at least one or two of the four ways mentioned by Sarala were not included in the Mahamandal's agenda. At least a home or an institution to offer shelter and protection to the 'distressed' women could have been attempted. Sarala and Rokeya thus did not link violence to their organizational activism, but they both reflected on the problem.

The second issue is communalism, a serious threat to the country today, and a disquieting concern for the women's movement.[41] It was rearing its ugly head during the time under discussion. How did Sarala respond to it? Does Sarala's depiction of Pratapaditya, an anti-Mughal zamindar, as a hero to bolster Bengali nationalism, entitle us to brand her as communal? At the personal level, Sarala enjoyed warm friendships with educated Muslim families, such as the family of Sujatali of Bangalore, Akbar Hydari of Bombay (he later became the Chief Minister of Hyderabad), and Syed Amir Ali of Bengal. She started learning Persian from the Maulvi, who used to teach the children of the Hydari family, with a view to reading Omar Khayyam in the original Persian.[42] At the organizational level, she sought Muslim support in her scheme of a pan-Indian women's movement. 'Any woman, regardless of caste, class or religion, was eligible to become a member of the Mahamandal'. When the Mahamandal was organized Muslim women played a part in it. Yet perhaps did she discursively exclude Muslim women because of her choice of heroes? However, Sarala regularly wrote articles urging Hindu–Muslim unity in *Bharati* and the *Hindusthan Review,* arguing that though India had been invaded by foreigners *starting with the Aryans,* after a while Indian civilization made insiders out of the outsiders. The Muslims were now insiders. Only the fundamentalists were trying to sow discord between the Hindus and the Muslims; they must not be allowed to get away with it. Quite early in her career, Sarala had placed the issue of Hindu–Muslim relations within a broad context. India as a colonized country was part of a larger conglomeration; the geopolitical mapping was significant. To survive the colonial onslaught the commonality between Hindus and Muslims must be appreciated and marked, Sarala said,

> We must clearly realize that in the encounter between the victor and the vanquished, the Hindus and the Muslims, have to eschew their mutual alienation in the interest of our defence against the grasping clutches of our enemies from the West. We have to highlight the distinctive features of the East as opposed to the West, and use this distinction to bring light to our otherwise darkened battlefield.[43]

Sarala put the whole question in the context of a East-West conflict, and the fundamental differences between Asia and Europe. Rokeya's attention was focused on Bengal. She does not seem to have considered the pan-Asianism that Sarala talked about, nor was she particularly bothered about the ethnic disaffinity between the East and the West. Such theoretical discussions might not have interested her. She was however not disturbed by the emerging Hindu–Muslim tension in Bengal politics, and relied on women to resolve it.[44] *Padmarag* is sure evidence, if indeed any is needed, that she believed in the possibility of affectionate coexistence between believers of all religions, and in women who could show the way to men. In Tarini Bhavan, Hindu, Muslim, and Christian women lived like sisters, enjoying a deep bond of mutual respect and love under the headship of a Hindu woman. In her Preface to the novel *Padmarag*, Rokeya uses a metaphor to state that for the truly devoted there was no difference between one religion and another.

Religion is like a three-storied mansion. The ground floor has many chambers housing Hindus with their many factions, such as Brahmins, Sudras, etc. Muslims in their many communities, like Shia, Sunni, Hanafi, Sufi, etc, and similarly, many Christians in their different denominations, Roman Catholics, Protestants, and the like. Go to the first floor; there are only Muslims, only Hindus, with no divisions into factions. On the second floor there is just one chamber inhabited by only people, all the same; there are no Hindus, no Muslims; all are worshipping only one God. In the final analysis, there is nothing—except the great God.[45]

Despite their limitations, both Sarala and Rokeya anticipated some of the crucial concerns of today's women activists, and raised some important questions. Most importantly, they built up women's networks, the basis of the women's movement. Rokeya's Anjuman was a local body, but Sarala's Mahamandal was the first all-India women's organization, and thus the precursor of later such organizations. The term 'feminist' is open to theoretical debate, but if we take it in its broadest sense to mean a woman or a man who is aware of at least some aspects of the oppression of women, and consciously tries to resist or fight against them, then both Sarala and Rokeya were feminists. Indeed, they were the earliest feminists in positions of leadership in twentieth century Bengal.

## 5. Conclusion

Sarala and Rokeya were both greatly concerned with women's issues, but they saw questions of gender through the lens of their own community, class, and culture. While there were major differences in their approach and ideology, they shared a common commitment towards the 'cause' of women. They had in common their colonial experience, the shared heritage of the language-based Bengali culture, and the comfort of personal financial security. Yet, they inhabited two very different social milieus and consequently their lives' work took place within different social dynamics. The nationalist Hindu social and political agenda and the slow burgeoning of Muslim community consciousness in Bengal implied disparate challenges for these two remarkable women.

Sarala spoke primarily to middle class Hindus in Bengal, and Rokeya to upper class Muslims, a large section of which denied their Bengali identity, and to middle class Muslims who were evolving a Bengali-Muslim identity. Sarala was a major precursor of feminist ideology, but in her agenda and organizational activity, her principal concern was Bengali-Hindu nationalism. Women provided a major, nonetheless secondary, impulse. Rokeya, on the other hand, was chiefly concerned with the status of women in Muslim society. Rokeya was primarily a feminist, Sarala primarily a nationalist.

Despite Sarala's own late marriage, she did not question child-marriage or polygamy. On the question of marriage itself, she was strangely silent. Rokeya spoke and wrote at length on marriage, divorce, and on the need for education before marriage. In the ultimate analysis, Sarala believed in women's inner strength and their innate potential, in tune with the Hindu religious dictum of women as shakti and the nineteenth century reformers' projection of women as the preservers of the home and the dharma. She was a romantic, impressed by the traditional domestic Hindu rituals performed in Bengali homes. In contrast, Rokeya was burdened by the helplessness of Muslim women. She was almost unique in her bold and direct attack on the precepts of Islam as taught by its guardians, and quite openly ascribed religious texts to male rather than divine origin. No woman, not even the intellectuals of the Sikha group, had dared to do so. It was their particular balance of conformity and non-conformity to the dominant views of their times that explains why Sarala secured admiration and support, and Rokeya received a mixed response from her contemporaries.

## Sarala Devi

Sarala was directly involved in the freedom movement against the British. Her political beliefs sprang from anti-colonialism and a deep resentment against the power of the colonial rulers at the cost of the colonized. This is one reason why the notion of power was in the forefront of her thoughts. Sarala's ideological perception of women stemmed from her acute political and social consciousness. Her principal thesis was that power was latent in women; it only needed to be awakened and activated. To her, the primary factor responsible for women's all-pervading degradation was women's own belief in the weakness of their sex. The lack of confidence in their own selves and the absence of respect for their own beings were rooted in the ignorance of their potential. For women, she believed, cognition of power would ensure acquisition of power. Her attempt, therefore, was to make women self-aware through education, build up women's power, and harness that power in the service of the nation.

The nationalist construction of women was a potent influence on Sarala's thoughts. The nationalist agenda regarding women had two clear features. On the one hand, it urged women to be good mothers and wives and maintain an ideal home as pivotal to the 'essence' of Indianness, and on the other, it exhorted them to be courageous and heroic in their personal character. The first formulation was based on the hypothesis that the outside world was 'the domain of the material' and unimportant. The home represented the 'inner spiritual self' of India and its 'true identity'. The former was the domain of the male, the latter the responsibility of the female. The spiritual was superior to the material, and the role of females was to nurture and protect the 'spiritual distinctiveness' of the nation. This duty was nothing new; it was in keeping with age-old Indian 'tradition'. The distinguished Aryan women of the 'golden' age of India's past had acted as the spiritual guides and guardians of the nation and its 'dharma'.[1]

The second blueprint emerged from the the material needs of the freedom struggle: the need for courage and support from both men and women. Boldness and physical fitness of the entire Indian population could alone effectively serve the national cause. It was argued that only courageous women could produce heroic sons, and could render timely assistance to the freedom struggle, directly or indirectly. Perhaps here was yet another contradiction (as there were many others) in the nationalist projection. Traditional concepts of femininity, including modesty, selfless service to the family and vigilance for the preservation of the spirituality and morality of the family would leave little space for physical exercises and heroic courage, except in the sphere of mental courage. The nationalists ignored this apparent contradiction. As Uma Chakravarty rightly remarks, 'boldness, bravery and physical fitness were accepted as female virtues if they served a political purpose'.[2] Partha Chatterjee confirms this line of argument: 'Once the essential femininity of women was fixed in terms of certain culturally visible spiritual qualities, they could go to schools, travel in public conveyances ... and in time take up employment outside the home.'[3] Political engagements would not be objectionable, provided moral qualities were kept at high plane. Sarala, by and large, was a believer in this philosophy.

Chakravarty however misses a vital point when she says, 'What is significant in the activities and concerns of Sarala Devi was the way in which the women never featured as an issue.'[4] We have seen throughout our discussion that Sarala was deeply involved with issues pertaining to women. What Sarala aimed at was creating both men and women physically and mentally strong for the nation. Men had to be trained to be strong and heroic, women already had power within them that had to be released. In Sarala's dictionary, freedom meant independence from colonial rule first and if it meant liberation from patriarchal rule, that consideration came second in her assertions and activities.

Yet let there be no doubt that Sarala was advocating concepts that must tear asunder the basis of patriarchy. When men averred that women were goddesses and the preservers of the spiritual qualities of the real India, and women echoed their words, it was one thing. It was quite another when a woman proclaimed to other women that they were the real power in the family and society, and that they must first be convinced of their power to be able to exercise it. If all women came truly to believe that they, 'and not men', were the real powers in the family and the larger society, hierarchical gender power relations would run the risk of being inverted.

Related to her analysis of the need for women to have power, was her call for Bengalis to display greater courage. She said in her autobiography, 'As I grew up, I came to realize with a shock that the Bengali character was cursed with faintheartedness. This stigma must be erased.'[5] She strove all her life to accomplish this objective. The following excerpt from one of her speeches encapsulates her attitude:

I will today gift you a magical charm, selected from the bottomless storehouse of

Bengal. This charm which has to be taught in secrecy will exorcise fear from your heart. Here it is, take careful note, it is just one word, *Courage*. Install this charm as a living Goddess in your heart, let it be your key force to guide your life, get rid of timidity, and then no one will be able to intimidate you ... Once you have realized the magnificence of courage, you will be ready to march on the path of progress.[6]

Courage for men and women alike was what Sarala urged, and what she found Bengalis to lack. For women especially, she advocated the cult of power. Her favourite image was that of Kali, which 'suggests as clearly as any symbolism can do the predominance of the Female Principle over the Male Principle.'[7] She repeatedly sought to inspire women with the concept of shakti, and asked them to regard themselves as part of the divine woman-power. Equally forcefully, she reminded women, after the current nationalist trend, that they must emulate the moral and spiritual qualities of the great women of ancient India.

Aware of the importance of organization and networking for building up power on the basis of shared understanding, Sarala was the first Indian woman to try to organize all women of India under a single umbrella. True, the actual scale was miniscule, given that the Mahamandal was a middle class women's organization, but the idea was not insignificant. No woman before Sarala had worked to create women's organizational strength at the national level, nor had held courage and heroism as the supreme ideals to be sought for by women (and also by men) in such inspiring terms.

Was Sarala unique? Or did she articulate more convincingly what other contemporary women were also saying and doing? Certainly, Sarala enjoyed a special position in the field of politics. She was the first woman leader in the Swadeshi movement, though a few other women also participated in it and later became important leaders during the Gandhian movement. Of Sarala's contemporaries, Hemaprabha Majumdar (1888–1962) and Basanti Devi (1880–1974) rose to eminence, but they stayed primarily concerned with the problem of colonial subjection.[8] Among those who dedicated themselves to the issue of women was Hemalata Sarkar (1868–1943), who founded a reputed school in Darjeeling. Suniti Devi (1864–1932), another contemporary, established a college at Coochbehar; Abala Basu was a celebrated educationist,[9] and Mrinalini Sen (1879–1972) struggled for the voting rights for women.[10] Krishnabhabini Das wrote and worked for women's education[11] and shouldered the responsibility of running Bharat Stree Mahamandal in Bengal during Sarala's absence in Punjab. All of them were remarkable in their own fields. Sarala, however, was a pioneer, in that she combined in her own self leadership in the struggle against both colonialism and gender oppression.

The low status of Hindu women had caught the attention of a number of women besides Sarala. As women became educated, they began to write. Many well-known authors, like Nirupama Devi (1883–1951) and Anurupa Devi (1882–1958) upheld 'traditional' ideas, extolling self-sacrificing mothers and sisters in their novels.[12] A few of them came out with strong criticism of existing customs like early marriage, polygamy, purdah, and denial of education to women. Kailasbashini Devi was the first in the nineteenth century to provide a graphic description of the degraded condition of Hindu women in her book *Hindumahilaganer Hinabastha* (1863). Mankumari Basu (1863–1943), a poet and an essayist, in her autobiography, *Amar Atit Jiban* (My Life), described her isolation in her in laws' home because she lacked household skills. Shailabala Ghoshjaya (1893–1973), a courageous writer, portrayed in *Sekh Andu* the love between a Hindu widow and a Muslim chauffeur, and in *Janma Aparadhini* (Guilty of Being Born) depicted the life of a woman neglected by her husband and tortured by her in-laws. Swarnakumari Devi portrayed the 'new' woman. Saratkumari Chaudhurani (1861–1920) wrote insightful essays on the women of Calcutta. She bluntly asked, 'Are our daughters objects of our love or not?',[13] and Kamini Roy questioned the entire contemporary method of bringing up and educating daughters.[14] Both these well-known writers and not-so-well-known housewives wrote fairly regularly in women's journals. It was easier for them to express their thoughts, their discontent or protest through the pen than verbally. For instance, one Charushila Mitra asked in *Bamabodhini Patrika*, 'Can men, who spend time with friends out of the house and are steeped in luxury, ever comprehend a woman's sad plight?'[15] In *Bharatamahila*, Sarajubala Dutta, its fiery editor, proclaimed that women 'must take upon themselves the responsibility of serving women'. Shatadalbasini Biswas, in a manner reminiscent of Rokeya, blatantly stated, 'The low position of women suits men' for allowing them to continue their domination over women. 'I want to tell educated men that women are, like them, human beings.' And yet, 'In a well-to-do family a wife is a commodity of luxury, and in a poor family she is a mere slave.'[16]

Sarala differed both from those who extolled women's uncomplaining self-sacrifice, and from those who blamed men for framing rules that enforced women's degeneration. On the one hand, she inspired women to be good mothers at home and good daughters to the nation, while on the other, she blamed women rather than men for their current problems. She repeatedly advocated in her essays *tej* or spirited courage.[17] Courage along with an unusual combination of three gifts—musical talent, literary skill, and leadership ability, made her what she was.

It is interesting to explore how Sarala was viewed and treated by her contemporaries. Was she appreciated for her courage and leadership and for her contributions to the nation? Or was she considered a threat to society? Contemporaries perceived Sarala as quite an unusual woman. There was public support for her outdoor activities. Malavika Karlekar points out that 'all-male organizations recognized her potential' and invited her to speak at various meetings. Sarala willingly obliged, and used these occasions to express her views.[18] The *Bengalee*, a widely circulated English language paper edited by Surendranath Banerjea, lent her wholehearted support and its editorials and news coverage contributed to a great extent to her popularity among the common people, especially the youth. When Sarala organized the Pratapaditya Utsav, the newspapers were lavish in praise of the initiative. The journal *Bangabasi* wrote, 'What wonderful sight did we perceive? ... Not too many speeches, not too much ado, only the invocation of Bengal's heroes, Bengali young men with arms in their hands, and a Bengali woman as their leader ... Has Goddess Durga appeared among us?' *Sanjivani* commented, 'We are very impressed by the sight of a woman presiding over an assembly of men'. When Sarala Devi started publishing a series of small books under entitled *Banger Bir* (The Heroes of Bengal), and introduced Udayaditya Utsav, the *Bengalee* lent enthusiastic support. 'Sarala Devi is springing new surprises on the country. We feel almost tired keeping pace with her. Every morning we ask ourselves, what next.'[19] Sarala seems to have continued the *utsav* when she later went to Punjab. In 1906, a function called Pratapaditya Hom (Homage to Prapaditya) was organized in Lahore. Punjabi and Bengali men and women were apparently present, and a young Punjabi girl sang a patriotic song, which charmed and inspired the audience. This was reported in *Bharati*, which asked,

How does one expect to kindle heroic sentiment in the country without paying homage to the past heroes of our land? Pratapaditya *utsav* should be organized on a large scale all over Bengal. The Pratapaditya *utsav* and the Birashtami *utsav* which Sarala Devi introduced brought considerable benefit to the country. She is not in Bengal now. Shall we not, therefore, celebrate Pratapaditya *utsav* and Birashtami *utsav* in Bengal?[20]

Several factors contributed to this positive public response. In the first place, we have to recall that during the Swadeshi movement many nationalist leaders subtly converted their socio-economic struggle against the British into a worship of the motherland. Nationalism assumed a religious form. The motherland became the Mother Goddess. Tanika Sarkar lucidly observes, 'Patriotism was subsumed within religion, the country became a vivid new deity added to the Hindu pantheon, and by a sleight of hand, became the highest deity from the moment of her deification'.[21] In Sarala's family, a song by her uncle Rabindranath evoked the image of Durga as motherland, and another of her relations, the reputed artist Abanindranath (1871–1951), popularized the painting of *Bharatmata* (Mother India) as Goddess.[22] Since women had traditionally nurtured religious faiths and rituals, the conversion of politics into religion made possible, even desirable, the acceptance of a political space for women. Borthwick comments, 'The mother-centred rhetoric of Hindu nationalism may help to explain how Sarala Devi gained recognition as a leader of militant nationalism in its early stages.'[23] Sarala excelled in this role. In the worship of the Mother Goddess that was India, she exhorted women to remember who they were—parts of the Goddess themselves—and urged men to be brave and strong in their worship of the country/Goddess.[24] That she did, significantly, through the medium of traditional Indian rituals like *hom* and *utsav* and in remembrance of Bengali heroes. It is no wonder then that the Bengali intelligentsia thoroughly approved.

When Sarala Devi organized the Pratapaditya Utsav, Bepin Chandra Pal (1858–1932), the nationalist leader, commented in *Young India*, 'As necessity is the mother of invention, Sarala Devi is the mother of Pratapaditya to meet the necessity of finding a hero for Bengal'.[25] Bepin Pal was right, and he made this point long before Terence Ranger and Eric Hobsbawm popularized their ideas on the invention of tradition.[26] Sarala was indeed 'inventing a tradition'. In history, the use or invention of rituals is a common enough phenomenon. Indeed, nationalist movements famously create new symbols or reinterpret old ones. Sarala invented Bengali heroes like Pratapaditya, and used the old symbolism of tying the *rakhi*, an accepted token of brotherhood, to bolster the pride of the Bengali people and cement bonds between Bengali youth. The inventions were acclaimed by those who understood their efficacy.

The tradition of shakti worship in Bengal, and the belief in Goddess Durga as the supreme power, smoothed the acceptance of Sarala's leadership. Sometimes Sarala was referred to in public parlance as Bengal's Joan of Arc, and sometimes she was likened to Goddess Durga herself. She herself played the part well, often dressing herself in eye-catching jewellery and with her long hair untied, continually invoking the name of Durga, and the religious tradition of female power in her speeches and writings. The attempts were noticed and they received favourable coverage from leading journals, such as *Prabasi* and *Modern Review*.

Sarala's talent and her character won for her high regard from revered men like Vivekananda and Gandhi, a factor that heightened her prestige. She wrote a piece on Vivekananda in *Bharati* that started a process of mutual admiration between him and Sarala. 'May the Lord grant that many women like you be born in this country and devote their lives to the betterment of the motherland,' Vivekananda wrote to her.[27] He requested her to go abroad to represent Indian womanhood and spread the message of the east to the west.[28] She did not go, but continued to be greatly attracted by his teachings. Sarala also developed a close relationship with Mahatma Gandhi. While they enjoyed a long correspondence, Gandhi's published works do not include his letters to Sarala; they remain with the family.[29] National political leaders, such as Chittaranjan Das (1870–1925) and Bepin Pal were Sarala's well-wishers,[30] while Lala Lajpat Rai, the nationalist leader in the Punjab, and Aurobindo Ghosh (1872–1950) were sympathetic fellow-travellers. Bankim Chandra Chattopadhyay wrote congratulatory letters to her on her compositions published in *Bharati*, and she worked with her uncle Rabindranath in the musical field.

Sarala was thus generally perceived as an extraordinary woman, who transcended the 'limitations' of most women. Her views on women did not provoke adverse criticism, partly because she remained basically within the parameters of nationalist discourse, and because she stepped on to a stage when the stage that had already, in a sense, been prepared. The Brahmos and 'progressive' Hindus had already been writing about women's lack of education, about the need of a new role for them, and for a general elevation of their condition. What Sarala did beyond this was to insist that women become confident of their power, which is the sine qua non of a women's movement, and to organize women at the all-India level. Contemporary women thought highly of her. Renuka Ray (1904–98), a reputed leader, observed in her autobiography that Sarala was regarded as 'a towering national leader of those days.'[31]

Yet, Sarala herself did not, in her personal life correspond to the 'nationalist construct of womanhood': the 'essential femininity' combined with responsible 'motherhood' were conspicuous by their absence. In her personal character, she deviated from Partha Chatterjee's explication of the nationalist construction of womanhood; she did not at all conform to the concept of '*lajjashila*'.[32] By all standards, whether of the 'golden age' or of contemporary times, at thirty-one or thirty-two years of age, Sarala should have been married with children and have become a 'good' mother and competent housewife, not a leader of youth clubs mixing uninhibitedly with men. For the appreciation she received here, I would argue, she owes a direct debt to Bankim Chandra Chattopadhyay whose celebrated novel *Devi Chaudhurani* (1884) created an eponymous female character who led a heroic band of men akin to Robin Hood's. The image of a brave female leader of men had thus already been internalized in the Bengali psyche;[33] and Sarala was often referred to as Devi Chaudhurani. She was Sarala Ghosal in those days, her marriage with Rambhuj not on the anvil, and no one then foresaw that her married surname would be Chaudhurani, and her name would officially become Sarala Devi Chaudhurani. The most interesting trait here was that she did not advise other women to be Devi Chaudhuranis or defy conventions as she did. She urged them to emulate the high-minded and heroic qualities of the women of the 'golden' age, in keeping with the design mapped out by the nationalists. Her concerns with women's issues, therefore, did not raise many eyebrows.

Finally, no assessment of Sarala should overlook the fact that she was a Tagore, albeit from her mother's side; she had Tagore blood in her. She had a share in the awe and reverence with which the family was generally regarded. The Tagore men and women had violated old customs, and created new ones. It was almost expected of them. Sarala also had the Tagore family charisma, and seems to have carefully nurtured it. The family connection helped her gain the recognition that she richly deserved. Her versatile talent was thus easy to admire, and her leadership was not hard to accept.

### BEGUM ROKEYA

Like Sarala, Rokeya thought deeply about power and politics, but hers was the politics of gender, and not that of anti-colonialism (although she supported the anti-colonial struggle) or of pan-Asian identity. The colonization that most moved her was that of women's minds by men, and her primary revolt was against gender injustice. Acutely conscious of hierarchical gender difference, she queried,

> May I ask, astronomer sir, why do we not find your wife with you? When you are engaged in measuring the distance between the earth and the sun or the stars, where is your wife occupied in the measurement of pillow covers?[34]

In Muslim theology, a woman is equal to half a man. 'According to Islamic belief a woman is worth only half a man, that is to say, two women equal a man,' said Rokeya,[35] and complained that Muslim males flouted even this dictum, and denied their daughters their rightful share on both counts, material and emotional, paternal property and affection. 'If the Prophet Muhammad asks you when the day of reckoning arrives, how have you all treated your daughters, what would you say?'[36] However, for Rokeya only a 'half' was not enough; it was not fair. Exhibiting rare courage she therefore advanced beyond religious prescriptions, and squarely demanded equality with men. 'When we talk about progress made by women, we think of equality with men. What other comparable standards have we got?'[37]

One wonders how Rokeya developed her ideas, confined as she was by abarodh in her childhood and strict purdah in her adulthood. She did not know much English to begin with. Although a voracious reader, it was not possible for her to be familiar with the writings on and by women in the Western world except for a selected few. She wrote only one book, *Dellicia Hatya* (Murder of Dellicia), based on a Western novel by Mary Correlli, but that was written much later than her masterpiece *Sultana's Dream*. Where did she imbibe the ideas presented in that *Dream*? The inevitable surmise is that protest against the gross injustice meted out to women and personally experienced by her, crystallized into a written rebellion. She must have been an intellectual of the rarest genre; her mind conceptualized the logic and the vision—and the dream.

However, Rokeya was an avid reader and had learnt both Urdu and Bengali well. She must have been familiar with, and influenced by, what was going on in the Muslim world of thought. She was keenly aware of her surroundings: the intellectual movement in the north led by the Aligarh School and the jagaran among Bengali Muslims.[38] As mentioned earlier, in contemporary Bengal, writings by scholars as well as articles in newspapers and journals, were giving birth to Bengali Muslim nationalism. While Imdadul Huq and Shirazi elaborated it in essays, Bulbul Chowdhury through dance and Abbasuddin through music, Rokeya took it to the women's arena. She was, as Abdul Mannan Syed observes, a part of the emergence of a new jagaran, of the birth of a new identity in multiple arenas.[39]

Rokeya was a devout Muslim, but she perceived the weaknesses in prevailing practices. Looking around at what she felt to be the pitiable condition of the women of the community, she blamed men for deceiving women in the name of Islam. For women's abanati, Rokeya identified two principal causes: the selfishness of men and the mental slavery of women. Unlike Sarala, however, she held men responsible for women's backwardness. In her view, women's mental slavery was the product of their ignorance and abarodh, both of which were men-ordained. However, Rokeya was faced with a moral issue which made her life far more difficult than it would otherwise have been. Belief in the principles of Islam and opposing orthodox mullahs meant for her a long, bitter battle, and a fine distinction between pristine Islamic dicta and mullahdom's proclamations. In actual day-to-day life, she had to make certain compromises, which must have troubled her deeply. For instance, she retained the purdah for herself, and even tacitly supported it despite her genuine objections to the custom. She observed purdah as a strategy to preserve her school, as she knew that non-observance would alienate many, who might not agree to send their children to her school. She said,

I am getting on in age and may die any day, but I do not wish the school which I have run for so many years to die with my death. This is the fear that haunts me, so I had to make a compromise in the interest of my school by observing purdah.[40]

Shamsunnahar Mahmud writes that 'Rokeya's protest was not necessarily trained against abarodh. She knew that it would erode on its own with the spread of education.'[41] I would argue, however, that it was abarodh that constituted the central focus of Rokeya's battle. While she approved of modesty and dignity in women's attire (as did Gyanadanandini and the Tagore women) and publicly endorsed limited observance of purdah, at heart she rejected both purdah and abarodh.[42] During Rokeya's time, some Muslim women in north and central India took the decision to discard purdah. Nazr Sajjad Hyder (b. 1890?) of Punjab, who wrote extensively, managed to free herself from purdah; Jahan Ara Shah Nawaz (1896–1979) dispensed with purdah, spoke at the Round Table Conference in London in the early 1930s, and was elected as a member of the Punjab Legislative Assembly in 1937; Masuma Begum (1902–90) of Hyderabad abandoned the purdah and was active in the AIWC; Rashid Jahan (1905–52) of Aligarh became a medical doctor and her sister Khatun Jahan became Principal of Aligarh Women's College, These were women who were carving new paths for themselves and defining new roles for Muslim women.[43] It was their example that caused Rokeya despair that while women in other parts of India were marching forward, Bengali women lagged far behind.

Rokeya appears to have been a fairly practical person with considerable administrative acumen. She exhibited shrewdness and pragmatism on several occasions, and made concessions when necessary. To her, the real issue was the *abanati* of Muslim women; the ways of achieving their unnati and advancing their education overshadowed every other consideration. She wrote, wept, despaired, and raged, and as a result of lifelong struggle made the beginning of a powerful women's movement.

Rokeya was not the only one among contemporary Muslim women to work for fellow women. For the promotion of women's education, Nawab Faizunnessa Chaudhurani, Khujasta Akhtar Banu and a few others had done pioneering work. Following in Rokeya's footsteps, Akhtar Imam (b. 1919), Fazilatunnessa Zoha (1905–76) and Daulatunnessa Khatun (1918–?) made significant contributions to the cause of education. In the sphere of literature, Rokeya had a distinguished predecessor in Nawab Faizunnessa Chaudhurani whose *Rupjalal*, a romantic work written partly in prose and partly in verse, was published in 1876. Among Rokeya's contemporaries, Azizunnessa wrote for *Islam Pracharak,* and Khairunnessa (1870–1912) for *Nabanoor.* Among those who immediately followed Rokeya, Shamsunnahar Mahmud was born in an aristocratic family and was an abarodhbasini in childhood. She, however, managed to pursue her studies and get a Bachelor's degree in 1932. Shamsunnahar's *Punyamoyee* (1925) was followed by *Begum Mahal* and *Rokeya Jiboni* (1937), her best known work. Begum Shaista Ikramullah (b. 1913) authored *From Purdah to Parliament*, Akhtar Imam wrote an important memoir, *Eden Theke Bethune*, and Anwara Bahar Chowdhury (1919–87) wrote a biography of Shamsunnahar Mahmud. Razia Khatun Chaudhurani (1907–34) published a number of essays and stories on women's education and purdah. In an essay entitled 'Samaj O Grihe Narir Abastha' (Women's Place at Home and Society), she wrote in a vein reminiscent of Rokeya, and doubtless influenced by her:

So long Muslim women had suffered all oppression in silence ... That we still remain alive is by itself a great wonder! We have a society to prevent cruelty to animals, and a considerate Government has now introduced death sentence for murder. And yet just no one spares a thought for us women, who are destined to rigid confinement within the stone walls of our homes, condemned to slow death by deprivation of any hope, happiness and promise.[44]

Three novels by Nurunnessa Khatun (1892–1975), *Bhagyachakra* (The Wheel of Destiny), *Bidhilipi* (Words of Fate), and *Niyoti* (Destiny) deserve special mention, because they portray love before marriage. According to Sonia Nishat Amin, this was 'a major change in the treatment of male-female interaction' in women's literature. Contemporary literature was replete with descriptions of romantic attraction, but not of the actual 'interaction between the sexes before marriage.'[45] It was however Rokeya, I will argue, who really pioneered this change before Nurunnessa did. Rokeya's *Padmarag* dwells on love at first sight between Siddika and Latif. Although technically married, they did not know each other when they met. Their mutual attraction must be treated as what Amin calls 'interaction between the sexes'. 'If the concept of love rather than duty as a basic ingredient of marriage and home life was new', and was 'a part of the emergent ideology of the domestic', it first made its appearance in Rokeya's essays and novel. What additionally set Rokeya apart from the authors mentioned above was her articulation of gender sensitivity with an unmatched force. Neither Nurunnessa nor Khairunnessa evinced the determination to protest against the injustice done to women, basically supporting the traditional ideology of womanhood.[46] Rokeya's writings point to the 'emerging views of the next generation': of Muslim women who gradually evolved their own viewpoints on purdah, polygamy, divorce, and other social issues, distinct from those of men in the generation of reform'.[47]

From her contemporaries Rokeya received quite a different response from the applause accorded to Sarala. What Rokeya said was rebellious, if not sacrilegious, and evoked severe criticism. Take the case of 'Strijatir Abanati' (Degradation of Women) for example. When it first appeared, it came as a shock to most readers, and some paragraphs had to be deleted or replaced before it was reprinted. Rokeya wrote, 'All that religion has done for women is to make their shackles of slavery stronger and stronger...Men have always propagated religious texts as edicts of God to keep us women under them'.[48] Nausher Ali Khan Yusufzai in an article in *Nabanoor*, asked, 'Women readers! Do you really believe that you are slaves? ... Was it really necessary to use such uncalled for unfair words [against men's use of religion]? Would there have been any problem in searching the causes of your degradation if such irrelevant words were not used?' His advice to Rokeya, and indeed to all women, was simple. 'By all means, be independent, if that is what you like, but do take care that you do not abuse your freedom.' S. A. Al Moosvi affirmed in the same journal, 'Women can never be equals of men ... That will be going against Nature.'[49] Even the literary critics of *Nabanoor*, where Rokeya wrote, often, commented that Rokeya's essays were influenced by Christian missionaries. 'The author of *Motichoor* is constantly whipping the society. We do not think that it will yield any fruitful result.'[50] *Mihir o Sudhakar* published a stronger condemnation:

She has made some very fallacious remarks on the time honoured sacred books of Islamic religion ... She has also averred that these sacred books are the work of mortal men. If she really thinks that her theory is true then one can only conclude that she can do no good to our country.[51]

Nor was the response from women favourable. One woman wrote, '... however powerful her language, the conclusions she arrived at are objectionable and in bad taste'. Another woman from Orissa warned that women's freedom, like everything else, must have a limit. A third one asked, 'Is it necessary to condemn men so rudely in order to attain women's progress?'.[52] Then, when *Bhrata Bhagni* was published, a woman bitterly complained, 'We recognize sister Hossain as the spokeswoman of our society. We do not expect to hear such things from her'.[53] Against *Abarodhbasini*, a reviewer wrote in the *Masik Mohammadi*, 'Her readers might have been more appreciative had the distinguished writer desisted from narrating fairy tales in the name of denouncing the purdah system'.[54]

Rokeya remained undaunted by such criticisms. The adverse evaluation by her readers did not put an end to her struggle, the disparagement of the mullahs did not affect her. She was, however, hurt, especially by the charges levelled at her school. She wrote to her cousin, 'Do you know, my sister, what has been my reward for all this hard work I do? All that I have ever received for my labours is a censorious watch over my activities by our people who are forever eager to pick holes in whatever I do.'[55] At her death, however, meetings were organized and tributes paid to her. One witness commented, 'True, today people are paying homage to her ... But for the last twenty-five years they have only condemned her and slandered her, and denounced her till her death. What claim can they have now to mourn her death?'[56]

Rokeya was dead. There was no problem mourning or praising her. Those sharp, satirical, hurtful writings were unlikely to be penned by any of her contemporaries.

### FINAL OBSERVATIONS

Given the differences in the responses of their contemporaries, how are Sarala and Rokeya judged today?

Discussion of Sarala is remarkably absent, despite her prominence during her lifetime. While she is mentioned in works on the Tagore family, and there are references to her in a few articles and monographs,[57] there has been no systematic research on the once-admired Devi Chaudhurani; nor has any in-depth dissertation been published on her political role in Bengal or in the Punjab.[58] No serious attempt been made in recent years to assess her pioneering contribution to the women's movement. The works of a number of women of the nineteenth and early twentieth centuries are being compiled and published now. Yet Sarala's essays that appeared in many journals, especially *Bharati*, lie scattered in the archives. Even Ghulam Murshid's latest work on the evolution of women's rights in Bengal over the past one hundred years, *Rasasundari Theke Rokeya*, does not include a chapter on Sarala, though it dwells on Rasasundari, Kailasbasini, Gyanadanandini, and Krishnabhabini. Gyanadanandini lacked Sarala's social consciousness, nor was she a leader, although she contributed to fashioning appropriate attire for women. Krishnabhabini wrote several articles advocating education for women and the improvement of women's position in society, but believed in the traditional roles for women. Rasasundari's is a fairy tale story of self-education. Kailasbasini exhibited social awareness, but no leadership or organizational qualities. In terms of personal achievement and social and political contribution, Sarala stands far above them.

Why has posterity not remembered Sarala in the way it should have done? One reason might have been that she was overshadowed by latter-day women political leaders. In the biplabi movement, where her earliest contributions lay, Pritilata Waddedar (1911–32) Suniti Chaudhury (1917–88), Shanti Ghosh (1916–89), and Kalpana Dutta (1913–95), who either died or risked their lives for the cause, became the celebrated revolutionary women in Bengal. In the freedom struggle led by Gandhi, women like Sarojini Naidu or Sucheta Kripalani (1908–74) occupied the centre-stage at the all India level. Basanti Devi and Jyotirmoyee Ganguli (1889–1943) became prominent in Bengal[59] while Sarala was living with her husband in Punjab. The freedom movement is now over, and Sarala's methods of bringing up strong men and women in the context of that movement are considered obsolete. Moreover, Sarala had propounded a particular Bengali nationalism. Her invocation of Bengali heroes and her passionate appeal to Bengali youth to match Rajput and Maratha heroism are pointers to this. She wrote articles in *Bharati*, asserting that the descendants of Lakshmansen, the ruler of Bengal, had actually established a Sena kingdom in Punjab, and claimed that she had undertaken extensive research on the subject.[60] Here she tried to fan Bengali nationalism with incidents from what she thought was history. Unfortunately for her, that brand of Bengali nationalism did not take deep root in Indian soil. Her 'invented' heroes were forgotten in their own land of Bengal, and when Subhas Chandra Bose (1897–?), a real life hero appeared,[61] Pratapaditya and Udayaditya lost all the glitter she had bestowed on them.

Besides, Sarala's involvement with women's issues might not initially have been considered disturbing, but it was not kindly looked upon when nationalism was at its height. Women political leaders of the nationalist movement who applied themselves to women's issues, tended to say in their interviews and autobiographies that during the freedom struggle they were concerned not with women's issues but with colonialism.[62] Many of them were involved with women's problems and with women's associations, but they avoided prioritizing them. In that climate of intense nationalism, any ideology that heightened an alternative identity, would have been perceived as a threat. Sarala's views, her initiation of an organization for women and led by women to focus on women's issues (as distinct from issues of nationalism) found little favour with those who had supported her role in the nationalist movement. Even her uncle Rabindranath was not sympathetic. 'Sarala spent some days at Shantiniketan, and upset everything. You know what the women missionaries are like. And Sarala is no ordinary missionary,' he wrote to Pramatha Chaudhuri in 1921.[63] Sarala's Mahamandal did not last long either. Its importance was marginalized by the All India Women's Conference (1927) and by latter-day women's wings of political parties.

In the field of contemporary literature, the mother (Swarnakumari) overshadowed the daughter. Moreover, editing *Bharati* appeared an insignificant enterprise when dazzlingly witty and brilliant journals like *Sabujpatra* appeared edited by men with Tagore family connections, or journals like *Prabasi* were published with the full support of the Tagore who mattered most, Rabindranath.[64] In the arena of music too, Rabindranath almost alone dominated the Bengali mind, leaving a little space only for Kazi Nazrul Islam (1898–1976), but little or none for his gifted niece, who sang brilliantly, created music, and collected melodies from various parts of India for use by her uncle. If being a Tagore gave Sarala a platform to launch her various initiatives, it also ensured that she stayed under the shadow of her illustrious relatives.

Sarala thus became a part of the past, acknowledged as a pioneer, and a fascinating personality with many contributions, but now dispensable, and so relegated to the dusty pages of history.

It is quite another story for Rokeya. She was born in undivided India, but her birthplace, Rangpur, is now in Bangladesh. Rokeya has emerged as the national model of a woman leader among the articulate and educated section in Bangladesh. This becomes clear if one analyses recent research on Rokeya. Rokeya published her books from 1905, and Shamsunnahar Mahmud wrote her biography in 1937. It was however only in 1973, after the birth of Bangladesh in 1971, that the first important volume, a collection of her writings, *Rokeya Rachanavali*, edited by Abdul Qadir, was published. The nineteen-eighties saw a number of important books written on her. Morshed Shafiul Hasan's work was published in 1982, Abdul Mannan Syed's in 1983, Motahar Hossain Sufi's in 1986, and Muhammad Shamsul Alam's in 1989. Most of these monographs were reprinted in the nineteen-nineties, indicating a growing interest in Rokeya's life and work.

Rokeya was a Bengali par excellence. Born in a family that valued only Urdu or Persian and denigrated Bengali, married to a Urdu-speaking man, she nurtured a passionate love for the Bengali language. Throughout her life she concentrated on Bengal, its language, its women. She claimed, 'Whatever may be the local language of other places, my concern is what should be the local language for Calcutta. After managing Sakhawat Memorial School for sixteen years, I have come to realise that the local Muslims are motherless, because they do not have a mother tongue.'[65] It may be recalled here that the language issue was the rallying point of Bengali nationalism that eventually culminated in the birth of Bangladesh.

Rokeya was a devout Muslim. At the same time she was thoroughly secular in the best sense of the term. On the occasion of the Id festival in 1905, at a moment when many Muslims and Hindus were distancing themselves from one another, Rokeya said,

> On such an auspicious day of the Id, must we forget our Hindu brethren? Is it too much to expect that on such an occasion Hindu brothers will join us? Are not all

children of Bengal one and the same? As the dark night of the moon is followed by the rising sun, let benediction enrich us after the end of an accursed period. Instead of fraternal conflict, let unsullied unity reign.[66]

Most importantly, Rokeya was the first Bengali Muslim woman who publicly articulated a strong protest against the injustice done to women and fought for women's equality with men. She burnt with a passion to reform the Muslim community, and women of the community. If we look at the overall movement for regeneration in the Muslim community of Bengal that took shape in the late nineteenth and early twentieth centuries, we realize that Rokeya provided major leadership in promoting the gender aspect of Bengali Muslim nationalism. According to her contemporary biographer, Shamsunnahar, 'From the very beginning until the last, Rokeya had one politics: *nari jagaran*'.[67] Motahar Hossain Sufi, a latter-day biographer comments, 'She was the first person to light the torch to set the Bengali Muslim women on their path to emancipation. Her place in the history of the jagaran of Muslim women of Bengal as a pioneer is now firmly secured.'[68] Maleka Begum, herself a reputed activist in today's Bangladesh, agrees with them and observes, 'Rokeya Sakhawat Hossain is hailed as the trailblazer in the cause of the awakening of Muslim women, because no one before her had shaken up the community so powerfully as she did with her movement, challenging the exploitation of, and discrimination against, women.'[69] Naturally, the women's movement in Bangladesh has found in her a role model, and, historically speaking, this movement, one of the strongest and most successful women's movements in the world, owes a tremendous debt to the pioneer, and it acknowledges the debt. In India, too, there is a growing appreciation of Rokeya. Susie Tharu and K. Lalitha's important work, *Women Writing in India*, has a major section on Rokeya.[70] A number of articles and seminars on the women's movement refer to her contributions. At the international level, those feminists who are familiar with *Sultana's Dream*, written originally in English, greatly admire Rokeya's wit, courage, and vision, and recognize her place in the women's movement of the world. She is thus not dispensable: her memory is cherished by the present generation of men and women.

Sarala Devi, once an inspiration to many, is a page in history; Begum Rokeya is a revived source of inspiration.

# Notes and References

## Chapter One

1. *Report of the Native Newspapers in Bengal*, State Archives, Government of West Bengal, Calcutta; see also Prashanta Kumar Pal, *Rabi-Jiboni* (The Biography of Rabindranath), vol. 5, Calcutta, 1397 BS, AD 1990), p. 60. The two words 'Sing Hindusthan' are translations of '*Gao Hindusthan*', the opening words of the Bengali song sung on the occasion.

2. Rokeya Sakhawat Hossain, 'Bayuyane Panchash Mile' (Fifty Miles in an Aeroplane), in Abdul Qadir (ed.), *Begum Rokeya Rachanavali* (henceforth, *Rachanavali*), Bangla Academy, Dhaka, 1993, p. 282.

3. Swarnakumari Devi, *Sekele Katha* (Stories of Olden Days), *Bharati*, Chaitra, 1322 BS, AD 1915. The *vaishnavi*s were acquainted with Puranic literature and religious verse, and taught these to the Tagore family women. Swarnakumari also mentions that Debendranath appointed teachers to teach Sanskrit, and even a European lady to teach English to the women of his family.

4. *Kahake* (1898) is considered by critics to be Swarnakumari's magnum opus. Many of her books were translated into several languages, including English.

5. *Bharati* became the premier Bengali journal after Sanjib Chandra Chattopadhyaya's *Bangadarshan* had disappeared. Swarnakumari was the first woman in Bengal to regularly edit a journal (1884). An earlier journal, *Binodini*, edited by Bhubanmohini Devi, ceased to exist after only a few issues. For Swarnakumari's success and popularity as the editor of *Bharati*, see Nistarini Devi, *Bharati O Bharatir Sampadika (Bharati and its editor)*, Jaladhar Sen, *Bharati Smriti (Bharati Remembered)*, *Bharati*, Baishakh, 1323 BS, AD 1916.

6. For a description of *Sakhi Samiti*, see Ghulam Murshid, *Reluctant Debutante*, Rajshahi, 1993. There is a list of members of the *Samiti* in App. IV.

7. For a first-hand account of this organization, see Hiranmoyee Devi, *Mahila Shilpasamiti* (The Centre for Arts and Crafts for Women), *Bharati*, Aswin, 1315 BS. The Shilpasamiti was a 'reincarnation of Sakhi Samiti' In 1906, it established Mahila Shilpashram to give shelter and vocational training to indigent widows. The original name of Mahila Shilpashram was subsequently changed to Bidhaba Shilpashram. Hironmoyee mentions that the samiti and the ashram had a support group of men who managed the work that 'women were unable to do'.

8. Since the marriage of his second daughter, Maharshi also insisted that the bridegroom-to-be for his daughter would have to be initiated into Brahmoism before marriage. Showing an independence of spirit, Janakinath refused to oblige, and maintained that there was no real difference between the Hindus and Brahmos as both worshipped the same God whether with images or without, and both belonged to the larger Hindu community. Sarala Devi Chaudhurani, *Jibaner Jharapata* (The Fallen Leaves of Life), Calcutta, 1982, henceforth *Jharapata*, p. 2.

9. For Hironmoyee Devi's role as editor of *Bharati*, see Hemendra Kumar Ray, *Bharatir Itihas* (The History of *Bharati*), *Bharati*, Baishakh, 1323 BS, AD 1916. As Sarala lived in Punjab during this period, Hironmoyee virtually edited it alone.

10. Under the patronage of the Tagores, Nabagopal Mitra, Manomohan Ghosh, Sisir Kumar Mallik, and others, Hindu Mela functioned from 1867 to 1880, and sought to shape a nationalist identity. It held annual exhibitions to display indigenous products, especially arts and crafts, *Jyotirindranather Jibonsmriti*, Vasanta Kumar Chattopadhyay (ed.), Calcutta, 1326 BS, AD 1919, pp. 49–50.

11. Satyendranath's letters to his wife bear adequate evidence of his belief in women's 'liberation'. Indira Devi Chaudhurani, *Puratani*, Calcutta, 1879 Sakabda, AD 1957. The bulk of the volume comprises letters from Satyendranath to his wife.

12. Gyanadanandini recalls:

After my marriage, my brother-in-law, Hemendranath deliberately took upon himself the task of teaching us. He was keen on teaching and taught his own daughters. We used to cover our heads and sit before him. Quite often we used to feel scared when he scolded us ... I learned my Bengali from him.

Indira Devi Chaudhurani, *Puratani*, p. 27.

13. The *Calcutta Christian Observer* commented:

One of the most influential natives of Calcutta, Debendranath Tagore, has added his own daughter to the long list of eighty female children already receiving instruction in the institution.

*Jharapata*, p. 207.

14. She was married at the age of seven, but received every opportunity for education at her in-laws'. She says that a maidservant of the Tagore family had selected her for marriage with Satyendranath! The family custom was to send a reliable maidservant armed with plenty of toys in quest of a suitable bride! Indira Devi Chaudhurani, *Puratani*, p. 19.

15. Swarnakumari Devi recalls that the scene of shame and sorrow at the family home was beyond description (Swarnakumari Devi, *Sekele Katha*). Gyanadanandini also ventured to attend a party at Government House without her husband, who had been taken ill. Members of the Tagore clan, especially Prasanna Coomar Tagore, were so enraged and ashamed that they left the party in a huff. Indira Devi Chaudhurani, *Puratani*, p. 33. She also went alone to England to visit her husband, taking her children along with her.

16. Swarnakumari Devi, *Sekele Katha*. Swarnakumari says that it was not possible to venture out in public draped only in a saree, and no other garment, which was the usual mode of dress for a Bengali woman. Gyanadanandini reminiscences, in 'Those days we used to wear only a saree. In winter we covered ourselves with

light wrappers', *Puratani*, p. 24. Usually, a long and simple piece of cloth was draped around the body of a Bengali woman. No undergarments were worn. This clothing was comfortable for the hot climate of Bengal, but not suitable for going out. For the significance of sartorial reform, see Himani Bannerji, 'Attired in Virtue: The Discourse on Shame (*lajja*) and Clothing of the *Bhadramahila* in Colonial Bengal', in Bharati Ray (ed.), *From the Seams of History: Essays on Indian Women*, Oxford University Press, New Delhi, 1995.

17. For an insight into the lives and activities of Tagore family women, see Chitra Deb, *Thakurbarir Andarmahal* (The Inner Quarters of the Tagore Household, Calcutta, 1993).

18. Sarala Devi Chaudhurani, 'Amar Balyajiboni' (My Childhood Days) in *Bharati*, Baishakh, 1312 BS, AD 1905).

19. Hironmoyee Devi, 'Kaifiyat' (An Apology) in *Bharati*, Baishakh, 1323 BS, AD 1918.

20. *Jharapata*, p. 28.

21. Usha Chakraborty, *Condition of Bengali Women Around the Second Half of the Nineteenth Century*, Calcutta, 1963, App. iv.

22. *Jharapata*, p. 104.

23. Chitra Deb, *Thakurbarir Andarmahal*, p. 165.

24. Sarala Devi, 'Janmaswar' (In Memory), *Bharati*, Jaishtha, 1323 BS.

25. Sumit Sarkar, *The Swadeshi Movement in Bengal, 1903–1908*, New Delhi, 1973, provides a fine analysis of the movement.

26. *Jharapata*, p. 95.

27. *Bharati* published a number of her songs with notations.

28. *Jharapata*, p. 33.

29. *See* Chitra Deb, *Thakurbarir Andarmahal*, pp. 164–5.

30. Indira Chowdhury, *The Frail Hero and Virile History: Gender and Politics of Culture in Colonial Bengal*, Delhi, 1998, is a good analysis of the contemporary view on the subject.

31. *Jharapata*, pp. 126–7. The Indian ceremony of rakhi symbolizes brotherhood and protection. Its use in the interest of the freedom movement was initiated by Sarala Devi, and popularized by Rabindranath Tagore during the heyday of the movement.

32. 'Anti-Partition Agitation: *Swadeshi* and Boycott', Freedom Papers, no. 47, West Bengal State Archives (henceforth WBSA).

33. *Jharapata*, pp. 135–42. Sarala also composed a song to be sung during the Utsav: see *Birashtamir Gan* (The Song for Birashtami), *Bharati*, Kartik, 1311 BS, AD 1904.

34. Prashanta Kumar Pal, *Rabi Jiboni*, vol. 5, p. 124.

35. 'Bangalir Pitridhan' (The Heritage of the Bengalis), *Bharati*, Jaistha, 1310 BS, AD 1903).

36. 'Kumar Udayaditya' , *Bharati*, Sravan, 1310 BS, AD 1903.

37. Prashanta Kumar Pal, *Rabi-Jiboni*, vol. 5, p. 170.

38. Ibid.

39. Rabindranath in an introduction to his novel, when it was reprinted, argued against the invention of such mythical heroes. Historical facts, he said, indicated

Pratapaditya as a cruel, arrogant, and incompetent man. It is a debatable question whether or not Sarala was deliberately distorting history. To her, what she said was a historical truth, not a misrepresentation of reality. She felt that Bengali heroes had existed; they might not have succeeded in the war, but had shown courage in resisting an imperial power. However, what is historically important is not the debate about the personal character of Pratapaditya, but the fact that Sarala was projecting, and upholding a form of Bengali Hindu nationalism, and was using Pratapaditya's story for the purpose.

40. A proposal to institute a Mir Qasim festival in Bengal was made by a local newspaper, *Jugantar*, 8 July 1906, Report of the Native Newspapers in Bengal.

41. Sarala Devi, 'Congress O Svayatta Shasan' (The Congress and the Issue of Autonomy), *Bharati*, Baishakh, 1312 BS, AD 1905.

42. Tirtha Mandal, *Women Revolutionaries of Bengal, 1905–1939*, Calcutta, 1991, pp. 51–2.

43. Sarala went to Mymensingh in 1905 to attend the Provincial Conference when she tried to organize the Samiti as 'an instrument of political work', and 'to infuse a martial spirit among its members' by introducing Birashtami Utsav and Pratapaditya Utsav. The Secretary of the Samiti, Kedarnath Chakravarty, 'was controlled by Sarala from Lahore'. 'Samitis and Associations of Mymensingh', Freedom Papers, no. 58, WBSA.

44. Bharati Ray, '*Swadeshi* Movement and Women's Awakening in Bengal, 1903–1910', *The Calcutta Historical Journal*, vol. 9, Jan.–June, 1985. See also Satish Pakrashi, *Agnidiner Katha* (Memoirs: Tales of Those Revolutionary Days), Calcutta 1947, esp. p. 93 and Bharati Ray, 'Women, Politics and Identity in Colonial Bengal, 1900–1947', in Bharati Ray and David Taylor (eds), *Politics and Identity in South Asia*, Kolkata, 2002.

45. Sarala Devi Chaudhurani, 'Bharater Hindu O Musalman' (The Hindus and Muslims of India), *Bharati*, Bhadra, 1310 BS, AD 1903.

46. Hemendra Kumar Ray, *Jander Dekhechhi* (Those Whom I Have Seen), Calcutta, 1355 BS, pp. 73–7. The noted author Sunil Gangopadhyay (b. 1934) in his novel *Pratham Alo*, vol. 2 (The First Dawn), Calcutta, 1997, pp. 602–3, sympathetically reconstructs the incident of Sarala's sudden marriage in Deoghar instead of in Calcutta with virtually no festivities. Her mother seems to have pressurized her in the context of her earlier romances, none of which had led to marriage.

47. J.C. Bagal, *Jharapata*, p. 196. Sarala ends her autobiography prior to her marriage. A short history of her later life was added to the book by J.C. Bagal.

48. Sarala wrote a brilliant poem 'Ahitagnika' (The Dedicated One) in *Bharati*, when she took up the responsibility of sole editorship. *Bharati*.

49. Hemendra Kumar Ray, 'Bharatir Itihas', *Bharati*, Baishakh, 1323 BS, AD 1916. See also Dinesh Chandra Sen, 'Sahityik Smriti' (Memories of a Litterateur) for Sarala's contributions to *Bharati*, op. cit.

50. This novel had been submitted to and rejected earlier by Ramananda Chatterjee, the editor of *Prabasi*. Sarala accepted it and thus contributed to the establishment of the reputation of Sarat Chandra Chattopadhyay, one of the most popular novelists of Bengal.

51. Aparna Basu and Bharati Ray, *Women's Struggle: A History of the All India Women's Conference, 1927–1990*, Delhi, 1990, dwells at length on the AIWC.

52. Sarala Devi published in *Bharati* a number of essays, which indicate her philosophical and religious temperament. See, for example, 'Chitravali' (The Pictures) which describes Mayavati and Kamana Devi ashram in the Himalaya, and reflects the influence of Hindu philosophy on her. *Bharati*, Shravan, 1323 BS, AD 1916.

See references in her autobiography to the spiritual quest that had taken her away from Brahmoism and that she often visited Vivekananda's ashram at Mayavati.

53. Motahar Hossain Sufi, *Begum Rokeya; Jibon o Sahitya (The Life and Literature of Begum Rokeya)*, Dhaka, 1986, pp. 1–4 and Shamsunnahar Mahmud, *Rokeya Jiboni* (The Biography of Rokeya), Dhaka, 1996, p. 14. Shamsunnahar Mahmud was Rokeya's contemporary. Her book was first published in 1937.

54. Shamsunnahar just mentions that Rahatunnessa was orthodox and was annoyed that Rokeya bothered her brother with her studies (Shamsunnahar Mahmud, *Rokeya Jiboni*, p. 21). Tahmina Alam, *Begum Rokeya Sakhawat Hossain: Chinta Chetanar Dhara O Samajkarma* (Begum Rokeya Sakhawat Hossain: Thoughts and Social Activities), Dhaka, 1996, p. 14, also says that Rahatunnessa was orthodox and a strong supporter of the purdah.

55. Motahar Hossain Sufi, *Begum Rokeya*, p. 4.

56. Rokeya Sakhawat Hossain, 'Lukano Ratan', *Rachanavali*, pp. 260–3, esp. p. 262.

57. Shamsunnahar Mahmud, *Rokeya Jiboni*, p. 19.

58. Abdul Mannan Syed, *Begum Rokeya*, Dhaka, 1996, p. 12.

59. Motahar Hossain Sufi, *Begum Rokeya*, p. 8.

60. Rokeya S. Hossain, *Abarodhbasini* (The Woman Confined) in *Rachanavali*, p. 47.

61. Ibid., pp. 447–8.

62. Rokeya Sakhawat Hossain, 'Dedication', *Padmarag, Rachanavali*, p. 289.

63. Shamsunnahar Mahmud, *Rokeya Jiboni*, p. 20.

64. Ibid., p. 11.

65. *Rachanavali*, p. 70. Rokeya goes on to say that in Calcutta she was running an Urdu-medium school where everyone spoke Urdu, yet she did not forget her Bengali due to his sister's kindness.

66. Shamsunnahar Mahmud, *Rokeya Jiboni*, p. 23.

67. Ghulam Murshid, *Rasasundari Theke Rokeya: Nari Pragatir Eksho Bachhar* (From Rasasundari to Rokeya: A Hundred Years of Women's Advancement), Dhaka, 1993, p. 134.

68. Muhammad Shamsul Alam, *Rokeya Sakhawat Hossain: Jibon O Sahityakarma* (Rokeya Sakhawat Hossain, Life and Literary Work), Dhaka, 1989, p. 110.

69. Letter dated 30 April 1931, cited in Moshfeqa Mahmud, *Patre Rokeya Parichiti* (Rokeya as Seen Through Her Letters), Dhaka, 1996, p. 23.

70. For a critical assessment of Rokeya's literary works, see Muhammad Shamsul Alam, *Rokeya Sakhawat Hossain*.

71. For a detailed discussion, see Abdul Mannan Syed, *Begum Rokeya*.

72. Anisuzzaman, *Muslim Manas O Bangla Sahitya* (The Muslim Psyche and Bengali Literature), Calcutta, 1971, p. 97.
73. Ibid., pp. 371 and 358.
74. Rokeya Sakhawat Hossain, *Rachanavali*, p. 75.
75. Rokeya Sakhawat Hossain, 'Muktiphal' in *Rachanavali*, pp. 198–220.
76. *Sandhya*, 11, 12 and 13 Nov. 1908, Report of the Native Newspapers in Bengal.
77. Rokeya Sakhawat Hossain, 'Nirupama Bir', in *Rachanavali*, pp. 526–7.
78. Rokeya Sakhawat Hossain, 'Baligarta' in *Rachanavali*, pp. 492–7.
79. Trans. Sukhendu Ray from Rokeya Sakhawat Hossain, 'Appeal' in *Rachanavali*, p. 524.
80. Bharati Ray, 'The Freedom Movement and Feminist Consciousness in Bengal, 1905–1929', in Bharati Ray (ed.), *From the Seams of History*, p. 193. For details of the struggle for votes for women, see Barbara Southard, *The Women's Movement and Colonial Politics in Bengal: The Quest for Political Rights, Education and Social Reform Legislation*, Delhi, 1995.
81. Letter dated 21.12.'31, cited in Moshfeqa Mahmud, *Patre Rokeya*, pp. 33–4.
82. Sarala, however, says that she chanced to read a poem in the pages of the *Bharati*, 'I have dedicated my life and soul to you, my motherland ... My music may not be powerful but if it touches a chord in even one single person, my life will be fulfilled.' Since then, she says, 'My young life of ten years became animated by overwhelming love of my country ... This song became my inspiration' Sarala Devi Chaudhurani, 'Janmaswar'.

## Chapter Two

1. In the world of the *antahpur* women must have had their own forms of fun and amusement, jokes and ribaldry, authority structure, and informal power, but they were generally denied formal power or public space.
2. Kamini Roy, *Balika Shikshar Adarsha* (The Goal of the Education for Girls), Calcutta, 1918, p. 21. Kamini Roy says, 'Discrimination between a son and a daughter is almost universal. In our country, if a couple is successful in producing a series of sons, the sons attract the benediction of long life from friends and relations. On the other hand, just two successive daughters is so unwelcome that the last born daughter is named either Khanto (Stop) or Ar Na (No more), or similar such appellation. A sole sister among many brothers may receive some attention of the family. And if a brother does not follow a sister's birth, then very often the unfortunate sister is blamed for the calamity.'
3. See A.S. Altekar, *The Position of Women in Hindu Civilisation*, Banaras, 1956; *Report of the Committee on the Status of Women in India*, Govt. of India, 1974; Neera Desai and Maithreyi Krishnaraj, *Women and Society in India*, Delhi, 1987, especially ch. 1; Bharati Ray, 'Beyond the Domestic/Public Dichotomy', in 'Women's History in Bengal, 1905–1947', in S.P. Sen and N.R. Ray (eds), *Modern Bengal: A Socio-Economic Survey*, Calcutta, 1988; M. Allen, 'The Hindu View of Women', in M. Allen & S.N. Mukherjee (eds), *Women in India and Nepal*, Australian University

Press, 1982; a relevant article based on autobiographies is Srabasi Ghosh, 'Birds in a Cage', *Economic and Political Weekly*, Oct. 1986, pp. 88–96. Bharati Ray, 'Bengali Women and the Politics of Joint Family, 1900–1947', *Economic and Political Weekly*, 26: 52, 28 Dec. 1991 looks at the joint family from the women's perspective. Hanna Papanek and Gail Minault (eds) *Purdah: Separate Worlds: Studies of Purdah in South Asia*, Delhi, 1982 is an excellent study of the custom of purdah, and the domestic/public dichotomy betwen men and women among both Hindus and Muslims.

4. Kailasbasini Devi, *Hindu Mahilaganer Hinabastha* (The Degraded Condition of Hindu Women), Calcutta, 1863, p. 2. This was the first book written by a woman in the nineteenth century analyzing the pitiable condition of contemporary Hindu women. She also wrote another book, *Hindu Abalakuler Bidyabhas O Tahar Samunnatir Upaya* (The Education of Hindu Women and Ways of Improvement), Calcutta, 1872, detailing women's social and educational status during her time. Kailasbasini was taught to read by her husband.

5. James Mill, *The History of British India*, London, 1840, pp. 445–7. For a recent article on contemporary English women's views on Indian women, see Janaki Nair, 'Uncovering the Zenana: Visions of Indian Womanhood in English Women's Writings, 1813–1940', *Journal of Women's History*, 2:1, 1990.

6. Amales Tripathi, 'The Role of Traditional Modernisers: Bengal's Experience in the Nineteenth Century', *Calcutta Historical Journal*, vol. 1983–4.

7. The issue has been competently dealt with in Meredith Borthwick, *The Changing Role of Women in Bengal, 1849–1905*, Princeton, 1984, pp. 26–108. See also K.N. Panikkar, 'The Intellectual History of Colonial India: Some Historiographical and Conceptual Questions', in S. Bhattacharya and Romila Thapar (eds), *Situating Indian History*, Delhi, 1986. For a recent insightful analysis, see Uma Chakravarti, 'Whatever Happened to the Vedic Dasi? Orientalism, Nationalism, and a Script for the Past', in Kumkum Sangari and Sudesh Vaid (eds) *Recasting Women*, New Delhi, 1989.

8. Editorial, *Sambad Prabhakar*, 9.8.1260 BS, AD 1853, in Benoy Ghosh (ed. & comp.), *Samayik Patre Banglar Samajchitra* (The Bengali Society as Reflected in Contemporary Newspapers and Journals), Calcutta, 1966, vol. 1, pp. 92–3. For an analytical history of Bengali newspapers and journals of the period, see Partha Chattopadhyaya, *Bangla Sanbadpatra O Bangalir Nabajagaran* (Bengali Newspapers and Renaissance in Bengal), Calcutta, 1988.

9. Shivanath Shastri, *Ramtanu Lahiri o Tatkalin Bangasamaj* (Ramatanu Lahiri and Contemporary Bengali Society), Calcutta, 1904, is an excellent contemporary portrayal. See also Syed Nurulla & J. P. Naik, *A History of Education in India During the British Period*, Bombay, 1951, and Aparna Basu, *Essays in the History of Indian Education*, Delhi, 1982, for a general overview. *Hundred Years of the Unversity of Calcutta, 1857–1957*, Calcutta, 1957, provides interesting details about the formation and early history of the university.

10. See Pradip Sinha, *Nineteenth Century Bengal: Aspects of Social History*, Calcutta, 1965, for a well-researched discussion.

11. In effect, as a result of the pull in two directions, Indian women were expected to combine in themselves the womanly qualities prized both in the

'modern' West and in the 'ancient' East. The models of both the women of the 'glorious past' as well as of Victorian Englishwomen were idealized. The image of the perfect Victorian lady did not correspond to the real life situations of the middle class women of Victorian England, as is clear from Mary Wollstonecraft's classic work, *Vindication of the Rights of Women*, London, 1875, and P. Branca, *Silent Sisterhood: Middle Class Women in the Victorian Home*, London, 1977. It may be of interest to recall that the ambivalence in the new construction of women's image is reflected in the otherwise brilliant indigenous Bengali literature. For instance, Madhusudan Dutta in *Meghnadbadh Kavya* (1861), portrayed Pramila as a stunningly brave woman, but she derived her strength from her pride in her husband and father-in-law. Bankim Chandra Chattopadhyay's Bhramar in *Krishnakanter Will* (1878), refused to forgive her husband for infidelity, but succumbed to the desire to see him on her deathbed.

12. See, for details, Nemai Sadhan Bose, *Indian Awakening and Bengal*, Calcutta, 1976; David Kopf, *The Brahmo Samaj and the Shaping of the Modern Mind*, Princeton, 1977. A contemporary documentation is Shivanath Shastri, *A History of the Brahmo Samaj*, 2 vols., Calcutta, 1911. For a history of social reforms, see also Charles Heimsath, *Indian Nationalism and Hindu Social Reform*, Princeton University Press, 1964, Kenneth Jones, 'Socio- Religious Movements and Changing Gender Relationships among Hindus of British India', in J. Bjorkman (ed.), *Fundamentalism, Revivalists and Violence in South Asia*, New Delhi, 1988, Kenneth Jones, *Socio-Religious Reform Movements in British India*, Cambridge University Press, 1989. Tapan Raychaudhuri makes an interesting observation in this context. 'Western, especially missionary, criticism of Hinduism had evoked a range of responses, reasoned or angry, ever since the days of Rammohan. Generally speaking, the responses had one characteristic in common—an implicit acceptance of the criteria by which the Western critics assessed Hindu belief and practices. Hence the anxiety to affirm the truly monotheistic character of Hinduism and the symbolic nature of the image-worship.' T. Raychaudhuri, *Europe Reconsidered*, New Delhi, 1988, p. 235.

13. *Rammohan Granthavali* (The Works of Rammohan), ed. Brajendranath Bandopadhyay and Sajanikanta Das, Calcutta, vol. 3, p. 45.

14. A recent analysis of the debate over Sati is Lata Mani, *Contentious Traditions: The Debate on Sati in Colonial India*, Delhi, 1998. Mani claims that the debates on the Sati were argued almost exclusively in terms of the scriptures and that what was at stake was not women's lives, but tradition.

15. The impact of Brahmoism on Indian society was manifest in two other perceptible ways. First, it began to produce a crop of Hindu missionaries whose principal motto was theological counter-aggression, e.g. the regeneration of Puranic Hinduism by Sasadhar Tarkachuramani (1851–1928), and the Neo-Vaishnavism of Bejoy Krishna Goswami (1841–99) Secondly, it also served to accentuate a sense of serious introspection, and to encourage objective, painstaking research into the annals of Hinduism. The Ramakrishna movement may also be regarded as a response to the Brahmo movement. See Amiya P. Sen, *Hindu Revivalism in Bengal, 1872–1905*, Oxford University Press, 1993, ch. 2, for Hindu–Brahmo relations.

16. Sekhar Bandyopadhyay, 'Caste, Widow-remarriage and the Reform of Popular Culture in Colonial Bengal' in Bharati Ray (ed.), *From the Seams of History*,

pp. 8–36, analyses the issue from the point of view of caste structure in Bengal. Benoy Ghosh, *Vidyasagar O Bangali Samaj* (Vidyasagar and the Bengali Society, Calcutta, 1366 BS, AD 1959) is a comprehensive study of Vidyasagar and his contributions.

17. Amiya P. Sen, *Hindu Revivalism*, ch. 5 is a brief, scholarly and analytical study of the movement.

18. S.P. Basu, *Vivekananda o Samakalin Bharatavarsha*, 4 vols. (Vivekananda and Contemporary India), Calcutta, 1975–80, is a good biography of Vivekananda. *Complete Works of Swami Vivekananda*, Mayavati Memorial Edition, 8 vols., Calcutta, 1972–3, is an authoritative compilation of his works. Bhupendranath Datta, *Swami Vivekananda: Patriot–Prophet*, Calcutta, 1954, is an important contemporary study on him.

19. *Samachar Darpan*, 3 March 1838, Brajendranath Bandopadhyay (ed. & comp.), *Sangbadpatre Sekaler Katha* (The Tales of Those Days as Reported in Newspapers), Calcutta, 1994, vol. 2, p. 99.

20. Author Ashapurna Devi in her prize-winning novel, *Pratham Pratisruti* (The First Step), Calcutta, 1964, portrays a nineteenth century family scenario where the wife not only accepts her husband's infidelity, but also proudly arranges his clothes for him to go out. The principal character of the novel, Satyavati, registers a strong condemnation.

21. See Bhudev Mukhopadhyay *Paribarik Prasanga* (On Family Matters), see also, Chandicharan Bandopadhyay, *Ma O Chele* (Mother and Son), Calcutta, 1887; Ishan Chandra Basu, *Stridiger Prati Upadesh* (Advice to Women), Calcutta, 1884; Pratap Chandra Majumdar, *Stri Charitra* (Women's Character), Calcutta 1898. Satyacharan Mitra, *Strir Prati Swamir Upadesh* (A Husband's Advice to His Wife), a Brahmo text published in 1884, is emblematic of didactic literature. See Judith Walsh, 'As the Husband, so the Wife: A Discussion of Satyacharan Mitra's *Strir Prati Swamir Upadesh*, An Advice to Women Text from Nineteenth Century Bengal', in *Journal of Women's Studies*, 2:1, 1997. Walsh shows how the purpose of the text was 'the redefinition of the wife', and how a woman, her thoughts, character and activities, moulded by her husband, was urged to serve the family and run the household in the context of the time. *The Journal of Women's Studies*, is edited by Bharati Ray and published by K.P. Bagchi, Calcutta.

22. Pyari Chand Mitra, 'Grihakatha, Strishiksha–Gyanakari Bidya' (On Home and Women's Education), in Anisuzzaman and Maleka Begum (eds), *Narir Katha*, Dhaka, 1994.

23. 'Antahpur Strisiksha-syllabi', *Bamabodhini Patrika*, Baishakh, 1273, Sravan 1276, & Aswin 1277 BS, AD 1870. The syllabi from the first to the fifth year comprised Bengali Readers, elementary arithmetic, the first steps of Bengali grammar, and some basic history, geography, and natural science. The reading list was supplemented by moral lessons. *Bamabodhini Patrika* (Journal for the Enlightenment of Women) was launched by the *Bamabodhini Sabha*, set up by a group of Brahmos for spreading zenana education. This was the primary women's journal of those days and continued publication for sixty years.

24. Rasasundari Devi, *Amar Jibon* (My Life), Calcutta, College Street Edition,

1987, pp. 41–2. For a good analysis of this book, see Tanika Sarkar, *Words to Remember: Rasasundari Devi, Amar Jiban: A Modern Autobiography*, New Delhi, 1999.

25. Shivanath Shastri, *Atmacharit* (Autobiography), Calcutta, 1991, p. 404.

26. Kailasbasini Devi notes in *Hindumahilaganer Hinabastha*, pp. 64–65, 'The fate of a woman who wishes to study is a great deal of pain and agony as she falls foul of everyone in the family. Her elders continuously pressurize her to desist from her efforts. She is victimized by her female neighbours through banter and ridicule, even to the extent of forbidding their unmarried daughters to talk to her. That is why very few girls opt to go to school. There are people who declare that widowhood is inevitable for a woman who learns to read and write; some others believe that once a woman goes in for education she will neglect her home; there are yet others who are convinced that an educated woman will neglect her husband, will be hungry for freedom, and may even take to lovers. Another school of thought claims that an educated woman through her developed intellect will behave like a man.' Kailasbasini also mentions that parents differentiate between sons and daughters in terms of education, because daughters' education has no economic utility. Asks Kailasbasini, 'Alas, was education designed only for money and not for knowledge?', Ibid., p. 3. See also W. Adam, *Reports on the State of Education in Bengal*, First and Third Reports, 1836, for a description of the nature of opposition to women's education in Bengal.

27. Translated by Sukhendu Ray from the original Bengali satirical poem. See Bharati Ray, 'Advances of Education: From Mortar and Pestle to Mortar-boards and Scroll', in Tilottama Tharoor (ed.), *Naari* (The Woman), Calcutta, 1990, p. 46. For a vivid description of real life social opposition to women's education in rural Bengal, see Sudakshina Sen, *Jiban Smriti* (Autobiography), Calcutta, 1939.

28. Shivanath Shastri, *Atmacharit*, p. 404. Shivanath Shastri also wrote as early as 1904 that among the modern women 'it was a matter of shame to be totally illiterate'. If unable to go to school they sought to educate themselves at home. Shivanath Shastri, '*Mahatma Bethune Ebang Bangadeshe Strisiksha*' (Mahatma Bethune and Education of Women in Bengal), *Prabasi*, Bhadra, 1311 BS, AD 1904.

29. Borthwick, *Changing Role*, pp. 60–108, is a good history of women's education in Bengal in the nineteenth century. For a brief summary, See Bharati Ray (ed.), *Sekaler Narishiksha: Bamabodini Patrika* (Women's Education of Yester Years), *Bamabodhini Patrika*, 1863–1922, Calcutta, 1994, Intro. pp. 19–34. Lakshmi Misra, *Education of Women in India, 1921–1966*, Bombay, 1966, deals with the history of women's education at the all-India level; Karuna Chanana (ed.), *Socialisation, Education and Women: Explorations in Gender Identity*, New Delhi, 1988, looks at the question from a modern standpoint and from women's perspective.

30. K. Nag (ed.), Bethune School and College Centenary Volume, 1849–1949, Calcutta, 1950, records details of the early schools, teachers and pupils. See also Rama Neogy, *Brahmo Balika Shikshalayer Itihas* (A History of Brahmo Girls' School) in *Brahmo Balika Shikshalaya Centenary Volume, 1890–1990*, Calcutta, 1994, pp. 9–39, for a description of the inception of another important girls' school; Malavika Karlekar, *Voices from Within: Early Personal Narratives of Bengali Women*, New

Delhi, 1991, dwells at length on the experiences of Dr Kadambini Ganguly, the first female Graduate of Calcutta University. Tapati Basu, 'Bangali Meyer Parashona' (The Education of Bengali Women), *Ananda Bazar Patrika,* Autumn Number, 1991, provides well-researched data on the educational institutions and female students in colonial Bengal.

31. Women themselves showed keen interest in education. Author Sarat Kumari Chaudhurani (1861–1920) records, 'Young women of Calcutta discuss books these days. "Have you read that particular book? I wept out my eyes when I read it", says one woman to another. A married woman met me in a social gathering and asked, "Do you know how to read and write? And some English as well"?' Sarat Kumari Chaudhurani, 'Kalikatar Strisamaj' (The Calcutta Society), *Bharati,* Bhadra, 1288 BS, AD 1881. Author Jyotirmoyee Devi (1894–1989) recalls that in some progressive families girls, even at home, 'used to study the English First Book'. *Smriti-Bismritir Taranga* (Memoirs), Calcutta, 1986, p. 28. The hesitant, but increasing, acceptance of English by the Bengali middle class for their sons and even daughters is depicted in Sarat Kumari Chaudhurani's popular novel, *Shubha Bibaha* (An Auspicious Wedding), Calcutta, 1905, pp. 20–1, through an imaginary conversation between two sisters.

| | |
|---|---|
| Elder Sister: | What can one do? Our sons prefer English-educated wives. This is a problem. |
| Younger Sister: | Since our sons are educated, how can they like uneducated wives? |
| Elder Sister: | Education is expensive. It is wiser to buy ornaments to marry off our daughters. |
| Younger Sister: | If the grooms prefer educated wives, we would have to pay less dowry. |

32. Ghulam Murshid, *Reluctant Debutante,* Rajshahi, 1983, p. 199. From a more feminist point of view, Suzie Tharu and K. Lalitha (eds), *Women Writing in India,* Delhi, 1991, vol. 1, p. 152, argue, 'Embedded in the explicit programme of the reform movement were massive ideological reconstruction of patriarchy and gender that underwrote the consolidation of imperial power ... the recasting of women into new models was not merely social, but political.' Perhaps Bhudev Mukhopadhaya (1827–90), an influential social reformer in the nineteenth century, had redefined women's role within the traditional patriarchy most forcefully. In an essay in *Paribarik Prasanga,* he ascribed the responsibility of running an efficient home to women. '*Grihakartrir kaaj sab*' (All housework is ultimately the housewife's). Bhudev Mukhopadhyay, *Bhudev Rachana Sambhar* (The Collected Works of Bhudev), (ed.) Pramatha Nath Bishi, Calcutta, 1369 BS, AD 1962.

33. The same theme continued in the twentieth century too. An extremely popular didactic treatise was Satish Chakravarty, *Lalana Suhrid* (A Friend of Women), Calcutta, 1911, one thousand copies of which were sold in a year and a half, a very large number by contemporary standards. The summum bonum of the advice was that women had to become educated and efficient to serve the family and husband. It may be of interest that *Lalana Suhrid* was later recommended by Muslim reformers as an ideal book for Muslim women.

34. The Bengali educated middle class had acted as the bulwark of British rule in India. They had admired the British, and had expected the British to help them in their development. However, as Hiren Mukherjee lucidly puts it, soon they realized that real improvement of India was 'incompatible with foreign domination'. After all, the driving force behind imperialistic expansion was not 'abstract missions of civilization, but the very concrete hunger for super profits'. Hiren Mukherjee, *India's Struggle for Freedom*, Calcutta, 1986, pp. 21, 91.

35. Pramatha Nath Bishi points out that it was Bhudev Mukhopadhyay who first conceived India, the motherland, in the image of a goddess in his *Pushpanjali* (1876), which was published earlier than Bankim's *Anandamath* (1882). Bankim was influenced by him. See Pramatha Bishi (ed.), *Bhudev Rachana Sambhar*, p. vi.

36. For details of women's role in the Freedom Movement, see Manmohan Kaur, *Role of Women in the Freedom Movement, 1857–1947*, Delhi, 1968; Bharati Ray, 'The Freedom Movement and Feminist Consciousness', Bharati Ray (ed.), *From the Seams of History*; Tanika Sarkar, 'Politics and Women in Bengal–The Conditions and Meaning of Participation', *Indian Economic and Social History Review*, vol. 21, no. 1, 1984; Geraldine Forbes, *Women in Modern India*, Cambridge University Press, 1998, pp. 121–56. See also Bhupendra Kishore Rakshit Roy, *Cholar Pathe*, Calcutta, 1930, a contemporary popular collection of short stories.

37. See Bharati Ray (ed.), Intro., *Nari o Parivar: Bamabodhini Patrika* (Women and the Family: *Bamabodhini Patrika*), Ananda Publishers, Calcutta, 2002.

38. See Anon, *Arya Parivar* (The Aryan Family), *Bamabodhini Patrika*, Agrahayan, 1308 BS, AD 1901; Bhavabhuti Vidyaratna, 'Pativratya' in *Bamabodhini Patrika*, Sravan and Bhadra, 1325 BS, AD 1918. *Bamabodhini Patrika* is replete with such essays.

39. Partha Chatterjee, 'The Nationalist Resolution of the Women's Question', in Kumkum Sangari and Sudesh Vaid, *Recasting Women*, pp. 235–43, esp. pp. 237–8.

40. A truly good wife, it was repeatedly hammered, would be so auspicious as to mark the eternal return of the cosmic principle embodied in the Goddess Lakshmi, the Goddess of domestic well-being, by whose grace the family, the extended family, and the entire clan would live and prosper. In an interesting essay, Dipesh Chakravarty analyses the concepts of Lakshmi and Alakshmi. Lakshmi symbolized dharma (right conduct), Alakshmi *adharma*. Lakshmi was an ideal housewife, Alakshmi either a *bibi* (westernized woman) or a *veshya* (prostitute). See Dipesh Chakravarty, 'The Difference-Deferral of a Colonial Modernity: Public Debates on Domesticity in British Bengal', in David Arnold and David Hardiman (eds), *Subaltern Studies* VIII (Oxford University Press, 1994).

41. Radhika Prasad Ghosh Chaudhury, 'Stri Niti Chatustaya' (The Four Rules for Women), *Bamabodini Patrika*, Baishakh, 1311 BS, AD 1904.

42. Partha Chatterjee, 'The Nationalist Resolution', pp. 239, 244. One may refer here to an interesting article written by Swadeshi (obviously, a pseudonym) and entitled, 'Save Your Women', published in *Modern Review*, August 1907, which implores the countrymen not to make women 'memsahibs', that is, westernized. They should be educated in the swadeshi way, and maintain the national tradition. *Modern Review*, edited by the Brahmo intellectual Ramananda Chatterjee, was

regarded as a 'modern' journal. Ramananda Chatterjee enjoyed Rabindranath's patronage. This caused some resentment on Sarala's part who thought that her uncle was favouring *Prabasi*, a Bengali periodical edited by Chatterjee, over *Bharati*, edited by her. This in turn annoyed Tagore. See Tagore's letter to Sarala, dated August 1907 Chithipatra (Correspondence) file 2, Rabindra Bhavan Archives, Visva Bharati, Shantiniketan.

43. Swami Vivekananda, while noting the basic differences between a woman's role in India and that of her Western counterpart, said that in India, she was the mother; in the West, her central function was as the wife. 'In India', said he, 'the mother is the centre of the family and our highest ideal. She is to us the representative of God, as God is the mother of the Universe.' Swami Vivekananda, *Complete Works*, vol. 2, pp. 506–7.

44. See Swarnaprabha Basu, 'Narir Grihadharma' (Women's Duties at Home), *Bamabodhini Patrika*, Agrahayan, 1315 BS, AD 1908; Mrs D.N. Das, 'Striloker Karya' (Women's Work), ibid., Chaitra, 1316 BS, AD 1907. It is significant that often highly educated women not only in their writings, but also in their behavioural pattern, tried to manifest their allegiance to traditional roles. An interesting example is that of Dr Kadambini Ganguly, the first lady doctor in Bengal, who used to knit lace seated in her carriage when on her rounds to visit her patients. She was also anxious to please her husband's relations by his first marriage. See Punyalata Chakravarti (1889–1974), *Chhelebelar Dinguli* (My Childhood Days), Calcutta 1381 BS, AD 1974, p. 12.

45. Charumati Devi, 'Strishikshar Upakarita' (The Utility of Women's Education), ibid., Kartick, 1322 BS, AD 1915; Charumati Debi's prize-winning essay, 'Sisuganer Akalmrityu O Jananir Kartavya' (Infant Mortality and Mothers' Duty), ibid., Kartick, 1319 BS, AD 1912.

46. Hemalata Sarkar, 'Narijatir Shiksha' (The Education of Women), *Bharatamahila*, Asadh, 1314 BS, AD 1907. Shatadalbasini Biswas, 'Amader Shishu' (Our Children), ibid., Baishakh, 1318 BS, AD 1911; Amodini Ghosh, 'Amader Shishu Siksha' (The Education of Our Children), ibid., Baishakh, 1316 BS, AD 1907. *Bharatamahila* was more political in character than other contemporary women's journals. Its editor, Sarajubala Dutta belonged to the Anushilan group of biplabis. The journal continued for 13 years.

47. See Bharati Ray, *Sekaler Narishiksha* (Women's Education of Yesteryears), pp. 34–9, for some examples and observations. Some women thought seriously regarding issues concerning solely women and the home and shared their views with other women. See, for example, Ambuja Sundari Das Gupta, 'Kasibasini' (The Woman Living in Banaras), *Bamabodhini Patrika*, Jaishtha-Asadh, 1312 BS, AD 1905; Sm. J. Sanyal, 'Hindu Grihe Badhu Jantrana' (The Sufferings of a Bride in a Hindu Home), op. cit., Aswin–Kartick 1318 BS, AD 1911. Three examples from three fairly well-circulated women's journals are: Anon, 'Balyabibaha', (Child Marriage), *Bharatamahila*, Falgun, 1315 BS, AD 1908; Nirupama Devi, 'Ekannabarti Paribare Ashanti Nibaraner Upay Ki' (How to Fight Disruption in a Joint Family), *Antahpur*, Paush, 1310 BS, AD 1903; Niharbala Devi, 'Bidhir Nirdesh' (The Destiny), *Paricharika*, Asadh, 1325 BS, AD 1918. *Antahpur*, founded in 1898 by the

founder-editor Banalata Devi (1880–1900), the daughter of the Brahmo reformer Sasipada Banerjee, was meant for women in antahpur and was well-received. *Paricharika* (New Series) started in 1923 and edited by Rani Nirupama Devi from Coochbehar was a renewal of the same journal (First Series: 1978) first edited by Pratap Chandra Majumdar. These women's journals, edited by women and intended for women readers, are historically important because one can trace through them the development of women's ideas, how women were sometimes echoing men's statements, sometimes discussing subjects ignored or marginalized by men but intertwined with their daily lives, and sometimes even challenging men's views, directly or by implication. Women's writings in women's journals certainly provide the richest source for an insight into their views. It may be mentioned here that modern feminists view motherhood in a light different from its mere glorification. See Maithreyi Krishnaraj in 'Motherhood: Power and Powerlessness', in J. Bagchi (ed.), *Indian Women: Myth and Reality*, Calcutta, 1995, for a brief analysis. On p. 35, Krishnaraj asks, 'What kind of rights should women claim as mothers?' Women are 'not only mothers', she asserts, 'women are also mothers'.

48. Malavika Karlekar, *Voices from Within*, p. 195.

49. Richard M. Eaton, *The Rise of Islam and The Bengal Frontier: 1204–1760*, Oxford University Press, 1994, pp. 297–8.

50. Ibid., pp. 298–300.

51. Begum Rokeya in *Abarodhbasini* and Shaista Ikramullah, *From Purdah to Parliament*, London, 1963, describe this constraining custom. Shaista Ikramullah observed the purdah from the age of nine. See also Hanna Papanek and Gail Minault (eds), *Separate Worlds*.

52. Sonia Nishat Amin, 'The Orthodox Discourse and the Emergence of the Muslim *Bhadramahila* in Early Twentieth Century', in Rajat Kanta Ray (ed.), *Mind, Body and Society: Life and Mentality in Colonial Bengal*, Oxford University Press, 1995, p. 394. See also Barbara D. Metcalfe, 'Islamic Reform and Islamic Women: Maulana Thanawi's Jewelry of Paradise', in T. Metcalfe (ed.), *Moral Conduct and Authority*, pp. 184–95.

53. Richard M. Eaton, *The Rise of Islam*, p. 298.

54. Sonia Nishat Amin, 'Orthodox Discourse', in Rajat Ray, *Mind, Body*, pp. 403–5, provides a succinct and analytical summary of the orthodox discourse.

55. Sonia Nishat Amin, 'The Early Muslim *Bhadramahila*: The Growth of Learning and Creativity, 1876–1939', in Bharati Ray, *From the Seams*, p. 108. The Hindu reformers came from social groups comprising the literate, commercial, professional urban middle class, as did the Muslim reformers. B.S. Cohn, *An Anthropologist Among the Historians*, Oxford University Press, 1987, in a perceptive study of the Benaras region analyses the economic factors of the formation of such groups that developed into the middle class (pp. 320–41).

56. Sonia Nishat Amin, 'Early Muslim *Bhadramahila*', in Bharati Ray, *From the Seams*, p. 109.

57. Kumkum Sangari and Sudesh Vaid, Intro., *Recasting Women*, p. 9.

58. Gail Minault while agreeing that there were many similar changes among the two communities, goes on to argue that in the process of articulating cultural

nationalism, the Muslim reformers reiterated what it meant to be an Indian Muslim and thus 'helped to create separate identities, to define what it meant to be either a Hindu or a Muslim, for both men and women'. Gail Minault, *Secluded Scholars: Women's Education and Muslim Social Reform in Colonial India*, Oxford University Press, 1998, p. 9. There were, therefore, some similarities and some differences between the reform movements of the two communities.

59. Maleka Begum, *Banglar Nari Andolan* (The Women's Movement of Bengal), Dhaka, 1989, pp. 49, 68. Bharati Ray has argued that the women's movement in Bengal started with the Swadeshi movement, see Bharati Ray, 'Freedom Movement and Women's Awakening in Bengal', *The Indian Historical Review*, vol. XII, 1985–6, pp. 145–7. Maleka Begum agrees. 'The women's movement in Bengal was initiated through patriotism ... Social consciousness and political consciousness, these two trends lent motivation to the women's movement in Bengal', *Nari Andolan*, pp. 12, 14.

60. See Rafiuddin Ahmed, *The Bengal Muslims, 1871–1906: A Quest for Identity*, Delhi, 1981, ch. 3.

61. See Rafiuddin Ahmed, 'Intro.' in Rafiuddin Ahmed (ed.), *Understanding the Bengal Muslims: Interpretative Essays*, Delhi, 2001, esp. p. 15. Ahmed argues that British rule created even among ordinary Bengali Muslims in rural areas 'a sense of deprivation that was uncommon to the Hindus'. They thought that the British had wrested power from 'them', as if to suggest that they had descended from ancestors who had ruled India long before the coming of the British! Essays in Ahmed's edited book offer persuasive explanations of how the Bengali Muslim mentality was gradually shaped. Unfortunately I came across the book only after the final proofs of this volume had gone to press.

62. Wakil Ahmed, *Unish Shataker Bangali Mussalmaner Chinta Chetanar Dhara* (The Thoughts of the Bengali Muslim in the Nineteenth Century), Dhaka, 1983, vol. 1, p. 33.

63. M.A. Rahim, *Banglar Musalmaner Itihas 1707–1947* ( A History of Bengali Muslims), Dhaka, 1989, pp. 62–4, contains a list of Muslims in Government offices.

64. Anisuzzaman, *Muslim Manas O Bangla Sahitya* (Muslim Mentality and Bengali Literature), Calcutta, 1971, p. 66

65. Wakil Ahmed, *Unish Shatake*, vol. 1, p. 36.

66. Abdul Karim, *Muhammedan Education in Bengal*, p. 4, cited in Wakil Ahmed, *Unish Shatake*, vol. 1, p. 34; see also M.A. Rahim, *Banglar Musalmaner*, pp. 125–7.

67. Anisuzzaman, *Muslim Manas*, p. 3. Shamsul Alam also says, 'The decade of the 1870s can be described as the period of the jagaran of the Muslim mind'. Muhammad Shamsul Alam, *Rokeya Sakhawat Hossain*, p. 47.

68. Wakil Ahmed, *Unish Shatake*, vol. 1, p. viii.

69. Anisuzzaman says that the beginninings of this nascent Muslim insurgence was somewhat scarred by the contrasting levels of attainments of the progressive Hindus, on the one hand, and the underdeveloped Muslims, on the other, to which were added many cultural disaffinities between the two communities. This led to a

parting of ways, each community choosing its own route to development. The unfortunate impact was manifest in the political arena. Anisuzzaman comments that this time saw the emergence of what we call the nationalist movement, which took roots amongst educated Hindus. Led by a particular religious community, the movement in many ways assumed the contours of Hindu ethos. Unable to identify with this development, the Muslims could not relate to it in their hearts. The desire to acquire political power came to them much later, and when it came, it took the form of demand for a separate state for the Muslims. Notwithstanding the sincere efforts of many in both the communities, the Hindus and the Muslims would not come together. See *Muslim Manas*, p. 6.

70. G.F.I. Graham, *The Life and Works of Sir Syed Ahmad Khan*, London, 1909, p 52. David Lelyveld, *Aligarh's First Generation: Muslim Solidarity in British India*, Princeton University Press, 1978, gives an insight about the Aligarh College, its founder, and the early group of teachers and scholars.

71. For Abdul Latif's life and works, see Enamul Haque (ed.), *Nawab Bahadur Abdul Latif: His Writings and Related Documents*, Dhaka, 1968. Jayanti Maitra, *Muslim Politics in Bengal, 1855–1906*, Calcutta, 1984, provides a brief summary and makes interesting comparisons between the political and social backgrounds of Sir Syed and Nawab Abdul Latif (pp. 102–23).

72. M.A. Rahim, *Banglar Musalmaner*, pp. 155–62. Non-Muslims could attend the Central Muhammedan Association. In 1879, one of the seven members of the Executive Council was a Hindu, Ganesh Chandra Chanda. The Association often participated in meetings organized by Hindus to articulate anti-colonial sentiments. In 1885, the British Indian Association of Surendranath Banerjea and the Central Muhammedan Association jointly convened a national conference. Anisuzzaman, *Muslim Manas*, p. 85.

73. Cited in Anisuzzaman, *Muslim Manas*, pp. 388–9. Significantly, Abdul Hamid Khan Yusufzai also complained that the community was specially 'indifferent to Bengali language', and that many Muslims disapproved of women learning any Bengali at all.

74. Sonia Nishat Amin, 'Early Muslim *Bhadramahila*', in Bharati Ray, *From the Seams*, p. 110.

75. Anisuzzaman, *Muslim Manas*, pp. 86–7; see also Sufia Ahmed, *Muslim Community in Bengal, 1884–1912*, Dhaka, 1974, pp. 10–15. Wakil Ahmed perceptively observes, 'The rulers, being aware of the rising strength of the Hindus, realized the need for pushing another backward community'. *Unish Shatake*, vol. 2, p. 84.

76. Emdad Ali, editorial, *Nabanoor*, cited in Wakil Ahmed, *Unish Shatake*, vol. 2, p. 17. Imdadul Haque, 'Hindu–Musalman O Bangasahitya' (The Hindus, Muslims, and Bengali Literature), *Bharati*, 1310 BS, AD 1903.

77. Anisuzzaman, *Muslim Manas*, p. 384.

78. These newspapers and journals played a pioneering role in facilitating a major social transformation. Geeta Chattopadhyay has done useful and detailed research on the history of journals in Bengal in the early twentieth century. Geeta Chattopadhyay, *Bangla Samayik Patrikapanji* (Bengali Journals), Vol. 1, 1900–1914, vol. 2, 1915–1930 (Calcutta, 1990, 1994).

79. With respect to Muslim middle class attempts at reform, Gail Minault observes, 'For a Muslim in favour of social, religious, or educational change, it helped to have the Prophet on your side'. *Secluded Scholars,* p. 60. It may be recalled that the Hindu–Brahmo reformers attempted to have the Hindu scriptures on their side. Even Vidyasagar, when advocating widow remarriage, quoted from the scriptures in his favour. Lata Mani shows how the reformers cited the scriptures in moving for the abolition of Sati.

80. For discussion on this issue of Muslim identity, see Salahuddin Ahmed, *Muslim Community in Bengal 1884–1912,* Dhaka, 1974; Rafiuddin Ahmad, *The Bengal Muslims*; Sufia Ahmed, Muslim Community in Bengal 1884–1912; Zoya Hasan (ed.), *Forging Identities: Gender, Communities and the State,* New Delhi, 1994; Dhurjoti Prosad De, *Bengal Muslims in Search of Social Identity 1905–47,* Dhaka, 1998.

81. Wakil Ahmed, *Unish Shatake,* vol. 2, p. 17.

82. Ibid., p. 165.

83. Morshed Shafiul Hasan, *Begum Rokeya,* p. 45. This was a genuine problem for the community. Rafiuddin Ahmed argues that for a Bengali Muslim, his 'socio-cultural identity' as well as the 'Islamic content of his personality' played a crucial role. It was the 'juxtaposition' of Islamic beliefs imported from outside and the 'local cultural conceptions' that shaped the perceptions of Bengali Muslims. See Intro., Rafiuddin Ahmed, *Understanding Bengali Muslims,* pp. 3–4.

84. Cited, ibid., p. 44.

85. For details, see ibid.

86. Abdul Mannan Syed, *Begum Rokeya,* p. 48.

87. Cited in Sonia Amin, 'Orthodox Discourse', in Rajat Ray, *Mind, Body,* p. 147.

88. For details, see Gail Minault, *Secluded Scholars,* pp. 33–54.

89. Ibid., pp. 62–95; see also Barbara D. Metcalfe, 'Islamic Reform and Islamic Women: Maulana Thanawi's Jewelry of Paradise', in T. Metcalfe (ed.), *Moral Conduct and Authority.*

90. Imdadul Huq, *Nabanoor,* cited in Wakil Ahmed, *Unish Shatake,* vol. 1, p. 132.

91. Ibid., in Morshed Shafiul Hasan, *Begum Rokeya,* p. 15.

92. Maleka Begum, *Banglar Nari,* pp. 43–4 describes the story lucidly. It may be mentioned here that Abdul Latif had four highly educated sons. It is not known whether he sent his only daughter to school.

93. Sonia Nishat Amin, 'Early Muslim *Bhadramahila*', in Bharati Ray, *From the Seams,* p. 114.

94. Wakil Ahmed, *Unish Shatake,* vol. 2, pp. 128–30.

95. Maleka Begum, *Banglar Nari,* pp. 44–9 provides a succinct summary of the history of, and the debates on, the early years of Muslim women's education. She also gives data on the number and ratio of Muslim girls vis-à-vis girls of other communities in schools in 1881–2.

96. About the date of the foundation of Eden School there is some confusion. According to Shamsul Alam, *Rokeya Sakhawat Hossain,* p. 61, the Brahmo leader

Brajasundar Mitra (1820–75) had established a school, which came to be known as Eden School from 1875. The number of Muslim women increased to 25 by 1911. This school later became one of the premier schools in Bengal. Akhtar Imam, *Eden Theke Bethune* (From Eden to Bethune), Dhaka, 1990, describes the school during her time.

97. These papers also provided a 'first platform' for new women writers. Sonia Amin, 'Early Muslim *Bhadramahila*', in Bharati Ray, *From the Seams,* p. 112.

98. Cited in Wakil Ahmed, *Unish Shatake,* vol. 2, 97, p. 132.

99. Bibi Taherunnisa, 'Bamaganer Rachana' (Section on Women's Writings), *Bamabodhini Patrika,* Falgun 1271 BS, AD 1864. She ends her essay by saying, 'My countrymen, do not remain indifferent to the education of women. If you want to make this world a happy world, first adorn women with education', Latifunnesa, 'Bangiya Musalman Mahilar Prati' (To Bengali Muslim Women), *Bamabodhini Patrika,* Asadh 1304 BS, AD 1897. *Bamabodhini Patrika* from its inception had a section entitled 'Bamarachana' (Writings by Women) to provide space for the contributions of new female writers.

100. Sonia Nishat Amin, 'Early Muslim *Bhadramahila*, in Bharati Ray, *From the Seams,* pp. 133–4.

## Chapter Three

1. Sarala Devi Chaudhurani, 'A Women's Movement', *Modern Review*, Oct. 1911.

2. Shashibhusan Das Gupta, *Bharater Shaktisadhana o Shakta Sahitya,* (Shakti Worship and Literature in India), Calcutta, 1970, is an excellent study. See also David Kinsley, *Hindu Goddesses* (Delhi, 1987).

3. Sarala Devi, 'Ahvan' (A Call), *Bharati,* Chaitra, 1324 BS, AD 1917.

4. Jharapata, p. 143.

5. Sarala Devi, 'Ramanir Karya' (Duties of Women), *Suprabhat,* Chaitra, 1316 BS, AD 1907.

6. Ibid.

7. Sarala Devi, 'Bharat Stree Mahamandal', (The Great Circle of Indian Women), *Bharati,* Chaitra, 1317 BS, AD 1910.

8. Sarala Devi, 'Bangali Paraye' (In the Bengali Locality), *Bharati,* Baishakh 1309 BS, AD 1902.

9. *The Complete Works of Swami Vivekananda,* Mayavati Memorial Edition, Calcutta, 1962–73, vol. 5, p. 231 & vol. 6, p. 489.

10. Sarala Devi, 'Bangali Paraye'.

11. Begum Rokeya, 'Ardhangi' (The Other Half), *Rachanavali,* p. 29.

12. Begum Rokeya, 'Strijatir Abanati' (The Degradation of Women), *Rachanavali,* p. 9.

13. Ibid.

14. Begum Rokeya, 'Griha' (The Home), *Rachanavali,* p. 64.

15. Begum Rokeya, 'Tin Kure' (Three Idle Men), *Rachanavali,* p. 486.

16. Begum Rokeya, Preface, *Abarodhbasini, Rachanavali,* p. 431.

17. Begum Rokeya, *Sultana's Dream, Rachanavali*, pp. 532–3.
18. Abdul Qadir, Intro., *Rachanavali*, pp. 11–2.
19. See this volume, p. 109.
20. Sarala Devi, 'Abhayamantra' (A Hymn for Courage), *Bharati*, Paush 1316 BS, AD 1907.
21. 'Chayan' (Collected Pieces), *Bharati*, Aswin, 1315 BS, AD 1908.
22. Sarala Devi, 'Abhaymantra', *Bharati*.
23. Ibid.
24. See chap. 2 of this volume.
25. Sarala Devi, 'Ramanir Karya', *Suprabhat*.
26. Ibid.
27. Sarala Devi, 'Bangali Paraye', *Bharati*.
28. Sarala Devi, 'Ramanir Karya', *Suprabhat*.
29. See Chapter 2 of this volume for a similarity with the nationalist discourse.
30. Sarala Devi, 'Bijoya Dasami', *Bharati*, Agrahayan, 1320 BS, AD 1913.
31. Sarala Devi, 'Ahvan', *Bharati*.
32. Sarala Devi, 'Udbodhan' (The Inauguration), *Bharati*, Baishakh, 1325 BS, AD 1918.

She further argued that knowledge which was confined to books and not translated into action was not worth acquiring, implying that this is what the Bengali youth was doing.

33. J.C. Bagal, *Jharapata*, p. 204.
34. Begum Rokeya, 'Strijatir', *Rachanavali*, p. 17.
35. Begum Rokeya, 'Ardhangi', *Rachanavali*, p. 34.
36. Begum Rokeya, 'Bhrata-Bhagni' (Brothers and Sisters), *Rachanavali*, p. 476.
37. Begum Rokeya, 'Ardhangi', *Rachanavali*, p. 35 and 'Burqa', *Rachanavali*, p. 51. Rokeya goes on to articulate one of her key beliefs that the lack of education made women unfit for independence, and that since they were unfit for it, they had lost it.
38. Cited in Shamsunnahar Mahmud, *Rokeya Jiboni*, p. 70.
39. Begum Rokeya, 'Burqa', *Rachanavali*, p. 52.
40. Begum Rokeya, 'Strijatir', *Rachanavali*, p. 18.
41. Begum Rokeya, 'Subeh Sadek', *Rachanavali*, p. 272.
42. Begum Rokeya, 'Abanati', *Rachanavali*, p. 21.
43. Hemantakumari Chaudhuri proposed mildly that indigent women could take up paid jobs as nurses. Hemantakumari Chaudhuri, 'Shushrusakarini' (Nurses) in *Antahpur*, Aug. 1900. Hemalata Sarkar clearly said that women should devote attention primarily to the home. If necessary, however, they could, sit at home and do some handwork in order to earn some money. Hemalata Sarkar, 'Narijatir Shiksha' (The Education of Women), *Bharatamahila*, Asadh, 1314 BS, AD 1907.
44. According to the Census of 1901, in Bengal just 1156 women worked as teachers, 67 as clerks, 849 were nurses, and 151 doctors. See Ghulam Murshid, *Reluctant Debutante*, p. 145. Muslim middle class women had not joined the workforce.

45. Begum Rokeya, *Padmarag, Rachanavali*, p. 414. This also indicates Rokeya's strong opposition to purdah and her keen desire to abolish the custom.
46. Ibid., p. 420.
47. Ibid., p. 357.
48. Begum Rokeya, 'Strijatir', *Rachanavali*, pp. 20–1.
49. For a detailed description of the school, see Tahmina Alam, *Begum Rokeya*, pp. 81–108.
50. Despite Rokeya's efforts, as late as 1927, out of 114 girls in the school, only two were Bengali speaking. Sonia Nishat Amin, 'Early Muslim *Bhadramahila*' in Bharati Ray, *From the Seams*, p. 120. This shows that the Muslim élite of Calcutta, whether they belonged to the aristocracy or the new professional middle class, favoured a pan-Islamic, pro-Urdu culture. Rokeya, however, continued to write in Bengali and tried to promote Bengali in her school, indicating her pride in her Bengali identity.
51. Shamsunnahar Mahmud, *Rokeya Jiboni*, p. 35.
52. Begum Rokeya, *Abarodhbasni*, p. 467.
53. Ibid., p. 468.
54. Shivnath Shastri, *Ramatanu Lahiri*, p. 140.
55. Begum Rokeya, 'Dhangsher Pathe', *Rachanavali*, pp. 276–7.
56. Cited in Shamsul Alam, *Rokeya Sakhawat Hossein*, p. 341.
57. Moshfeka Khatun, *Patre Rokeya*, pp. 34–5. Rokeya was opposed to the system of unilateral *talak*, as well as child marriage and marriage of old men to young girls. See Begum Rokeya, 'Biye Pagla Buro' (The Old Man Greedy for Marriage), *Rachanavali*, pp. 502–7 Similar criticism was voiced in the new genre of 'progressive' Muslim journals/newspapers.
58. Begum Rokeya, 'Ardhangi', *Rachanavali*, p. 35.
59. Begum Rokeya, 'Abanati', *Rachanavali*, p. 20.
60. Sarala Devi, 'Bangali Paraye'.
61. Sarala Devi, 'Sinher Bibare' (In the Lion's Den), *Bangabani*, 3:1, Falgun-Sravan, 1330 BS, AD 1923.
62. Begum Rokeya, 'Abanati', *Rachanavali*, p. 11.
63. Begum Rokeya, 'Sugrihini' (A Good Housewife), *Rachanavali*, pp. 36–42.
64. Ghulam Murshid, *Rasasundari Theke*, p. 145.

## Chapter Four

1. For a history of the early women's organizations, see Meredith Borthwick, *Changing Role*, pp. 271–307; Latika Ghosh, 'Social and Educational Movements for Women and by Women', in K. Nag (ed.), *Bethune College*, pp. 129–69; Rajat Sanyal, *Voluntary Associations and the Urban Public Life in Bengal* (Calcutta, 1980) for associations outside Calcutta.
2. Sarala Devi, 'Bharat Stree Mahamandal', *Bharati*.
3. Sarala Devi, 'Bangali Paraye', *Bharati*.
4. Ibid.

5. Sarala Devi, 'Bharat Stree Mahamandal', *Bharati*.
6. Ibid.
7. Ibid.
8. Ibid.
9. Sarala Devi, 'A Women's Movement', *Modern Review*.
10. Ibid.
11. Ibid.
12. Sarala Devi, 'Bharat Stree Mahamandal', *Bharati*.
13. Sarala Devi, 'A Women's Movement', *Modern Review*.
14. Ibid.
15. Krishnabhabini Devi was 'known to the public as the beloved and revered Mrs D.N. Das of the *Bharat Stree Mahamandal*'. On her death, the *Bengalee* on 5 March 1919 commented, 'In her the East, while imbibing the good of both the East and the West, retains the stamp of oriental genius and character.' Cited in *Navyabharat*, Falgun 1325 BS, AD 1919.
16. Sarala Devi, 'A Women's Movement', *Modern Review*.
17. Sarala Devi, 'Bharat Stree Mahamandal', *Bharati*.
18. Sarala Devi, 'A Women's Movement', *Modern Review*.
19 Sarala Devi, 'Bharat Stree Mahamandal', *Bharati*.
20. Ibid.
21. For details, see Mrinalini Sen, *Knocking at the Door*, Calcutta, 1954 and Barbara Southard, *The Women's Movement and Colonial Politics in Bengal: The Quest for Political Rights, Education and Social Reform Legislation*, Delhi, 1995.
22. See Bharati Ray, 'The Freedom Movement and Feminist Consciousness in Bengal', in Bharati Ray (ed.), *From the Seams of History*. Ashalata Sen, *Sekaler Katha* (Stories of Bygone Days), Calcutta, 1990, pp. 15–22, provides interesting details about her organization in Dhaka.
23. *Jayasree*, first published in 1931 and edited by Lilabati Nag (Ray), regularly published information about Dipali's meetings. For the history of this important journal and this important association, see Amalendu Bose (ed.), *Jayasree Subarna Jayanti Volume* (Centenary Volume), Calcutta, 1983.
24. Begum Rokeya, 'Strijatir', *Rachanavali*, p. 20.
25. Begum Rokeya, 'Subeh Sadek', *Rachanavali*, p. 272.
26. Ibid., p. 271.
27. Ibid.
28. Ibid., p. 272.
29. Begum Rokeya, *Padmarag, Rachanavali*, p. 357.
30. This paragraph is based on Gail Minault, *Secluded Scholars*, pp. 285–91.
31. Shamsunnahar Mahmud, *Rokeya Jiboni*, pp. 50–1.
32. Cited in Tahmina Alam, *Begum Rokeya*, Parishista (App.), p. 137.
33. Ibid., pp. 137–9.
34. Gail Minault, *Secluded Scholars*, pp. 291–3.
35. For a more detailed account, see Tahmina Alam, *Begum Rokeya*, pp. 117–22.
36. Ibid., p. 122.

37. Begum Rokeya, 'Bhrata-Bhagni', *Rachanavali*, p. 469.
38. Sarala Devi, 'Bangali Paraye', *Bharati*.
39. In Ladyland, Sultana was told that men were kept indoors because

> It is not safe for us to come out as long as men are about the streets, nor is it so when a wild animal enters a market place.

Begum Rokeya, *Sultana's Dream, Rachanavali*, p. 533.
40. Sarala Devi, 'Nari Nirjatan', *Bharati*, 1331 BS, AD 1927.
41. See Tanilka Sarkar and Urvasi Butalia (eds), *Women and the Hindu Right*, New Delhi, 1998.
42. Sarala Devi, *Jharapata*, pp. 78–9.
43. Sarala Devi, 'Bharater Hindu o Mussalman' (The Hindus and Muslims of India), *Bharati*, Bhadra 1310 BS, AD 1903.
44. See Rokeya's allegorical novel, *Muktiphal*, in *Rachanavali*.
45. Begum Rokeya, 'Nibedan' (Preface), *Padmarag, Rachanavali*, p. 291.

## CONCLUSION

1. For a more detailed discussion, see this volume, chapter 2.
2. Uma Chakravarty, 'Vedic Dasi', in Kumkum Sangari and Sudesh Vaid, *Recasting*, p. 62.
3. Partha Chatterjee, 'Nationalist Resolution', in ibid., p. 247.
4. Uma Chakravarty, 'Vedic Dasi', in ibid., p. 65.
5. Sarala Devi, *Jharapata*, p. 136.
6. Sarala Devi, 'Abhayamantra', *Bharati*.
7. Ashok Rudra, 'Cultural and Religious Influences', in Devaki Jain (ed.), *Indian Women*, Delhi, 1978.
8. For a brief assessment of their contributions, see J.C. Bagal, 'Rashtriya Andolone Bangamahila' (Bengali Women in the Freedom Movement), in K. Nag, *Bethune School.* See also Bharati Ray, 'Women, Politics and Identity in Colonial Bengal, 1900–1947', in Bharati Ray and David Taylor (eds), *Politics and Identity in South Asia*, Calcutta, 2002.
9. See *Nari Shiksha Samiti Centenary Volume*, Calcutta, 1996.
10. Mrinalini Sen, *Knocking at the Door*, Calcutta, 1954.
11. Krishnabhabini Das, *Englande Bangamahila* (A Bengali Woman in England, Calcutta, 1997), gives a good account of her views on women.
12. See, for instance, Anurupa Devi, *Ma* (Mother), and Nirupama Devi, *Didi* (Elder Sister).
13. Sarat Kumari Chaudhurani, 'Adarer na Anadarer'? (Are Daughters Lovable or Not?), *Sadhana*, 1298 BS, AD 1891, B. Bandopadhyay, *Sarat Kumari Rachanavali*.
14. Kamini Ray, 'Balika Shiksha'. See also her highly interesting poem 'Thakurmar Chithi' (A Letter from a Grandmother), Calcutta, n.d., where she presents arguments between a grandmother, emphasizing the old ideology, and the granddaughter representing the viewpoint of modern young women.
15. Charushila Mitra, 'Uttar' (A Reply), *Bamabodhini Patrika*, Agrahayan, 1319 BS, AD 1912.

16. Shatadalbasini Biswas, 'Narishaktir Apachaya' (Waste of Woman Power), ibid., Jaishtha, 1317 BS, AD 1910.

17. Hemendra Kumar Ray, *Jander Dekhechhi*, p. 18 observes that there was remarkable similarity between the words of Vivekanada and Sarala. What Sarala said about courage (cited in this volume, p. 100) was reminiscent of Vivekananda's lifelong advocacy of fearlessness.

18. Malavika Karlekar, *Voices from Within: Early Personal Narratives of Bengali Women*, Delhi, 1991, p. 187.

19. Cited in Sarala Devi, *Jharapata*, pp. 128–9.

20. Srish Chandra Dhar, 'Punjabe Pratapaditya Utsav' (The Pratapaditya Festival in Punjab), *Bharati*, Asadh 1313 BS, AD 1906; Srish Chandra Dhar, 'Marathaye Shivaji Utsav', (Shivaji Festival in Maharashtra), *Bharati*, Jaishtha, 1313 BS, AD 1906.

21. Tanika Sarkar, 'Politics and Women in Bengal—The Conditions and Meaning of Participation', in *The Indian Economic and Social History Review*, vol. 21, Jan.–March 1984, p. 98.

22. Sister Nivedita commented on this significant painting in *Modern Review*, 1911. See also Sister Nivedita, *Complete Works*.

23. Meredith Borthwick, *Changing Role*, p. 340.

24. Sarala's advocacy of physical courage and even her clubs for training young men in physical fitness and the martial arts had also the stamp of social approval. Indira Chowdhury has analyzed the 'colonial categorization of the Bengali as effeminate' and the nationalist attempts to counter the allegation. On the one hand, body-building was popularized, and on the other, historiography was 'remodelled' to reclaim a heroic past for Bengal. Sarala worked within this parameter; she invented heroes and designed rituals for the purpose of 'nation-making'. See Indira Chowdhury, *The Frail Hero and Virile History*, Delhi, 1988, esp. ch. 2.

25. Sarala Devi, *Jharapata*, pp. 128. Sunil Gangopadhyay in his novel *Prathom Alo*, vol. 2, pp. 246–50, describes imaginatively and faithfully Sarala'a unique appeal to the contemporary public, especially the youth of Bengal.

26. See Eric Hobsbawm and Terence Ranger (eds), *The Invention of Tradition*, Cambridge University Press, 1983.

27. Vivekananda to Sarala, 6 April 1897, *Letters of Swami Vivekananda*, Almora, 1948, p. 364.

28. Vivekananda wrote to Sarala on 24 April, 1897: 'I am a humble mendicant, an itinerant monk; I am helpless and alone. What can I do? you have the power of wealth, intellect and education; will you forego this opportunity?' ibid., p. 371.

29. I am grateful to Tapati Sen Gupta for this information.

30. Sarala Devi, *Jharapata*, pp. 160–2, 144.

31. Renuka Ray, *My Reminiscences*, Calcutta, 1982, p. 16.

32. Partha Chatterjee, 'Nationalist Resolution', Kumkum Sangari and Sudesh Vaid, *Recasting*, p. 242. For a nineteenth century exposition of the concept, see Bhudev Mukhopadhyay, *Paribarik Prabandha*.

33. Borthwick, however, seems to take the argument too far when she says that

Bankim's heroines, depicted as brave fighters in the service of their country, 'through their heroism', presented a 'challenge to Bengali males to assert their masculinity in the defense of the country ...'. M. Borthwick, *Changing Role*, pp. 339–40. Uma Chakravarty, indirectly accepting this argument, says that Sarala 'presented a challenge to Bengali males'. *Recasting*, p. 64. Perhaps this was not a case of challenging men or their masculunity, but offering leadership at a time of crisis in the style of the mythical Durga, so ingrained in the Bengali thinking.

34. Begum Rokeya, 'Ardhangi', *Rachanavali*, p. 30.
35. Ibid., p. 32.
36. Begum Rokeya, 'Abanati', *Rachanavali*, p. 20.
37. Begum Rokeya, 'Ardhangi', *Rachanavali*, p. 33.
38. See this volume, ch. 2.
39 Abdul Mannan Syed, *Begum Rokeya*, p. 48.
40. Cited in Morshed Shafiul Hasan, *Begum Rokeya*, p. 32.
41. Shamsunnahar Mahmud, *Rokeya Jiboni*, p. 69.
42. Perhaps Rokeya had to publicly endorse the use of some purdah because she had to placate 'conservative' Muslims whose support was essential for the survival of her school. However, she could never reconcile herself to the humiliation of abarodh that she had suffered in her childhood, or to the strict purdah that she had to abide by all her life. In a presidential speech at the Bengal Women's Educational Conference, she said with all the bitterness at her command:

You have done me a signal honour by inviting such an insignificant person like me to preside over this function, for which I am indeed very grateful. Nevertheless, I must say that you made a mistake in doing so. All my life I have been cocooned inside an iron safe under the rigours of a harsh purdah system. I never had the opportunity to go out and mix well with the outside society. I do not even know what are the functions of a President—should she smile, should she cry? Please be prepared for many pitfalls into which I may find myself.

Begum Rokeya, 'Bangiya Nari Shiksha', *Rachanavali*, p. 253. So saying, Rokeya proceeded to deliver a brilliant speech on education. It may be mentioned here that Sarala had no problem with regard to chairing any meeting. On the contrary, she would almost expect to do so if present on the occasion. Her education and family background had prepared her well for a leadership position in any cultural or political conference.

43. For a short summary of their lives, see Gail Minault, *Secluded Scholars*, pp. 269–83.
44. Razia Khatun Chaudhurani, 'Samaje o Grihe Narir Abastha', in Anisuzzaman and Maleka Begum (eds), *Narir Katha* (Women's Story), Dhaka, 1994, p. 211. Rokeya had made a similar observation, i.e. there were organizations to prevent cruelty to animals, but none such existed for women. See 'Bangiya Nari Shiksha Samiti' in *Rachanavali*, p. 254. Interestingly, such a thought was first expressed by Bankim Chandra Chattopadhyay in his article, 'Samya' (Equality).

There is no dearth of organizations in our country. We have associations and societies, clubs and leagues. Some are concerned with politics, some are dedicated to social and civic affairs; there are bodies devoted to religious matters; some others have questionable motives. Yet, there is none devoted to women. No one can ill-treat an animal for there is a society for the prevention of cruelties to animals, but there is just no organization to look after the interests of women who constitute half the population of Bengal. Much money is expended on schools, hospitals, animal shelters, etc. But cannot something be done to reform the zoo that is Bengal?

*Bankim Rachanavali*, vol. 2, 1361 BS, AD 1954, p. 406.

    45. Sonia Nishat Amin, 'Early Muslim *Bhadramahila*' in Bharati Ray, *From the Seams*, pp. 142–3.

    46. Tahmina Alam, *Begum Rokeya*, pp. 69–70.

    47. Gail Minault, *Secluded Scholars*, p. 262.

    48. Begum Rokeya, 'Strijatir', cited in Abdul Qadir, Intro., *Rachanavali*, p. 12.

    49. Ibid.

    50. Cited in Anisuzzaman, *Muslim Manas*, p. 377.

    51. Cited in Wakil Ahmed, *Unish Shatake*, vol. 2, p. 10.

    52. Cited in Morshed Shfiul Hasan, *Begum Rokeya*, pp. 39–40.

    53. Cited in Abdul Qadir, Intro., *Rachanavali*, p. 13.

    54. Ibid., p. 17.

    55. Rokeya's letter dated 8. 9. 1915, Cited in Moshfeka Mahmud, *Patre Rokeya*, p. 14.

    56. Cited in Motahar Hossain Sufi, *Begum Rokeya*, p. 17.

    57. See, for instance, Prashanta Kumar Pal, *Rabi-Jiboni*.

    58. Tapati Sen Gupta, a college teacher in Calcutta, is writing a dissertation, yet to be submitted, on Rokeya's political role.

    59. See Kamala Das Gupta, *Swadhinata Sangrame*, for short biographical sketches of these women.

    60. Sarala Devi, 'Palayan O Palayaner Par' (The Flight and After), *Bharati*, Bhadra, 1323 BS, AD 1916 and 'Bangiya Senrajganer Uttar Charit' (The Later History of the Sena Kings of Bengal), *Bharati*, Magh 1323 BS, AD 1916.

    61. Subhash Chandra Bose, who escaped abroad from home confinement and built the Indian National Army, is highly revered in Bengal with an almost romantic adoration.

    62. The Oral History Transcripts preserved at the Nehru Memorial Museum and Library, New Delhi, contain many such interviews. See especially the oral transcripts of Sucheta Kripalani and Renuka Ray.

    63. Rabindranath Tagore to Pramatha Chaudhuri, dt. 18 Kartick 1328 BS, *Chithipatra* (Correspondences), file no. 2, Rabindra Bhavan Archives, Visva Bharati, Shantiniketan.

    64. Ramananda Chatterjee, the editor of *Prabasi*, enjoyed Rabindranath's patronage. This caused some resentment in Sarala, who thought that her uncle was favouring *Prabasi* more than *Bharati*, edited by her. This, in turn, annoyed Tagore. See Tagore's letter to Sarala, dated, 8 May 1926, 'Chithipatra' (file name) Sarala Devi Chaudhurani, Rabindra Bhavan Archives.

    65. Begum Rokeya, 'Bangiya Nari Shiksha', *Rachanavali*, p. 258. No wonder,

Mohitlal Majumdar, the reputed litterateur observed, 'She was a true Bengali woman'. Cited in Abdul Mannan, *Begum Rokeya*, p. 17.

66. Begum Rokeya, 'Id Sammilan' (The Assemblage on the day of the Id), *Rachanavali*, p. 236.

67. Shamsunnahar Mahmud, *Rokeya Jiboni*, p. 68.

68. Motahar Hossain Sufi, *Begum Rokeya*, p. 1.

69. Maleka Begum, *Banglar Nari*, p. 85.

70. Susie Tharu and K. Lalitha, *Women Writing in India*, vol. 1, Delhi, 1991, pp. 340–52.

# Biographical Notes

The following pages give brief biographical notes on some of the men and women who figure in this story and who participated actively in the social, political, and cultural movements of the time. Most of them were contemporaries of Sarala Devi and Rokeya Hossain. However, the list is by no means comprehensive; the selection is subjective. Alphabetically arranged by first name, these notes sketch the barest outline of the lives mentioned.

ABALA BASU (1864–1951)
Daughter of the reputed Brahmo reformer Durgamohan Das, she married the celebrated scientist Jagadish Chandra Bose (1887). Educated in Bethune School, she passed out of the Medical College in Madras (1882). A committed educationist, she founded Nari Shiksha Samiti in 1919, Vidyasagar Bani Bhavan for teacher's training in 1925, and assisted in the establishment of several other schools.

ABANINDRANATH TAGORE (1871–1951)
A great-grandson of Prince Dwarakanath Tagore, he revived and rejuvenated the traditional Indian method of painting. Regarded as the most important influence in contemporary Indian art, he created many paintings, and was the author of a number of interesting books.

ABDUL HAMID KHAN YUSUFZAI (1845–1910?)
Born in Mymensingh, he served as a manager of the Estate of Delduar. A reputed educationist, reformer, and author, he edited the fortnightly journal *Ahmadi*. His book, *Udashi*, a volume of poems, won wide acclaim. He participated in the Swadeshi movement and worked in association with Surendranath Banerjee.

ABDUL KARIM, *Sahitya Bisharad* (1869–1953)
Born in Chittagong district, he started his career as a teacher. He was a keen researcher, and concentrated on *Punthi* literature. He collected about two

thousand handwritten *punthi*s in Bengali and Sanskrit, and wrote extensively about them. He also co-edited the monthly journal *Sadhana* for some time.

ABDUL LATIF, NAWAB (1828–93) Khan Bahadur, C.I.E.
Born in Faridpur, he was educated in Calcutta Madrassah, and became a Deputy Magistrate in 1849, Magistrate in 1852, and a Justice of Peace in 1853. In 1862 he became the first Muslim member of the Bengal Legislative Assembly. He was one of the pioneers in spreading 'modern' ideas amongst the Muslims in Bengal. His aim was to spread education, especially English education, amongst the Muslims. He founded the Mohammedan Literary Society in Calcutta in 1863.

AKHTAR IMAM, BEGUM (1919–)
An eminent student of Eden School. Her book *Eden Theke Bethune* provides a vivid account of Eden School, Bethune School and College, and contemporary students, shedding light too on her own contemporary society.

ANURUPA DEVI (1882–1958)
A granddaughter of Bhudev Mukhopadhyay, she made her entry into the field of literature through her novel *Poshya Putra*, published in *Bharati*. She subsequently became an extremely popular author and came to be known by the epithet *Sahitya Samragyi*.

ANWARA BAHAR CHOWDHURY (1919–87)
She became a protagonist of the women's movement in Calcutta and Dhaka in the 1940s and 1950s. She wrote a biography of Shamsunnahar Mahmud.

ASHALATA SEN (1894–1986)
She became involved at a young age with the Swadeshi movement. Later, she joined the non-cooperation movement and formed Gandaria Mahila Samiti to assist indigent women. In 1946, she was elected as a member of the Bengal Legislative Assembly.

AUROBINDO GHOSH (1872–1950)
A political leader and philosopher, he started his career as a professor at Baroda College in 1893, and later, became the Principal of National College (1906). A dedicated nationalist, and editor of the English daily *Bande Mataram*, he was accused in the sensational Alipore Bomb case and imprisoned. After he was released he began editing *Karmoyogin* and *Dharma*, but later left politics and founded a now famous ashram in Pondicherry.

### AZIZUNNESSA BEGUM
She was one of the first women whose writings were published in *Islam Pracharak*. She also translated Oliver Goldsmith's, *The Hermit*, in Bengali in 1884.

### BANKIM CHANDRA CHATTOPADHYAY (1838–94)
Born in Kanthalpara in 24 Parganas district, he was one of the most influential intellectuals of nineteenth century Bengal. His publications, that stirred contemporary readers, include *Durgeshnandini, Anandamath, Devi Chaudhurani, Kamalakanter Daptar*, and many others. He founded and edited the journal *Bangadarshan*, an influential publication.

### BASANTI DEVI (1880–1974)
Educated at Loreto House and married to Chitta Ranjan Das at the age of seventeen, she joined the nationalist movement. In 1921, she was imprisoned for a few hours along with Urmila Devi and Suniti Devi for hawking khadi on the streets. She edited the periodical *Banglar Katha*, and presided at the Bengal Provincial Conference of the Congress in 1922.

### BHUDEV MUKHOPADHYAY (1827–1890)
An educationist, a social reformer, and regarded as one of the architects of Hindu revivalism, he was a member of the Hunter Commission, and a member of the Bengal Legislative Assembly. He edited the *Education Gazette*, assisted the foundation of a number of schools, supported women's education, and published several books of which *Paribarik Prasanga* (On Family Matters) is the best known.

### BRAHMAMAYEE DEVI (1846–76)
At the age of four, she was married to nine year old Durgamohan Das. One of the first generation of educated women, she was taught at home by her husband, and was known for her generosity and social service.

### CHANDRAMUKHI BASU (1860–1944)
A Bengali Christian, she shared the honour with Kadambini Ganguli of becoming the first female graduate of Calcutta University in 1883, and passed her MA in 1884. Appointed first as Assistant Superintendent of Bethune College, she became a professor, and then the first Principal of the College in 1888 when the collegiate section was separated from the school. She retired in 1901. She married a Kashmiri Pandit, Kesharananda Mamagayen.

### Debendranath Tagore, Maharashi (1817–1905)

Son of Dwarakanath Tagore, father of Rabindranath Tagore, he was the founder of Tattobodhini Sabha in 1839, and published *Tattobodhini Patrika* in 1843 and *Indian Mirror* in 1861. He embraced Brahmoism in 1843, and became a philosopher–leader of the community. After Keshub Chandra Sen's formation of a new Brahmo Samaj in 1866, his Samaj became known as the Adi Brahmo Samaj. A social reformer, he supported widow remarriage, and protested against polygamy and child marriage.

### Dilwar Hossain Ahmed (1840–1912)

Born in Dagnan village of Hooghly district, he graduated from Presidency College, Calcutta (1861) and first joined the Alipore Court as a Deputy Magistrate. An educationist and 'liberal' thinker, he worked for reform of Muslim law, became a member of the Asiatic Society, and of the Central Book committee. He also became Vice-President of the Calcutta Muhammedan Union and Central National Muhammedan Association. In 1893 he was awarded the title Khan Bahadur.

### Durgamohan Das (1841–1897)

An advocate by profession, a Brahmo in belief, he was a social reformer. He supported widow remarriage, married off his young and widowed stepmother, and when he was widowed, married a widow (the mother of Atul Prasad Sen). An ardent supporter of women's education, he took a leading part in the foundation of Hindu Mahila Bidyalay (1873), and Banga Mahila Bidyalay (1876).

### Dwarakamath Tagore, Prince (1794–1846)

Adopted son of his uncle, Ramlochan, he was proficient in English and French. He was a rich industrialist, a zamindar, and the founder of Union Bank. He was a friend of Rammohan Roy, and a patron of Hindu College.

### Faizunnessa Chaudhurani, Nawab (1847–1905)

A zamindar of Paschimgaon in Comilla district, she administered land and property after the death of her father, worked for social welfare, and received the title Nawab from Queen Victoria. Proficient in Arabic, Persian, and Sanskrit, she was the pioneer of Muslim women's education in Bengal. She set up a school which later became Faizunnesa Degree College. She also founded, at her own expense, eleven primary schools, a middle English school, and a Sanskrit *tol* at her own home. She was a member of Sakhi Samiti founded by Swarnakumari Devi. Her personal life was however unhappy because her co-wife dominated their husband. Her semi-autobiographical work, *Rup Jalal*, was published from Dhaka in 1876.

### FAZILATUNNESSA ZOHA (1905–76)
The first Muslim woman to receive a Bachelor's degree from Calcutta University (1925), and later a Master's at Dhaka University (1927), she received acclaim from many, including Nazrul Islam, who dedicated a poem in her honour. A student of Eden School and Bethune College, she became Head of the Department of Mathematics, and then Vice-Principal of Bethune College. 'Modern' in outlook, she chose her husband while studying abroad.

### GYANADANANDINI DEVI (1852–1941)
She was married to Satyendranath Tagore, son of Debendranath Tagore, at the age of seven, and was taught at her in-laws home. She accompanied her husband to Bombay, and later visited him in England, defying all conventional family norms. In 1885, she started the journal *Balak*, which was the first journal for children edited by a woman. She is best remembered as an innovator of dress reform for Bengali *bhadramahilas*.

### HEMALALTA SARKAR (1868–1943)
Daughter of the Brahmo leader Shivanath Shastri, she married Dr Bepinbehari Sarkar and went to Nepal with him. She wrote *Nepale Banganari* and *Bharatavarsher Itihas*. She founded Maharani Girl's School in Darjeeling, and was also the first elected woman member of Calcutta Corporation.

### HEMANTAKUMARI CHAUDHURI (1868–1950)
Daughter of the Brahmo reformer and educationist Nabin Chandra Ray. she was born in Lahore, and studied in Bethune School. She was proficient in Hindi, Bengali, Sanskrit, and English, but did not take any degree examination. Married at the age of seventeen, she founded a girl's school in Shillong where her husband was posted. She edited the Hindi journal *Sugrihini* for six years from 1888, and *Antahpur* from 1901–4. Later, she settled in Patiala and founded Victoria Memorial School there.

### HEMAPRABHA MAJUMDAR (1888–1962)
She joined the Congress in 1921 and took charge of Nari Karma Mandir (Temple for Service to Women), founded by Urmila Devi, and formed the Mahila Karmi Sansad (Women's Workforce). She assisted the steamer strike in Chandpur and Goalanda in 1921. One of the five founder–members of C.R. Das-led Swaraj Party, she became a member of the Bengal Provincial Legislature, and later in 1939 joined the Forward Bloc.

### HIRONMOYEE DEVI (1870–1925)
Daughter of Swarnakumari Devi and Janakinath Ghosal, she was educated in Bethune School. In 1883, she married Phanibhusan Mukhopadhyay, a Professor of Botany. She wrote a number of poems and essays, edited *Bharati* along with Sarala Devi, and ran the Sakhi Samiti along with her mother, and founded Bidhaba Shilpashram in 1906.

### ISMAIL HOSSAIN SHIRAZI (1880–1931)
Born in Pabna, poverty prevented him from pursuing higher education, but through his own unremitting efforts became simultaneously a poet, a politician, a social reformer, a physician, and one of the pioneers of the new age among Muslims in Bengal. He was the author of many books, of which *Anil Prabaha* was proscribed by the British Government. He participated in the non-cooperation and Khilafat movements.

### JYOTIRMOYEE GANGULI (1889–1945)
Daughter of Kadambini Ganguly, she was a nationalist, an educationist, a social worker, and was associated with a number of women's organizations in India and Sri Lanka. She organized a women's volunteer corps during the Calcutta session of the Congress (1920), and lent courageous assistance to Subhas Bose during an attack by mounted police (1931).

### KADAMBINI GANGULY (1861–1923)
She was one of the first two women graduates of Calcutta University in 1883, and entered medical college in 1884, becoming the first female medical student, but was unable to secure a medical degree because she failed in the paper on medicine. She went to Britain in 1892 for further training, worked for a while in Lady Dufferin Hospital, and later took to private practice. She married Brahmo leader and educationist, Dwarakanath Ganguly. She was also one of the first female delegates to the Congress session in Bombay.

### KAIKOBAD (1858–1952)
He was born in the Nawabgunj in Dhaka, and his real name was Muhammade Kasem Al Quoreshi. His first book of poems, '*Biraha Bilap*', was published in 1870 when he was only twelve. He published profusely, acquired a considerable reputation as an author, and strove to project Islamic tradition through the medium of literature.

### KAILASBASINI DEVI (1837–?)
A Hindu woman, married early, she had no formal schooling, but was educated at home by her husband Durga Charan Gupta. She published

three books, *Hindumahilaganer Hinabashtha, Hindumahilakuler Bidyabhyas O Tahar Samunnati*, and *Biswasobha*. She was the first woman to describe the degenerate condition of contemporary Hindu women.

### Kalpana Dutta (1913–1995)
The best known *biplabi* woman of Bengal, she was a colleague of Surya Sen in the Chittagong armoury raid. Although she was sentenced to life imprisonment, she was released in 1939. Later, she joined the Communist movement and married P.C. Joshi.

### Kamini Roy (1864–1933)
One of the first generation of educated Brahmo women, she graduated with Honours in Sanskrit from Calcutta University in 1885 and joined Bethune College as a teacher. At the age of twenty-five, she published *Alo O Chaya* (Light and Shadow), a volume of poems, and became one of the most highly considered female poets of her time. She was also involved in politics, and in the movement for women's right to vote.

### Karimunnessa Khanam (1855–1922)
Rokeya's elder sister, she spent her childhood in *abarodh*, but managed to learn Bengali from her brother. She pursued her studies after marriage, and financed and patronized the periodical *Ahmadi* published from Tangail.

### Kazi Imdadul Huq (1882–1926)
Born in the Kazi family of Khulna, he studied in Presidency College, Calcutta. Starting his career as a teacher in Calcutta, he became a professor in the Teacher's Training College, Dhaka, and then Secretary of the Dhaka Intermediate and Secondary School Board. He wrote several thoughtful essays and books, and was one of the architects of 'jagaran' in the Muslim community of Bengal.

### Kazi Nazrul Islam (1899–1976)
A distinguished poet of Bengal, he was greatly admired and appreciated by Hindus and Muslims alike. Known as the 'Rebel Poet', he inspired thousands of young people with patriotism, and ideals of social equality and justice. The songs composed and put to music by him, known as Nazrul Geeti, are extremely popular to this day. He lost his mental balance in the latter part of his life.

### Keshab Chandra Sen (1838–84)
Educated in Hindu College, he joined the Brahmo Samaj in 1857 and rose

to be a reputed Brahmo leader. He however parted company with Debendranath Tagore on the issue of his daughter's marriage, and in 1861 established Bharatavarshiya Brahmo Samaj. He was one of the most enthusiastic supporters of women's education, and established the Normal School for women.

### KHAIRUNNESSA BEGUM (1870–1912)
One of the first generation of Muslim women writers, she wrote for *Nabanoor*. Her essays indicate her deep political insight. In 'Swadesh Anurag', she urged Muslim women to boycott foreign goods and assist the Swadeshi movement. Her *Satir Patibhakti* (A Model Wife's Devotion to her Husband) was emblematic of the didactic literature written for women by a woman. It lists the duties of a good wife and a model woman.

### KHUJASTA AKHTAR BANU SUHRAWARDY (1874–1919)
A highly educated lady, she translated several novels from Urdu into Bengali, and founded the Suhrawardiya Girls' School in Calcutta in 1909.

### KRISHNABHABINI DAS (1864–1919)
Married at the age of nine to Debendranath Das, she later went to England with her husband, leaving her little daughter with her in-laws. She published her book *Englande Bangamahila* (1885), which was proscribed for her views on women's liberation. After her return to Bengal she lost her husband and her daughter. She devoted herself to social work, and looked after Bharat Stree Mahamandal during Sarala Devi's absence from Bengal. She contributed many articles to *Bamabodhini Patrika*, *Bharati*, and other journals.

### KUMUDINI MITRA (1882–1943)
Daughter of Brahmo reformer and nationalist, Krishna Kumar Mitra, the editor of *Sanjivani*, and Lilabati Mitra, she graduated from Bethune College in 1903. She was active in the Swadeshi movement, especially as a writer, wrote a number of books, and edited the nationalist women's journal *Suprabhat* from 1907–17, and the journal *Bangalakshmi* from 1925–7. She married Sachindranath Bose in 1914.

### KUMUDINI KHASTAGIR (1865–?)
Born in Chittagong, daughter of Annada Charan Khastagir, she was educated in Bethune College. She began her career as a teacher in Bethune School, then joined Bethune College, and served as the Principal of the college from 1902–12. She got married in 1897.

### Lajjabati Basu (1874–1942)
Daughter of the celebrated Brahmo reformer Rajnarayan Basu, she remained unmarried. She wrote many poems and essays and regularly contributed to *Pradip, Prabasi, Sahitya, Navyabharat*, but did not publish any of her writings in book form.

### Lila Roy (1900–70)
She graduated from Bethune College, but passed MA degree from Dhaka University. She founded Dipali Sangha in 1923, and in 1926, formed the Dipali Chhatri Sangha, the first female students' organization in India to inculcate in them a political consciousness. She was the founder-editor of *Jayasree*. She joined Shree Sangha, a biplabi organization, married Anil Roy, and both of them subsequently joined the Forward Bloc.

### Mankumari Basu (1863–1943)
Niece of the famous Bengali poet Michael Madhusudan Dutta, she became a well-known poet herself. Married at the age of ten she was widowed at the age of nineteen. She was the author of many books which by and large upheld the traditional view about women.

### Mir Musharraf Hossain (1847–1911)
A Sayiid, was born in Kushtia, in Nadia district, and served as the manager of the Delduar estate. A distinguished writer, he published twenty-five books, the best known among which were *Bishad Sindhu* and *Gazi Miar Bastani*. His play, *Jamidar Darpan*, woven around the theme of the peasant rising in Pabna in 1872–3, marked him out as a politically progressive writer.

### Mrinalini Sen (1879–1972)
At the age of thirteen, she married Raja Indra Chandra Sinha of Paikpara, and was soon widowed. In 1905, she married Nirmal Chandra, second son of Keshub Chandra Sen, and went to London with her husband. On return, she became an activist in the movement for women's right to vote, and one of the leaders of Bangiya Nari Samaj.

### Muhammad Riyazuddin Ahmed (1862–1933)
Born in a suburb of Barisal, he chose journalism as a career. He served as the editor of the weekly, *Mussalman*, and edited the monthly *Islam Pracharak* for thirteen years. He belonged to the 'Sudhakar' group of literatteurs and was a supporter of Pan-Islamism.

## MUHAMMAD YAKUB ALI CHOWDHURY (1888–1940)
Born in Faridpur, he was a reputed journalist. He was intimately associated with *Kohinoor*, a progressive journal, and joined the Khilafat movement.

## NAUSHER ALI KHAN YUSUFZAI (1864–1924)
An author and social reformer, he was born in Tangail district. His principal concern was how to regenerate the Muslim community in Bengal and how to foster Hindu–Muslim unity. He contributed many thoughtful essays in *Islam Pracharak*, *Nabanoor*, and *Mihir o Sudhakar*. His best known book is on the system of higher education in Bengal (*Uccha Bangla Siksha Bidhi*, 1901).

## NIRUPAMA DEVI (1883–1951)
Born in Berhampore in Murshidabad district, she was widowed at an early age. A popular author, she published many books. She derived inspiration from Sarat Chandra Chattopadhyay, but her novels extol only the traditional, sacrificing model of womanhood.

## NURUNNESSA KHATUN, BIDYABINODINI (1892–1975)
Born in an aristocratic family in Murshidabad, she was confined to the *andarmahal* at the age of eight but encountered no opposition to studious pursuits. She married a liberal lawyer and travelled extensively with him. She wrote several novels describing the lives of the Muslim *bhadramahilas*, and obtained the title of Bidyabinodini for her contribution to literature.

## PRITILATA WADDEDAR (1911–32)
One of the first generation of women biplabis, she became involved in the Chittagong Armoury Raid (1930), and was chosen to lead a group to attack the European Club in Pahartali (1932). She committed suicide after her mission had achieved partial success.

## PRIYAMBADA DEVI (1871–1930)
Daughter of Prasannamoyee Devi, who had been married to a Kulin, Priyambada spent her childhood in her maternal grandfather's home. She graduated from Bethune College (1892), married Taradas Bandopadhyay but was soon widowed. She became a poet and a social worker, and was long associated with Bharat Stree Mahamandal.

## PYARICHAND MITRA (1814–80)
Educated in Hindu College, he fell under the influence of Derozio. He wrote many books in English and Bengali. His *Alaler Gharer Dulal*, written

under the pseudonym Tekchand Thakur, by using colloquial language set a new trend in Bengali literature.

### Rabindranath Tagore (1861–1941)
Son of Debendranath Tagore, he was a renowned literatteur, philosopher, artist, and educationist. The first Asian to be awarded the Nobel Prize for literature in 1913 for the English translation of *Gitanjali*, a book of poems in Bengali, he renounced his Knighthood in protest against the military atrocities in Jalianwallabag in 1919. He wrote profusely, and composed the genre of songs, known as Rabindra Sangeet, and exercised tremendous influence over Bengali language and literature and also on the Bengali life and culture. With the money he received with the Nobel Prize, he founded a model educational institution at Shantiniketan, the Visva Bharati of today.

### Rammohan Roy, Raja (1772–1833)
An extremely erudite scholar of philosophy and religious studies, proficient in Arabic, Persian, English, and Bengali, he founded Atmiya Sabha in 1815, which became the Brahmo Samaj in 1828. He preached monotheism, spearheaded the movement for the abolition of sati, and advocated women's education. He was one of the foremost pioneers of the nineteenth century social reform movement in Bengal.

### Rasasundari Devi (1809–99)
Born in Pabna, she was married at the age of twelve, and went to live in Ramdiya village in Faridpur district. She taught herself to read, learned how to write from her son, and published autobiography entitled *Amar Jiban* in 1868.

### Razia Khatun Chaudhurani (1907–34)
A writer and social worker, she was married to an idealistic politician, Ashrafuddin Ahmed Chaudhury of Comilla. Her writings, like Rokeya's, mostly focused on women, especially women's education and status. She was an ardent supporter of the advancement of women's status, but was opposed to 'Westernization'.

### Saratkumari Chaudhurani (1861–1920)
Daughter of Shashi Bhusan Basu, she was married at the age of ten to Akshay Chandra Chaudhury. She received her education at Lahore and known as Lahorini. She was closed to the Tagore family and contributed articles to *Bharati, Sabuj Patra, Sadhana*. *Shubha Bibaha*, published in 1906, is her most acclaimed work.

SAROJINI NAIDU (1879–1949)
Daughter of Dr Aghorenath Chattopadhyay, she was born in Hyderabad, and studied at Gurton College, University of Cambridge. A superb orator, an accomplished poet, she was also a politician. She became President of the Congress in 1925, joined the Civil Disobedience movement and the Salt Satyagraha under Gandhi, and after Indian Independence became the Governor of Uttar Pradesh.

SATYENDRANATH TAGORE (1842–1923)
Son of Debendranath, and husband of Gyanadanandini Devi, he was the first Indian in the Indian Civil Service. Educated at Presidency College, he was an enthusiastic supporter of women's 'liberation' and education. He also became an Acharya of the Brahmo Samaj in 1906, and edited *Tattobodhini Patrika*. He published a number of books in English and Bengali. He started Hindu Mela with a view to promoting nationalism.

SHAILABALA GHOSHJAYA (1894–1974)
Born in Burdwan, she was married to Narendramohun Ghosh at the age of thirteen. A reputed author, she wrote a number of books, the best known among which is *Sekh Andu* (1914). Her *Janma Aparadhini* is also a striking novel depicting the oppression of women in the family.

SHAISTA SUHRAWARDY IKRAMULLAH, BEGUM (1915–2000)
Educated in an English-medium school in Calcutta, she obtained a PhD from London. Her book *From Purdah to Parliament* delineates a pen-picture of the contemporary Muslim society, especially its women. She refers to the seclusion of women in her nawabi family home. Her childhood was however spent in a railway colony near Calcutta where her father served as District Medical Officer. She came out of strict purdah, and later joined parliamentary politics.

SHAMSUNNAHAR MAHMUD (1908–64)
A writer, educationalist, teacher, and social worker, a close associate of Begum Rokeya, and later a parliamentarian in East Pakistan, she was an aristocratic family of Noakhali, and was an abarodhbasini during her childhood. At the age of nine she was taken out of Dr Khastagir Girls' School because of purdah, but she pursued her studies at home under a private tutor, passed the Matriculation examination creditably, and obtained a Bachelor's degree with distinction from Calcutta University (1932). She joined Brabourne College as a teacher, and wrote a number of books, of

which the best known is *Rokeya Jiboni*, the first biography of Begum Rokeya. She also worked for Anjuman-i-Khawatin-i-Islam.

SHANTI GHOSH (1916–1989)
A *biplabi* at a very young age during her school days, she, along with Suniti Chowdhuri, shot at Stevens, District Magistrate of Comilla (1931). She was tried and sentenced to life imprisonment. In 1939, on Gandhi's intervention, she was released. Shanti proceeded to pursue her studies, and in 1942 married Chiraranjan Das and became a member of the Bengal Provincial legislature.

SHIVANATH SHASTRI (1847–1919)
An educationist, social reformer, and Brahmo leader, he started his career as the Headmaster of South Suburban School in Calcutta. A widely respected educationist, he was one of the initiators of the foundation of City School (1879). He supported women's education and widow remarriage, and was the founder of Sadharan Brahmo Samaj.

SUCHETA KRIPALANI (1908–74)
She passed her MA in History from Delhi University (with a first class first), and began teaching at the University in Benares. She joined the Congress, became Secretary of the Women's Section in 1941, a member of the Congress Working Committee in 1947, and the Chief Minister of Uttar Pradesh in 1963. She was the first woman Chief Minister in India. She married Acharya Kripalani.

SUNITI CHOWDHURI (1917–88)
She was imprisoned for ten years for shooting the British Magistrate of Comilla (1931). Later she became a physician and married Pradyot Ghosh, a trade union leader.

SWARNAPRABHA BASU (1869–1918)
Born in Bikrampur, she went to school in Calcutta. She married the leading Brahmo leader Ananda Mohan Bose, and was one of the first women to be actively involved in women's associations. She contributed articles to *Bamabodhini Patrika* and *Bharatamahila*. She was a member of the general committee of the Sadharan Brahmo Samaj.

SWARNAKUMARI DEVI (1855–1932)
Daughter of Debendranath Tagore, sister of Rabindranath Tagore, and mother of Sarala Devi Chaudhurani, Swarnakumari was married at the age

of twelve. She was educated at home, and achieved fame as a poet, novelist, and social worker. For over fifteen years, she edited the monthly, *Bharati*. She founded Sakhi Samiti, a women's association, in 1886, with a view to educating and assisting indigent women, especially widows. The Samiti organized an exhibition of women's handicrafts for three days in the Bethune School campus, which attracted considerable attention in those days. She was a delegate to the Indian National Congress session in Bombay in 1889.

SYED AHMED KHAN, Sir (1817–1898)
Born in Delhi, he began his career in the service of the British in India and rose to the rank of a subordinate judge. He had a deep appreciation of the values of Western culture devoted himself to the task of propagating English education among the Indian Muslims. He founded the Muhammedan Anglo-Oriental College in Aligarh in 1875. In 1920 the College was raised to the status of a university, called the Aligarh Muslim University.

SYED AMIR ALI (1849–1928)
Born in Hooghly, he passed MA and BL from Calcutta University. In 1873, he qualified as a Bar-at Law in London and started practising at the Calcutta High Court. He wrote a number of books and founded the Central National Muhammedan Association in 1877 in order to propagate political and social awareness amongst Bengali Muslims. Along with Nawab Abdul Latif, he shared the honour of being the pioneer in familiarizing educated Muslims with Western thought. In 1890, he became the first Muslim Justice of Calcutta High Court, and in 1909, the first Indian member of the Privy Council.

SYED NAWAB ALI CHOWDHURY (1863–1929)
A reputed zamindar of Mymensingh, he was associated with the political, cultural, and social developments of the country. He financed the paper *Mihir o Sudhakar*, built a press for its publication, and was also a patron of *Islam Pracharak*. He was the author of *Vernacular Education of Bengal* (1900) and *Primary Education in Rural Areas* (1906). He received the titles Khan Bahadur in 1917, Nawab in 1917, and CIE in 1924. In 1921 he became a minister in the Bengal Provincial Government.

SYED SHAMSUL HUDA (1862–1922)
Born in Comilla, he studied at Hooghly College and Presidency College, Calcutta, and won fame, first as an advocate in Calcutta High Court and later as a judge. He was associated with educational and cultural activities, helped the foundation of Koreya Muslim Boy's School, and served as a

member of the governing body of Sakhawat Memorial School. He received the title of Nawab in 1913 and KCII in 1915; in 1922 he became President All India Muslim League.

SYED WAJED HOSSAIN (1870–1934)
An advocate of Calcutta High Court, he took a keen interest in the development of Muslim education. He was one of the principal initiators of the Bengal Provincial Muslim Education Society (1903), and acted as its Secretary for many years. He also assisted in the establishment of the first Madrassah for Muslim girls in Calcutta in 1897.

VIVEKANANDA, SWAMI (1863–1902)
Son of Biswanath Dutta, Narendranath became a devoted disciple of Ramakrishna, and after his death founded Belur Math (1899). He travelled widely in India and abroad to preach his philosophy and religion. His speech at the Conference on Religion in Chicago (1893) made history. He wielded enormous influence over the lives and thoughts of men and women in India, and was one of the most widely acclaimed Indians of his time.

# Bibliography

### ARCHIVAL MATERIALS

*For details of files, and numbers, see Notes.*

*a) Nehru Memorial Museum and Library, New Delhi.*

Oral History Transcript; Oral History Project; Transcripts of Freedom Fighters.

*b) Rabindra Bhavan Archives, Visva Bharati, Shantiniketan.*

Chithipatra: Letters of Rabindranath Tagore.

*c) West Bengal State Archives, Kolkata.*

Freedom Papers (State Committee for Compilation of History of Freedom Movement in India, Bengal Region).

Report on the Native Newspapers in Bengal, 1902–1931.

### PRINTED GOVERNMENT RECORDS/REPORTS

*Census of India, 1911,* vol. 5, Bengal, Part 1 (Report).

W. Adam, *On the State of Education in Bengal,* First and Third Reports, Calcutta, 1836.

*Report of The Committee on The Status of Women in India,* Government of India, New Delhi, 1974.

### BENGALI WORKS

*Arranged alphabetically by the author's first name. For English translation of titles see Notes. The Bengali calendar,* BS, *is roughly 593 years behind* AD. *1 January of a Christian calendar approximately corresponds to 15th of Paush, i.e. the ninth month of the Bengali calendar.*

Abanindranath Thakur O Rani Chanda, *Gharoa,* Visvabharati Granthalay, Calcutta, 1358 BS.

# BIBLIOGRAPHY

Abdul Mannan Syed, *Begum Rokeya,* Abasar Prakashan Sanstha, Dhaka, 1996; first published, 1983.

Abdul Qadir (ed.), *Begum Rokeya Rachanavali,* Bangla Academy, Dhaka, 1984.

Abhijit Sen, *Agranthita Rokeya,* Naya Udyog, Calcutta, 1998.

Akhtar Imam, *Eden Theke Bethune,* Dhaka, 1990.

Ambuja Sundari Das Gupta, 'Kashibasini', *Bamabodhini Patrika,* Jaishtha-Asadh, 1312 BS.

Amalendu Bose (ed.), *Jayasree Subarna Jayanti Volume,* Calcutta, 1983.

Amodini Ghosh, 'Amader Shishu Shiksha', *Bharatamahila,* Baishakh, 1316 BS.

Anisuzzaman, *Muslim Manas O Bangla Sahitya, 1757–1918,* Muktadhara, Calcutta, 1971.

Anisuzzaman and Maleka Begum (eds), *Narir Katha,* Mudrak, Dhaka, 1994

Anon, 'Arya Parivar', *Bamabodhini Patrika,* Agrahayan 1308 BS.

Anon, 'Balyabibaha', *Bharatamahila,* Falgun, 1315 BS.

Arati Gangopadhyay, *Banglar Itihase Narir Bhumika O Sangram,* Gana Unnayan Parshad, Calcutta, 1992.

Ashalata Sen, *Sekaler Katha,* Firma K.L.M. Pvt Ltd., Calcutta, 1990.

Ashapurna Devi, *Pratham Pratisruti,* Mitra & Ghosh Publishers Pvt Ltd., Calcutta, 1403 BS.

Bankim Chandra Chattopadhyay, *Bankim Rachanavali,* 2 vols., Sahitya Sansad, Calcutta, vol. 2, 1361 BS.

Basanta Kumar Chattopadhyay, *Jyotirindranather Jibonsmriti,* Prajna Bharati, Calcutta, 1982.

Benoy Ghosh (ed.), *Samayik Patre Banglar Samajchitra (1840–1905),* vols. 1–5, Bengal Publishers Private Ltd., Calcutta, 1961–7.

—— *Vidyasagar O Bangali Samaj,* vols. 1–3, Orient Longman, Calcutta, 1973.

Bhababhuti Vidyaratna, 'Pativratya', *Bamabodhini Patrika,* Sravan & Bhadra, 1325 BS.

Bharati Ray (ed.), *Sekaler Narishiksha: Bamabodhini Patrika,* Calcutta University Press, Calcutta, 1994.

—— (ed.), *Nari O Parivar: Bamabodhini Patrika,* Ananda Publishers, Kolkata, 2002.

Bhudev Chaudhuri, *Bangla Sahityer Chhotogalpa O Galpakar,* Modern Book Agency, Calcutta, 1962.

Bhudev Mukhopadhyay, *Bhudev Rachana Sambhar,* Pramatha Nath Bishi (ed.), Mitra & Ghosh, Calcutta, 1962.

Bhupendra Kishore Rakshit Ray, *Chalar Pathe,* Yugamantra Publishing House, Calcutta, 1930.

Bibi Teherunnesa, 'Bamaganer Rachana', *Bamabodhini Patrika,* Falgun 1271 BS.

Brajendranath Bandopadhyay (ed.), *Sangbadpatre Sekaler Katha,* 2 vols., Bangiya Sahitya Parishad, Calcutta, vol. 2, 1401 BS, 1340 BS.

—— *Banga Sahitye Nari,* Bangiya Sahitya Parishad, Calcutta, 1357 BS.

—— *Sahitya Sadhak Charitamala,* 10 vols., Bangiya Sahitya Parishad, Calcutta, 1364–70 BS.

# BIBLIOGRAPHY • 157

Chandicharan Bandopadhyaya, *Ma O Chhele,* Sahitya Sansad, Calcutta, 1887.
Charumati Devi, 'Strishikshar Upakarita', *Bamabodhini Patrika,* Kartick, 1322 BS.
—— 'Sisuganer Akalmrityu O Jananir Kartavya', *Bamabodhini Patrika,* Kartick 1319 BS.
Charushila Mitra, 'Uttar', *Bamabodhini Patrika,* Agrahayan, 1319 BS.
Chitra Deb, *Thakurbarir Andarmahal,* Ananda Publishers, Calcutta, 1397 BS.
—— *Antahpurer Atmakatha,* Ananda Publishers, Calcutta, 1984.
Ghulam Murshid, *Rasasundari Theke Rokeya: Nari Pragatir Eksho Bachhar,* Bangla Academy, Dhaka, 1993.
Gita Chattopadhyay, *Bangla Samayik Patrikapanji,* vol. 1, 1900–14, & vol. 2, 1915–30, Bangiya Granthagar Parishad, Calcutta, 1990 & 1994.
Dinesh Chandra Sen, 'Sahityik Smriti', *Bharati,* Baishakh, 1323 BS.
Gyanadanandini Devi, 'Smritikatha', in Indira Devi (ed.), *Puratani,* Calcutta, 1957.
Gyanesh Maitra, *Nari Jagriti O Bangla Sahitya,* National Publishers, Calcutta, 1987.
Hemanta Kumari Chaudhury, 'Shusrushakarini', *Antahpur,* Bhadra, 1306–7 BS, Aug. 1900.
Hemalata Sarkar, 'Narijatir Shiksha', *Bharatamahila,* Asadh, 1314 BS.
Hemendra Kumar Ray, *Jander Dekhechhi,* Indian Associated Publishing Co., Calcutta, 1955.
—— 'Bharatir Itihas', *Bharati,* Baishakh, 1323 BS.
Hiranmoyee Devi, 'Mahila Shilpashram', *Bharati,* Aswin, 1315 BS.
—— 'Kaifiyat', *Bharati,* Baishakh, 1323 BS.
Imdadul Huk, 'Hindu–Mussalman O Banga Sahitya', *Bharati,* Baishakh, 1310 BS
Indira Devi Chaudhurani, *Puratani,* Indian Associated Publishing Co. Pvt. Ltd., Calcutta, 1957.
Ishan Chandra Basu, *Stridiger Prati Upadesh,* Victoria Press, Calcutta, 1884.
J. Sanyal (Sm), 'Hindu Grihe Badhu-jantrana', *Bamabodhini Patrika,* Aswin-Kartick, 1318 BS.
Jaladhar Sen, 'Bharati Smriti', *Bharati,* Baishakh, 1323 BS.
Jay Krishna Mitra, *Ramanir Kartavya,* Giribala Mitra, Calcutta, 1890.
Jogesh C. Bagal, Postscript, in Sarala Devi Chaudharani, *Jibaner Jharapata,* Rupa, Calcutta, 1382 BS.
—— 'Rashtriya Andolone Banga Mahila', in K. Nag (ed.), Bethune School and College Centenary Volume, Calcutta, 1949.
Jyotirmoyee Devi, *Smriti-Bismritir Taranga,* Nirmal Book Agency, Calcutta, 1986.
—— *Jyotirmoyee Devir Rachana Sankalan,* 5 vols. vol. 1, Subir Ray Chowdhury (ed.), Dey's Publishing, Calcutta, 1991; vol. 5, Gaur Kishore Ghosh (ed.), Calcutta, 1995.
Kailasbasini Devi, *Hindumahilaganer Hinabashtha,* Durga Charan Gupta, Calcutta, 1863.
—— *Hindu Abalakuler Bidyabhas O Tahar Samunnatir Upaya,* Calcutta, 1865.
Kamala Das Gupta, *Swadhinata Sangrame Banglar Nari,* Basundhara Prakashani, Calcutta, 1963.

Kamala Das Gupta, *Rakter Akshare,* Navana, Calcutta, 1954.
Kamini Roy, *Balika Shikshar Adarsha: Atit O Bartaman,* Sudhir Kumar Sen, Calcutta, 1918.
—— *Thakurmar Chithi,* Sisir Kumar Neogy, Calcutta, 1924.
Krishnabhabini Das, *Krishnabhabini Daser Englande Bangamahila,* Simanti Sen, Stree (ed.), Calcutta, 1996.
Latifunnesa, 'Bangiya Musalman Mahilar Prati', *Bamabodhini Patrika,* Asadh 1304 BS.
Latika Ghosh, 'Social and Educational Movements for Women and by Women', in K. Nag (ed.), *Bethune School and College Centenary Volume,* Calcutta, 1949.
Lila Majumdar, *Aar Konokhane,* Mitra & Ghosh, Calcutta, 1374 BS.
—— *Pakadandi,* Ananda Publishers, Calcutta, 1986.
M. A. Rahim, *Banglar Musalmander Itihas, 1757–1947,* Ahmad Publishing House, Dhaka, 1989.
Maleka Begum, *Banglar Nari Andolan,* Dhaka University Press, Dhaka, 1989.
Michael Madhusudan Dutt, *Rachanavali,* Kshetra Gupta (ed.), Sahitya Sansad, Calcutta, 1977.
Morshed Shafiul Alam, *Begum Rokeya: Samay O Sahitya,* Bangla Academy, Dhaka, 1996.
Moshfeka Mahmud: *Patre Rokeya Parichiti,* Sahitya Prakash, Dhaka, 1996.
Motahar Hossein Sufi, *Begum Rokeya: Jiban O Sahitya,* University Press, Dhaka, 1986.
Muhammad Idris Ali, *Bangladesher Upanyas Sahitye Maddhabitta Shreni,* Bangla Academy, Dhaka, 1985.
Muhammad Shamsul Alam, *Rokeya Sakhawat Hossein: Jibon O Sahityakarma,* Bangla Academy, Dhaka, 1989.
Nasiruddin Mohammad, *Bangla Sahitye Saogat Jug,* Nurjahan Begum, Dhaka, 1985.
Niharbala Devi, 'Bidhir Nirdesh', *Paricharika,* Asadh, 1325 BS.
Nirupama Devi, 'Ekannabarti Paribare Ashanti Nibaraner Upaya ki?, *Antahpur,* Paush, 1310 BS.
Nistarini Devi, 'Bharati O Bharatir Sampadika', *Bharati,* Baishakh, 1323 BS.
Partha Chattopadhyay, *Bangla Sangbadpatra O Bangalir Nabajagaran,* Mandal & Sons, Calcutta, 1988.
Peary Chand Mitra, 'Grihakatha, Stree Shiksha—Gyanakari Bidya', in Anisuzzaman and Maleka Begum, (eds), *Narir Katha,* Mudrak, Dhaka, 1994.
Prashanta Kumar Pal, *Rabi Jiboni,* Ananda Publishers, Calcutta, 5 vols., vol. 5, 1397 BS.
Pratapchandra Majumdar, *Stri Charitra,* published by the author, Calcutta, 1898.
Punyalata Chakravarty, *Chhelebelar Dinguli,* New Script Publishers, Calcutta, 1381 BS.
Rabindranath Thakur, *Rabindra Rachanavali,* Centenary Volume, Govt. of West Bengal, Calcutta, 1368 BS.

Radhika Prasad Ghosh Chaudhury, 'Stree Niti Chatustoy', *Bamabodhini Patrika*, Baishakh, 1311 BS.
Rama Neogy, 'Brahmo Balika Shikshalayer Itihas', in Rama Neogy (ed.), *Brahmo Balika Shikshalay Centenary Volume, 1890–1990*, Calcutta, 1994.
Ramendrasundar Trivedi, *Ramendra Rachanavali*, Brajendranath Bandopadhyay and Sajanikanta Das (eds), Bangiya Sahitya Parishad, Calcutta, 1959.
Rammohan Roy, *Rammohan Granthavali*, Brajendranath Bandopadhyay and Sajani Kanta Das (eds), Calcutta, vol. 3.
Rani Chanda, *Abar Mar Baper Bari*, Viswabharati Grantha Bibhag, Calcutta, 1972.
Rathindranath Majumdar, *Rabindra Kabye Naribhavana*, The Book Trust, Calcutta, n.d.
Rasasundari Devi, *Amar Jibon*, College Street Edition, Calcutta, 1987. First published 1868.
Razia Khatun Chaudhurani, 'Samaje O Grihe Narir Sthan', in Anisuzzaman and Maleka Begum (eds), *Narir Katha*, Mudrak, Dhaka, 1994.
Rokeya Sakhawat Hossain, *Motichoor*, 2 vols. vol. 1, Gurudas Chatterjee, Calcutta, 1314 BS, vol. 2, published by the author, 1328 BS.
—— *Rachanavali*, Abdul Qadir (ed.), Bangla Academy, Dhaka, 1993.
Sankari Prasad Basu, *Vivekananda O Samakalin Bharatavarsha*, 4 vols, Mondal Book House, Calcutta, 1975–80.
Sarala Devi Chaudhurani, *Jibaner Jharapata*, Rupa, Calcutta, 1382 BS.
—— 'Amar Balyajiboni', *Bharati*, Baishakh, 1312 BS.
—— 'Birashtamir Gan', *Bharati*, Kartick, 1311 BS.
—— 'Bangalir Pitridhan', *Bharati*, Jaishtha, 1310 BS.
—— 'Kumar Udayaditya', *Bharati*, Sravan, 1310 BS.
—— 'Congress O Svayatta Shasan', *Bharati*, Baishakh, 1312 BS.
—— 'Ahitagnika', *Bharati*.
—— 'Chitravali', *Bharati*, Shravan, 1323 BS.
—— 'Janmaswar', *Bharati*, Jaishtha, 1323 BS.
—— 'Bharater Hindu O Mussalman', *Bharati*, Bhadra, 1310 BS.
—— 'Sinher Bibare', *Bangabani*, *3:1*, Falgun–Sravan, 1330–1 BS.
—— 'Ahvan', *Bharati*, Chaitra, 1324 BS.
—— 'Ramanir Karya', *Suprabhat*, Chaitra, 1316 BS.
—— 'Bharat Stree Mahamandal', *Bharati*, Chaitra, 1317 BS.
—— 'Bangali Paraye', *Bharati*, Baishakh, 1309 BS.
—— 'Abhayamantra', *Bharati*, Paush, 1316 BS.
—— 'Bijoya Dashami', *Bharati*, Agrahayan, 1320 BS.
—— 'Udbodhan', *Bharati*, Baishakh, 1325 BS.
—— 'Nari Nirjatan', *Bharati*, 1311 BS.
—— 'Palayan O Palayaner Par', *Bharati*, Bhadra, 1323 BS.
—— 'Bangiya Senrajaganer Uttar Charit', *Bharati*, Magh, 1323 BS.
Sarat Chandra Chattopadhyay, *Sarat Rachanavali*, Centenary Volume, Sarat Samiti, Calcutta, 1385 BS.

Sarat Kumari Chaudhurani, 'Kalikatar Strisamaj', *Bharati*, Bhadra, 1288 BS.
—— *Shubha Vivaha*, Calcutta, Pustak Bipani, 1983; first published 1905.
—— 'Adorer Na Anadorer', in *Sarat Kumari Rachanavali*, B. Bandopadhyay (ed.), Bangiya Sahitya Parishad, Calcutta, 1357 BS, AD 1950.
—— *Sarat Kumari Chaudhuranir Rachanavali*, Brajendranath Bandopadhyay (ed.), Bangiya Sahitya Parishad, Calcutta, 1357 BS.
Satish Chandra Chakravarty, *Lalana Suhrid*, Gurudas Chattopadhaya & Sons, Calcutta, 1911.
Satish Pakrashi, *Agnidiner Katha*, Navajivan Prakasani, Calcutta, 1947.
Satyacharan Mitra, *Strir Prati Swamir Upadesh*, Victoria Printing Works, Calcutta, 1884.
Satyendranath Tagore, *Amar Balyakatha o Amar Bombai Prabas*, Kantik Press, Calcutta, 1915.
Shailabala Ghoshjaya, *Sekh Andu*, Gurudas Chattopadhyay & Sons, Calcutta, 1917.
—— *Janma Aparadhini*, Kar, Majumdar & Co, Calcutta, 1919.
Shamsunnahar Mahmud, *Rokeya Jiboni*, Sahitya Parishad, Dhaka, 1996. First published, 1937.
Shashibhusan Das Gupta, *Bharater Shaktisadhana o Shakta Sahitya*, Sahitya Sansad, Calcutta, 1970.
Shatadalbasini Biswas, 'Amader Shishu', *Bharatamahila*, Baishakh, 1318 BS.
—— 'Narishaktir Apachay', *Bharatamahila*, Jaishtha, 1317 BS.
Shibnarayan Ray, 'The Sikha (1927–32) Movement—A Note on Bengali Muslim Intelligence', *The Radical Humanist*, vol. 41:9, 1977.
Shivanath Shastri, *Ramatanu Lahiri o Tatkalin Banga Samaj*, New Age Publishers, Calcutta, 1955.
—— *Atmacharit*, Sadharan Brahmo Samaj, Calcutta, 1991.
—— 'Mahatma Bethune Ebang Bangadeshe Strisiksha', *Prabasi*, Bhadra, 1311 BS.
Srimati, 'Grihaswamir Kartavya', *Bamabodhini Patrika*, Agrahayan, 1325 BS.
Srish Chandra Dhar, 'Marathaye Shivaji Utsav', *Bharati*, Jaishtha, 1313 BS.
—— 'Punjabe Pratapaditya Utsav', *Bharati*, Asadh, 1313 BS.
Subodh Chandra Sen Gupta (ed.), *Sansad Bangali Charitabhidhan*, 2 vols, Sahitya Sansad, Calcutta, 1994 &1996.
Sudakshina Sen, *Jibon Smriti*, Art Press, Calcutta, 1939.
Sunil Gangopadhyay, *Pratham Alo*, 2 vols., Ananda publishers, Calcutta, 1996–7.
Suniti Gupta, 'Ramanir Karyakshetra', *Bharatamahila*, Bhadra, 1320 BS.
Swarnakumari Devi, 'Sekele Katha', *Bharati*, Chaitra, 1322 BS.
Swarnaprabha Basu, 'Narir Grihadharma', *Bamabodhini Patrika*, Agrahayan 1315 BS.
Tahmina Alam, *Begum Rokeya Sakhawat Hossein: Chinta-Chetanar Dhara o Samajkarma*, Bangla Academy, Dhaka, 1996. First published, 1992.
Tapati Basu, 'Bangali Meyer Parashona', *Ananda Bazar Patrika*, Autumn Number, 1991.
Wakil Ahmed, *Unish Shataker Bangali Mussalmaner Chinta Chetanar Dhara*, 2 vols, Bangla Academy, Dhaka, 1983.

## Journals (Selected Years)
For details of dates and numbers, see Notes.

*Antahpur* (Calcutta)
*Bamabodhini Patrika* (Calcutta)
*Bangabani* (Calcutta)
*Banglar Katha* (Calcutta)
*Bharati* (Calcutta)
*Bharatamahila* (Calcutta, Dhaka)
*Jayasree* (Calcutta)
*Mahila* (Dhaka)
*Navyabharat* (Calcutta)
*Paricharika* (Koch Behar)
*Prabasi* (Calcutta)
*Sadhana* (Dhaka)
*Suprabhat* (Calcutta)

## English Works
### Books
Arranged alphabetically by the author's last name.

Agnes, Flavia, *Law and Gender Inequality: The Politics of Women's Rights in India*, Oxford University Press, New Delhi, 1999.
—— 'Gender Justice' in Bharati Ray (ed.), *Women and Politics: France, India and Russia*, Calcutta, K.P. Bagchi, 2000.
Ahmed, Aziz, *Studies in Islamc Culture in the Indian Environment*, Clarendon Press, Oxford, 1964.
Ahmed, Rafiuddin, *The Bengal Muslims 1871–1906, A Quest for Identity*, Oxford University Press, New Delhi, 1981.
—— (ed.), *Understanding Bengal Muslims: Interpretative Essays*, Oxford University Press, New Delhi, 2001.
Ahmed, Salahuddin, *Muslim Community in Bengal 1884–1912*, Dhaka, 1974.
Ahmed, Sufia, *Muslim Community in Bengal 1884–1912*, Oxford University Press, Dhaka, 1964.
Allen, Michael and S. N. Mukherjee (eds), *Women in India and Nepal*, Australian National University, Australia, 1982.
Altekar, A.S. *The Position of Women in Hindu Civilisation*, Benaras, 1956.
Amin, Sonia Nishat, 'The Early Muslim *Bhadramahila:* The Growth of Learning and Creativity, 1876 to 1939', in Bharati Ray (ed.), *From The Seams of History: Essays on Indian Women*, Oxford University Press, New Delhi, 1995.
'The Orthodox Discourse and the Emergence of the Muslim *Bhadramahila* in

Early Twentieth Century Bengal, 1900–47', in Rajat Kanta Ray (ed.), *Mind, Body and Society*, Oxford University Press, New Delhi, 1995.

Arnold, David and David Hardiman (eds), *Subaltern Studies*, vol. 8, Oxford University Press, New Delhi, 1994.

Bagchi, Amiya K., *Private Investment in India, 1900–1939*, Cambridge University Press, Cambridge, 1972.

Bagchi, Jasodhara (ed.), *Indian Women: Myth and Reality*, Sangam Books, Calcutta, 1995.

Bandopadhyay, Sekhar, 'Caste, Widow-remarriage and the Reform of Popular Culture in Colonial Bengal', in Bharati Ray (ed.), *From the Seams of History: Essays on Indian Women*, Oxford University Press, New Delhi, 1995.

Bannerji, Himani, 'Attired in Virtue: The Discourse on Shame (*lajja*) and Clothing of the *Bhadramahila* in Colonial Bengal', in Bharati Ray (ed.), *From the Seams of History: Essays on Indian Women*, Oxford University Press, New Delhi, 1995.

Banerjee, Sumanta, *The Parlour and the Street: Elite and Popular Culture in Nineteenth Century Bengal*, Seagull Books, Calcutta, 1989.

Barrett, Michele, *Women's Oppression Today: Problems in Marxist Feminist Analysis*, Verso, London, 1985.

Basu, Amrita, *Two Faces of Protest: Contrasting Modes of Women's Activism in India*, University of California Press, Berkeley, 1992.

Basu, Aparna, *Essays in the History of Indian Education*, Concept Publishing House, New Delhi, 1982.

——— and Bharati Ray, *Women's Struggle: A History of the All India Women's Conference 1927–1997*, Manohar Publications, Delhi, 1990.

Bhattarchaya, Sabyasachi and Romila Thapar (eds), *Situating Indian History*, Oxford University Press, New Delhi, 1986.

Borthwick, Meredith, *The Changing Role of Women in Bengal, 1849–1905*, Princeton University Press, Princeton, 1984.

Bose, Nemai Sadhan, *The Indian Awakening and Bengal*, Firma K.L. Mukhopadhyay, Calcutta, 1960.

Branca, P., *Silent Sisterhood: Middle Class Women in the Victorian Home*, London, 1977.

Butalia, Urvashi, *The Other Side of Silence*, Kali for Women, New Delhi, 1998.

Chakravarty, Dipesh, 'The Difference-Deferral of a Colonial Modernity: Public Debates on Domesticity in British Bengal' in David Arnold and David Hardiman (eds), *Subaltern Studies*, VII, Oxford University Press, New Delhi, 1994.

Chakravarty, Papia, *Hindu Response to Nationalist Ferment*, Subarnarekha, Calcutta, 1992.

Chakrabarti, Sambuddha, 'Changing Notions of Conjugal Relations in Nineteenth Century Bengal', in Rajat Kanta Ray (ed.), *Mind, Body and Society: Life and Mentality in Colonial Bengal*, Oxford University Press, New Delhi, 1995.

Chakravarti, Uma, 'Whatever happened to the Vedic Dasi? Orientalism, Nationalism and a Script for the Past', in Kumkum Sangari and Sudesh Vaid (eds), *Recasting Women: Essays in Colonial History*, Kali for Women, New Delhi, 1989.

Chakravarty, Usha, *Condition of Bengali Women Around the Second Half of the Nineteenth Century*, published by the author, Calcutta, 1963.

Chanana, Karuna (ed.), *Socialisation, Education and Women: Explorations in Gender Identity*, Orient Longman, New Delhi, 1988.

Chatterjee, Partha, *Nationalist Thought and the Colonial World: A Derivative Discourse?* Oxford University Press, New Delhi, 1986.

—— 'The Nationalist Resolution of the Women's Question', in Kumkum Sangari and Sudesh Vaid (eds), *Recasting Women*, Kali for Women, New Delhi, 1989.

Chowdhury, Indira, *The Frail Hero and Virile History: Gender and Politics of Culture in Colonial Bengal*, Oxford University Press, New Delhi, 1998.

Cohn, B.S., *An Anthropologist Among the Historians*, Oxford University Press, Delhi, 1987.

Das, Suranjan, *Communal Riots in Bengal*, Oxford University Press, New Delhi, 1991.

Datta, Bhupendra Nath, *Swami Vivekananda: Patriot-Prophet*, Nababharat Publications, Calcutta, 1954.

De, Amalendu, *Roots of Separatism in Nineteenth Century Bengal*, Calcutta, 1974.

De, Dhurjati Prosad, *Bengal Muslims in Search of Identity 1905–47*, Dhaka University Press, Dhaka, 1998.

Desai, Neera (ed.), *A Decade of Women's Movement in India*, Himalaya, Bombay, 1988.

—— and Maithreyi Krishnaraj, *Women and Society in India*, Ajanta Publications, Delhi, 1987.

Devendra, Kiran, *Status and Position of Women In India*, Shakti Books, New Delhi, 1985.

Dube, Leela and Rajni Palriwala (eds), *Structures and Strategies: Women, Work and Family*, Sage Publications, New Delhi, 1990.

Eaton, Richard M., *The Rise of Islam and the Bengal Frontier, 1204–1760*, Oxford University Press, New Delhi, 1994.

Eck, Diana L. and Devaki Jain (eds), *Speaking of faith: Cross-Cultural Perspectives on Women, Religion and Social Change*, Kali for Women, New Delhi, 1986.

Engels, Dagmar, 'The Age of Consent Act of 1891: Colonial Ideology in Bengal', *South Asia Research*, vol. 3:2, Nov. 1985.

Forbes, Geraldine, *Women in Modern India*, Cambridge University Press, Cambridge, 1998.

Fraser, Mary, *Unruly Practices: Power Discourse and Gender in Contemporary Social Theory*, University of Minnesota Press, Minneapolis, 1989.

Freeman, Jo (ed.), *Women: A Feminist Perspective*, Mayfield Publishing Co., California, 1975.

Gandhi, M.K., *Women and Social Justice*, Navajivan Publishing Hosue, Ahmedabad 1954.

—— *Collected Works*, Publishing Division, Ministry of Information and Broadcasting, Govt of India, Delhi, 1958.

Gandhi, Nandita and Nandita Shah, *The Issues at Stake: Theory and Practice in the contemporary Women's Movement in India*, Kali for Women, New Delhi, 1992.

Ghose, Sankar, *The Renaissance to Militant Nationalism in India*, Allied Publishers, Pvt. Ltd., Bombay, 1969.

Ghosh, Srabasi, 'Birds in a Cage', *Economic and Political Weekly*, Oct. 1986.

Gordon, Leonard A., *Bengal: The Nationalist Movement 1876–1940*, Columbia University Press, New York, 1974.

Graham, G.F.I., *The Life and Works of Sir Syed Ahmad Khan*, Oxford University Press, New Delhi, 1974.

Hasan, Zoya, 'Muslim Women and the Debate on Legal Reforms', in Bharati Ray and Aparna Basu (eds), *From Independence Towards Freedom*, Oxford University Press, New Delhi, 1999.

—— (ed.), *Forging Identities: Gender, Communities and the State*, Kali for Women, New Delhi, 1994.

Heimsath, Charles H., *Indian Nationalism and Hindu Social Reform*, Princeton University Press, Princeton, 1964.

Hobsbawm, Eric and Terence Ranger (eds), *The Invention of Tradition*, Cambridge University Press, Cambridge, 1983.

Hossainur Rahman, *Hindu–Muslim Relations in Bengal, 1905–47*, Bombay, 1974.

*Hundred Years of the University of Calcutta, 1857–1957*, University of Calcutta, Calcutta, 1957.

Hunter, W.W., *The Indian Mussalmans*, London, 1876.

Haq, Enamul (ed.), *Nawab Bahadur Abdul Latif: His Writings and Related Documents*, Dhaka, 1968.

Ikramullah, Shaista, *From Purdah to Parliament*, Crescent Press, London, 1963.

Inden, Ronald, *Imagining India*, Basil Blackwell, Oxford, 1990.

Jahan, Roushan, *Inside Seclusion: The Abarodhbasini of Rokeya Sakhawat Hossain*, Women for Women, Dhaka, 1981.

Jain, Devaki, *Indian Women*, Publication Division, Ministry of Information and Broadcasting, Govt. of India, New Delhi, 1978.

Jawardane, Kumari, *Feminism and Nationalism in the Third World*, Kali for Women, New Delhi, 1986.

Joardar, Hasina and Safiuddin Joardar, *Begum Rokeya, the Emancipator*, Nari Kalyan Sangha, Dhaka, 1980.

Jones, Kenneth, 'Socio-Religious Movements and Changing Gender Relationships Among Hindus in British India', in J. Bjorkman (ed.), *Fundamentalism, Revivalists, and Violence in South Asia*, New Delhi, 1988.

—— *Socio-Religious Reform Movements in British India*, Cambridge University Press, Cambridge, 1989.

Joshi, V.C. (ed.), *Rammohun Roy and the Process of Modernization in India*, Vikas Publishing House, New Delhi, 1975.

Kaur, Manmohan, *Women in India's Freedom Struggle*, Sterling Publishers Pvt. Ltd., New Delhi, 1985.

Karim, Abdul, *Social History of the Muslims in Bengal*, Dhaka, 1959.

Karlekar, Malavika, *Voices from Within: Early Personal Narratives of Bengali Women*, Oxford University Press, New Delhi, 1991.

Kasturi, Leela and Vina Mazumdar (eds), *Women and Indian Nationalism*, Vikas Publishing House, New Delhi, 1994.

Kaviraj, Sudipta, *The Unhappy Consciousness: Bankim Chandra Chattopadhyay and the Formation of Nationalist Discourse in India*, Oxford University Press, New Delhi, 1995.

Kinsley, David, *Hindu Goddesses: Visions of the Divine Feminine in the Hindu Religious Tradition*, Motilal Banarasidass, Delhi, 1987.

Kopf, David, *The Brahmo Samaj and the Shaping of the Modern Indian Mind*, Princeton University Press, Princeton, 1979.

Krishnaraj, Maithreyi, *Women's Studies in India: Some Perspectives*, Popular Prakashan, Bombay, 1986.

―― 'Motherhood: Power and Powerlessness', in Jasodhara Bagchi (ed.), *Indian Women: Myth and Reality*, Sangam Books, Calcutta, 1995.

Lelyveld, David, *Aligarh's First Generation: Muslim Solidarity in British India*, Princeton University Press, Princeton, 1978.

Liddle, Joanna and Rama Joshi, *Daughters of Independence: Gender, Caste and Class in India*, Kali for Women, New Delhi, 1986.

Maitra, Jayanti, *Muslim Politics in Bengal, 1855–1906*, K.P. Bagchi, Calcutta, 1984.

Mandal, Tirtha, *Women Revolutionaries of Bengal*, Minerva, Calcutta, 1991.

Mani, Lata, *Contentious Traditions: The Debate on Sati in Colonial India*, Oxford University Press, New Delhi, 1998.

Mazumdar, Sudha, *A Pattern of Life: The Memories of an Indian Woman*, Manohar, New Delhi, 1977.

Mazumdar, Vina, *Education and Social Change*, Indian Institute of Advanced Studies, Simla, 1972.

McGuire, John, *The Making of a Colonial Mind: A Quantitative Study of the Bhadrolok in Calcutta 1857–1885*, Australian National University, Canberra, 1983.

Metcalf, Barbara D., 'Islamic Reform and Islamic Women: Maulana Thanawi's Jewelry of Paradise', in T. Metcalfe (ed.), *Moral Conduct and Authority*.

Mies, Maria, Veronica Bennholdt-Thomson and Claudia von Werlhof, *Women: The Last Colony*, Kali for Women, New Delhi, 1988.

Mill, James, *The History of British India*, vol. 1, James Madden, London, 1840.

Minault, Gail, *Secluded Scholars: Women's Education and Muslim Social Reform in Colonial India*, Oxford University Press, New Delhi, 1998.

―― (ed.), *The Extended Family: Women and Political Participation in India and Pakistan*, Chanakya Publications, Delhi, 1981.

Misra, B.B., *The Indian Middle Classes: Their Growth in Modern Times*, Oxford University Press, Oxford, 1961.

Misra, Lakshmi, *Education of Women in India, 1921–1966*, Macmillan, Bombay, 1966.

Mukherjee, Hiren, *India's Stuggle for Freedom*, Manisha, Calcutta, 1986.

Mukherjee, S.N., *Sir William Jones*, Cambridge University Press, Cambridge, 1968.

Murshid, Ghulam, *Reluctant Debutante*, Sahitya Sansad, Rajshahi, 1983.

Nag, Kalidas (ed.), *Bethune School and College Centenary Volume, 1849–1949*, Saraswati Press, Calcutta, 1949.

Nair, Janaki, 'Uncovering the Zenana: Visions of Indian Womanhood in English Women's Writings, 1813–1940', *Journal of Women's History*, 2:1, 1990.

Nelson, Barbara and Najma Chowdhury (eds), *Women and Politics Worldwide*, Oxford University Press, New Delhi, 1997.

Niranjana, Tejaswini, P. Sudhir and Vivek Dharaswar (eds), *Interrogating Modernity: Colonialism and Culture*, Seagull, Calcutta, 1993.

Noble, Margaret Elizabeth, (Sister Nivedita), *The Complete Works of Sister Nivedita, 1867–1911*, vols.1–4, Sister Nivedita Girls' School, Calcutta, 1967.

Panikkar, K.N., 'The Intellectual History of Colonial India: Some Historiographical and Conceptual Questions', in S. Bhattacharya and R. Thapar (eds), *Situating Indian History*, Oxford University Press, New Delhi, 1986.

Papanek, Hannah and Gail Minault (eds), *Separate Worlds: Studies of Purdah in South Asia*, Oxford University Press, New Delhi, 1982.

Ray, Bharati (ed.), *From the Seams of History: Essays on Indian Women*, Oxford University Press, New Delhi, 1995.

—— 'Women of Bengal: Transformations in Ideas and Ideals, 1900–47', *Social Scientist*, vol. 19, May–June, 1991.

—— 'Swadeshi Movement and Women's Awakening in Bengal, 1903–1910', *The Calcutta Historical Journal*, vol. 9, Jan–June, 1985.

—— 'Bengali Women and the Politics of Joint Family', *Economic and Political Weekly*, 26:52, 28 Dec. 1991.

—— 'The Freedom Movement and Feminist Consciousness in Bengal, 1905–1929', in Bharati Ray (ed.), *From the Seams of History*, 1995.

—— 'Advances of Education: From Mortar and Pestle to Mortar-boards and Scroll', in Tilottama Tharoor (ed.), *Naari*, Calcutta, 1990.

—— 'Freedom Movement and Women's Awakening in Bengal', *The Indian Historical Review*, vol. XII, 1985–6.

—— (ed.), *Women and Politics: France, India and Russia*, K.P. Bagchi, Calcutta, 2000.

—— and Aparna Basu (eds), *From Independence Towards Freedom: Indian Women Since 1947*, Oxford University Press, New Delhi, 1999.

—— and David Taylor (eds), *Politics and Identity in South Asia*, K.P. Bagchi, Kolkata, 2002.

Ray, Rajat Kanta, *Social Conflict and Political Unrest in Bengal, 1875–1927*, Oxford University Press, New Delhi, 1984.

—— (ed.), *Mind, Body and Society: Life and Mentality in Colonial Bengal*, Oxford University Press, New Delhi, 1995.

Ray, Raka, *Fields of Protest: Women's Movements in India*, University of Minnesota Press, Minneapolis, 1999.

Ray, Renuka, *My Reminiscences: Social Development during the Gandhian Era and After*, Allied Publishers, New Delhi, 1982.

Ray, Sibnarayan, 'The Sikha Movement: A Note on Bengali Muslim Intelligence', *The Radical Humanist*, vol. 41, no. 9, 1977.

Ray Chaudhuri, Tapan, *Europe Reconsidered: Perceptions of the West in Nineteenth Century Bengal*, Oxford University Press, New Delhi, 1988.

Robb, Peter (ed.), *The Concept of Race in South Asia*, Oxford University Press, New Delhi, 1978.

Rowbotham, Sheila, *A Century of Women: The History of Women in Britain and the United States*, Viking, UK, 1997.

Roy, Manisha, *Bengali Women*, Chicago University Press, Chicago, 1975.

Roy, Soma and Sarbani Ghosal, *Images, Perspectives: Golden Jubilee Commemorative Volume, Nari Seva Sangha, 1944–1994*, Calcutta, 1994.

Rudra, Ashok, 'Cultural and Religious Influences', in Devaki Jain (ed.), *Indian Women*, Publications Department, Government of India, Delhi, 1978.

Said, Edward, *Orientalism*, Routledge and Kegan Paul, London, 1978.

Sangari, Kumkum and Sudesh Vaid (eds), *Recasting Women: Essays in Colonial History*, Kali for Women, New Delhi, 1989.

Sanyal, Rajat, *Voluntary Associations and the Urban Public Life in Bengal*, Riddhi, Calcutta, 1980.

Sarkar, Sumit, *The Swadeshi Movement in Bengal, 1903–1908*, People's Publishing House, Delhi, 1973.

Sarkar, Tanika, 'Politics and Women In Bengal: The Conditions and Meaning of Participation', *The Indian Economic and Social History Review*, 21:1, 1984.

—— 'The Hindu Wife and the Hindu Nation: Domesticity and Nationalism in Nineteenth Century Bengal', *Studies in History*, vol. 8:2, 1992.

—— 'Hindu Conjugality and Nationalism in Late Nineteenth Century Colonial Bengal', Jasodhara Bagchi (ed.), *Indian Women: Myth and Reality*, Sangam Books, Calcutta, 1995.

—— *Words to Remember: Rasasundari Devi, Amar Jiban, A Modern Autobiography*, Kali for Women, New Delhi, 1999.

—— and Urvashi Butalia (eds), *Women and the Hindu Right*, Kali for Women, New Delhi, 1998.

Shastri, Shivanath, *A History of the Brahmo Samaj*, 2 vols. Calcutta, 1911.

Scott, Joan, Wallach (ed.), *Feminism and History*, Oxford University Press, Oxford, 1996.

Sen, Amiya P., *Hindu Revivalism in Bengal, 1872–1905*, Oxford University Press, New Delhi, 1993.

Sen, Ilina, *A Space Within the Struggle*, Kali for Women, New Delhi, 1990.

Sen, Mrinalini, *Knocking at the Door*, Calcutta, published by Samir Dutta, 1954.

Sen, S.P., *Dictionary of National Biography*, 4 vols, Institute of Historical Studies, Calcutta, 1972.

—— and N.R. Ray, *Modern Bengal: A Socio-Economic Survey*, Naya Prokash, Calcutta, 1990.

Sen, Samita, 'Motherhood and Mothercraft: Gender and Nationalism in Bengal', *Gender and History*, vol. 5:2, 1993.

Sinha, Mrinalini, *Colonial Masculinity: The 'Manly' Englishman and the 'Effeminate' Bengali in the late Nineteenth Century*, Manchester University Press, Manchester, 1995.

Sinha, Pradip, *Nineteenth Century Bengal: Aspects of Social History*, Firma K. L. Mukhopadhyay, Calcutta, 1965.

Sister Nivedita, *Complete Works*, 4 vols., Sister Nivedita Girls' School, Calcutta, 1967.

Southard, Barbara, *The Women's Movement and Colonial Politics in Bengal: The Quest for Political Rights, Education and Social Reform Legislation*, Manohar Publishers, Delhi, 1995.

Srinivas, M.N., *The Changing Position of Indian Women*, Oxford University Press, New Delhi, 1978.

Stree Shakti Sanghatana, *We Were Making History: Life Stories of Women in the Telengana People's Struggle*, Kali for Women, New Delhi, 1989.

Sarodamani, K. (ed.), *Women, Work and Society*, Indian Statistical Institute, Calcutta, 1985.

Swadeshi, 'Save Your Women', *Modern Review*, August 1907.

Syed Nurulla and J.P. Naik, *A History of Education in India*, Macmillan & Co. Ltd., Bombay, 1951.

Thapar, Romila, 'Imagined Religious Communities? Ancient History and the Modern Search for a Hindu Identity', *Modern Asian Studies*, vol. 23:2, 1989.

Tharu, Suzie and K. Lalitha (eds), *Women Writing in India*, 2 vols, Oxford University Press, New Delhi, 1991.

Tripathi, Amales, *The Extremist Challenge*, Calcutta, 1967.

—— 'The Role of Traditional Modernisers: Bengal's Experience in the Nineteenth Century', *The Calcutta Historical Journal*, 1983–4.

Viswanathan, Gauri, *Masks of Conquest: Literary Study and British Rule in India*, Faber & Faber, London, 1990.

Vivekananda, Swami, *Complete Works*, Mayavati Memorial Edition, 8 vols, Calcutta. 1962–73.

—— *Letters of Swami Vivekananda*, Almora, Advaita Ashram, Mayavati, 1948; first published 1940.

Wollstonecraft, Mary, *A Vindication of the Rights of Women*, London, 1875.

## Periodicals (Selected Years)

*For dates and numbers, see Notes.*

*Calcutta Historical Journal* (Calcutta)
*Economic and Political Weekly* (Bombay)
*Indian Economic and Social History Review* (Delhi)
*Indian Historical Review* (Delhi)
*Journal of Women's Studies* (Calcutta)
*Modern Review* (Calcutta)

# Index

Abala Basu, 7, 26, 86, 100, bio.140
Abanindranath Tagore, 103, bio.140
*abarodh*, 19–20, 43, 106–8, *see also* Rokeya Sakhawat Hossain
Abbasuddin Ahmed, 50
Abdul Hafiz Gazhnavi, 18
Abdul Halim Gazhnavi, 18–19
Abdul Hamid Khan Yusufzai, 18, 47, 49, bio.140
Abdul Karim, 23, 49, bio.140–1
Abdul Karim Gazhnavi, 18
Abdul Latif, Nawab, Khan Bahadur bio.141
   Muhammedan Literary Society, 47
   policy of 'modernization', 17, 46, 48
   support to English education, 47–9
   women's education, 53
Abul Asad Ibrahim Saber
   education of, 17
   family, 17–18
   support to 'modernization', 17–18
   and Rokeya's education, 20–3, 27
Akbar Hydari, Sir, 95
Akhtar Imam, Begum, 107, bio.141
Aligarh College, 50, 89–90, 106
Aligarh Girls' School, 89
Aligarh Women's College, 108
All India Muslim Educational Conference, 53, 90
All India Women's Conference, 15, 86, 89, 111
Amir Hossain Chowdhury, 19
Anjuman-i-Khawatin-i-Islam(AKI)
   aims, 89–90
   formation, 89, 92
   meeting in Calcutta, 91–2
   limitations, 89
   and Rokeya, 26, 90–4, 96
   significance, 92–3, 96
Annie Besant, 4, 25
Anurupa Devi, 101, bio.141
Anushilan Samiti, 10–12, 58
Anwara Bahar Chowdhury, 107, bio.141
Arya Samaj, 13, 15
Ashalata Sen, 87, bio.141
Ashraf Ali Thanavi, Maulana, 44, 51
Ashrafunnissa, Begum, 51
Aurobindo Ghosh, 17, 104, bio.141
Azizunnessa, Begum, 55, 107, bio.142
Azizunnissa, Begum, 51

Bangiya Nari Samaj, 26
Bankim Chandra Chattopadhyay, 9, 104–5, bio.142
Basanti Devi, 87, 111, bio.142
Begum of Bhopal, 81, 89
Bengal Provincial Muslim Education Society, 50
Bengal Women's Education League, 86
Bethune School and College, 4–5, 7, 36–7, 54, 73–4
Bharat Stree Mahamandal, *see also* Sarala Devi Chaudhurani
   aims, 81–2, 84
   activities, 83, 84–5, 100

formation, 15, 26, 80–1, 89
secular character, 84
limitations, 83, 86, 94–5, 100, 111
significance, 84–7, 96, 100
Bhudev Mukhopadhyay, 34, bio.142
*biplabi* movement, 10, 12–3, 24–5, 34, 110–1
Brahmamoyee Devi, 35, bio.142
Brahmo Samaj, 32–3
Bulbul Chowdhury, 50

Calcutta Girls' Madrassah, 54
Calcutta Muhammedan Union, 50
Calcutta University, 31
Central Muhammedan Association, 47
Chandramukhi Bose, 7, 37, bio.142
Chittaranjan Das, 104

Dayanand Saraswati, 57
Debendranath Tagore, 3–6, 78, bio.143
Deoband School, 50
Dhaka College, 53
Dilwar Hossain Ahmed, 49–50, bio.143
Durgamohan Das, 7, 37, bio.143
Dwarakanath Tagore, 5, bio.143
Dwijendranath Tagore, 5

Eden School, 54, 107

Faizunnessa Chaudhurani, Nawab, 54–5, 107, bio.143–4
Faizunnessa Degree College, 54
Faizunnessa Girls' Pilot High School, 54
Fazilatunnessa Zoha, 107, bio.144
Firdaus Mahal, Nawab, 54

Gandhi, Mahatma, 14–5, 25, 38, 103–4
Ghulam Wahib Chaudhury, 18
Gyanadanandini Devi, 5–6, 77, 107, 110, bio.144

Hemalata Sarkar, 7, 42, 100, bio.144
Hemantakumari Chaudhuri, 71

Hemaprabha Basu, 7
Hemaprabha Majumdar, 87, 100, bio.144
Hemendranath Tagore, 5–6
Hindu School, 31, 46
Hindu women, *see also* Sarala Devi Chaudhurani and nationalist movement
condition of, 28–30, 42–4, 61–2
didactic literature on, 39–41
education of, 7, 28–9, 33–7, 51, 86
social reform, 33–7
zenana educaton, 35, 83
writings by, 4–6, 14–5, 29, 35, 41–2, 55, 100–1
Hironmoyee Devi, 4, 6–7, 15, bio.145
Homyera, Begum, 19
Hossainuddin Chaudhury, 17

Indian National Congress, 1, 8–9, 12, 14–5, 24–5, 80–1
Indira Devi Chaudhurani, 6, bio.144
Ismail Hossain Shirazi, 23, 49, 55, 106, bio.145
Iswar Chandra Gupta, 36
Iswar Chandra Vidyasagar, 5, 33, 36–7, 57

Jagadish Chandra Basu, 7
Jahan Ara Shah Nawaz, 107
Jainul Abedin, 50
Janakinath Ghosal, 4
Jyotirindranath Tagore, 3, 5–6
Jyotirmoyee Ganguli, 111, bio.145
Jyotsna Ghosal, 4, 6

Kadambari Devi, 6
Kadambini Ganguli, 4, 37, 71, bio.145
Kaikobad, 23, bio.145
Kailasbasini Devi, 29, 41, 101, 110, bio.145–6
Kalpana Dutta, 111, bio.146
Kamini Roy, 7, 26, 28, 71, 77, 101, bio.146
Karimunnessa Khanam, bio.146
education of, 18, 20

love of Bengali language, 18
  influence on Rokeya, 18, 21, 23, 27
Kazi Imdadul Huq, 23, 48–9, 52, 55, 106, bio.146
Keramat Ali, 44
Khalilur Rahman Abu Jaigam Saber, 18
Kazi Nazrul Islam, 112, bio.146,
Kumidini Khastagir, 7, bio.147
Kumudini Mitra, 58, 86, bio.147
Khairunnessa Begum, 55, 107–8, bio.147
Khatun Jahan, Begum, 107
Khwaja Altaf Hussain Hali, 51
Khujasta Akhtar Banu Suhrawardy, 107, bio.147
Khilafat movement, 93
Krishnabhabini Das, 77, 82–3, 100, 110, bio.147

Lady Brabourne College, 19
Lajjabati Basu, 7, bio.148
Latifunnessa Begum, 53
Lila Roy, 86–7, bio.148

Madanmohan Tarkalankar, 36–7
Maharani School, 8
Maleka Begum, 113
Mankumari Basu, 44, 101, bio.148
Masuma Begum, 107
Maulvi Abdul Hakim, 53
Mir Musharraf Hossain, 23, 47, 49, bio.148
Mrinalini Devi, 6
Mrinalini Sen, 86, 100, bio. 148.
Muhammad Riyazuddin Ahmed, 49, bio.148
Muhammad Yakub Ali Chowdhury, 49, bio.149
Muhammedan Literary Society, 47
Muslim Balika Madrassah, 53–4
Muslim nationalism, 45–7
  Bengali Muslim nationalism
    growth of, 46–9, 56
    and periodicals, 18, 23–4, 48–50, 54–5
  quest for identity, 49–50, 79
  and Rokeya, 106, 113
  social reform, 44–5, 47–50
  and women's education, 51–6
Muslim League, 24
Muslim Suhrid Sammelani, 53
Muslim women, *see also* Rokeya Sakhawat Hossain
  condition of, 19, 42–4
  didactic literature on, 44
  education of, 43–4, 50–5
  *jagaran*, 45, 106, 113
  organizations of, 87– 96, 107, 113
  social reform, 48
  writings by, 44–5, 48, 55, 107–9

Nafis Dulhan Sherwani, 89–92
nationalist movement, *see also* Rokeya Sakhawat Hossain and Sarala Devi Chaudhurani
  beginning of, 38
  discourse on women, 33–4, 38–41, 58–9, 65–6, 98–9,
  and response of women, 41–2
  Hindu identity, 30–3, 56
  revolutionary (*biplabi*) movement, 12–3, 34
  Swadeshi movement, 8–13, 38, 102–4
  women's participation in, 4, 38, 111
Nausher Ali Khan Yusufzai, 23, 49, 109, bio.149
Nazir Ahmad, 51
Nirupama Devi, 101, bio.149
Nivedita, Sister, 15, 34
Nurunnessa Khatun, Bidyabinodini, 108–9, 111, bio.149

Pritilata Waddedar, 110, bio.149
Priyambada Devi, 84, bio.149
Pyarichand Mitra, 35, 53, bio.149–50

Rabindranath Tagore, 3, 5–6, 9, 11, 103–4, 111, 113, bio.150

Rahatunnessa Sabera Chaudhurani, 17, 22
Rajnarayan Basu, 7
Ramakrishna Paramhansa, 33–4
Rambhuj Dutta Chaudhury, 13–4, 105
Rammohan Roy, Raja, 5, 32, 37, 57, bio.150
Rasasundari Devi, 35, 51, 110, bio.150
Rashid Jahan, Begum, 108
Razia Khatun Chaudhurani, 108, bio.150
Rokeya Sakhawat Hossain, Begum, *see also* AKI, and Sarala Devi
   childhood of, 19–20, 22
   death of, 26, 110
   education of, 20–1, 27, 44
   family, 16–9, 27, 44
   marriage of, 21–2
   on men's education, 69–70
   love of Bengali language, 23, 76, 106, 112
   perception by contemporaries of, 98, 109–10
   perspectives on women's issues, 2–3, 27, 60–4, 76–7, 93–4, 106–7
      *abarodh*, 17, 19–20, 27, 62, 69–70, 106, 108, 113
      *Abarodhbasini*, 17, 22–3, 62, 97, 106
      gender equality, 23–4, 27, 60–2, 70, 76, 93, 97 87–8, 105–6, 113
      gainful employment for women, 71–3
      women's marriage, 71–2, 75, 97
      *Motichoor*, 21–3, 60, 77
      *Padmarag*, 20, 23, 72–3, 88–9, 96, 108
      purdah, 27, 62, 69–70, 73–4, 92, 106–8
      *Sultana's Dream*, 23, 62–3, 70, 106
      women's education, 64, 69–75, 77, 107
   women's movement, pioneer of, 26, 87–93, 96, 107–13
   and women's suffrage, 25–6
   religion, 3, 22, 61, 88, 97–8, 105–6, 109–10, 112
   and Sarala, 2–3, 16, 24, 26–7, 56–7, 60–1, 68, 70–1, 75–7, 88, 93–8, 105, 110, 113
   secularism, 24, 95–6, 113
   support to nationalist movement, 24–5, 93, 105
   and Bengali Muslim nationalism, writings by, 22–5, 60–4, 69–75, 88–9, 94

Sakhawat Hossain, 1–2, 21–2, 26–7
Sakhawat Memorial Girls' School, 19, 22, 26, 73–4, 106–7, 112
Sakhi Samiti, 4–5, 78
Sarajubala Dutta, 101
Sarala Devi Chaudhurani, *see also* Bharat Stree Mahamandal and Rokeya Hossain
   and biplabi movement, 10, 12–3, 34, 70–1, 103, 110–1
   Birashtami Utsav, 9
   childhood of, 6–7
   editorship of *Bharati*, 4, 14–5
   education of, 7, 26
   employment of, 8
   family, 2–7, 26–7, 44, 105, 110, 112
   and Gandhi, 14–5
   Lakshmir Bhandar, 15,
   marriage of, 97
   music, 1, 8–9
   nationalism, 8, 14, 12, 13–4, 26–7, 57, 68, 97–101, 103, 110–1
   and nationalist discourse, 48–9, 58–9, 66–7, 98–100, 104–5
   on men's education, 68
   promotion of martial culture, 9–12, 70, 99
   and Nivedita, 15, 34
   perception by contemporaries, 102–4

perspectives on women, 2–3, 27, 57–60, 76–7, 93–4, 101
belief in woman power, 57–60, 67–8, 78–80, 94, 97–100, 103
on violence against women, 94
women's education, 64–8, 70, 77
women's organization, 1, 15, 78, 80–7, 96, 100, 104
political involvement, 1, 8–14, 24, 100
Pratapaditya Utsav, 10–1, 102–3, 111
religion, 3, 13, 15–6, 57–8, 66–7, 79–80, 97, 100, 103
secularism, 81, 84, 95
Siksha Sadan, 15, 68, 84
Udayaditya Utsav, 11–2, 102, 111
writings by, 9–11, 14–5, 58–60, 64–8, 76, 78–82, 94, 110–2
Sarala Ray, 86
Sarat Chandra Chattopadhyay, 15
Saratkumari Chaudhurani, 101, bio.150
Sarojini Naidu, 25, 87, 111, bio.151
Satyendranath Tagore, 5–6, bio.151
Shailabala Ghoshjaya, 101, bio.151
Shaista Suhrawardy Ikramullah, Begum, 107, bio.151
Shamsunnahar Mahmud, 17, 20–1, 44, 90, 107–8, 112–3, bio.151–2
Shanti Ghosh, 111, bio.152
Shivanath Shastri, 7, 35–7, 74, bio.152
social reform, *see also* women's education 29–37, 44–6, 48–51, 56, 74
Suhrid Samiti, 13
Sucheta Kripalani, 111, bio.152
Suniti Chaudhury, 110, bio.152
Swadeshi movement, 8–13, 24, 38, 100, 102–3
Swarnakumari Devi, bio.152–3
Bharat Stree Mahamandal, 83
Bidhaba Shilpashram, 4
editorship of *Bharati*, 3
education of, 3
Indian National Congress, 4
marriage, 4–5
on Gyanadanandini Devi, 6
Sakhi Samiti, 4
writings by, 3–4, 41, 101, 111
Swarnaprabha Basu, 42, 71, 75, bio.152
Syed Ahmed Khan, Sir 17, 46–8, 50–1, bio. 153
Syed Amir Ali, bio.153
Central Muhammedan Association, 47
support to 'modernization', 17, 47–8
and women's education, 53
Syed Emdad Ali, 48–9, 55
Syed Nawab Ali Chowdhury, 49, bio. 153
Syed Shamsul Huda, 49–50, 153–4
Syed Wajed Hossain, 50, bio.154
Sayyid Mumtaz Ali, 51

Taherunnessa, 55
Tayyiba Begum Khediv Jung, 91–2

Vivekananda, 15–6, 33–4, 37, 59, 101, 103–4, bio.154

Wahabi movement, 46
Wahid Jahan, Begum, 89–91
women's education, *see also* Rokeya Sakhawat Hossain and Sarala Devi Chaudhurani
lack of, 28–9, 43–4, 51–2
progress of, 31–7, 50–5, 83
opposition to, 35–6
zenana education, 35, 83
women's movement, *see also* Sarala Devi and Rokeya Sakhawat Hossain
AKI, 89–93
Bharat Stree Mahamandal, 80–96
nineteenth century associations, 78, 86

Zahiruddin Muhammad Abu Ali Saber, 16–7, 19–21

OUP 5006/17/09/02